W9-ACG-353

The Sustainability Curriculum

The Challenge for Higher Education

Edited by
John Blewitt
and
Cedric Cullingford

London • Sterling, VA

First published by Earthscan in the UK and USA in 2004

ISBN: 1-85383-949-3 paperback
       1-85383-948-5 hardback

Typesetting by JS Typesetting Ltd, Wellingborough, Northants
Printed and bound in the UK by Cromwell Press Ltd, Trowbridge
Cover design by Danny Gillespie

For a full list of publications please contact:

Earthscan
8–12 Camden High Street, London, NW1 0JH, UK
Tel: +44 (0)20 7387 8558
Fax: +44 (0)20 7387 8998
Email: earthinfo@earthscan.co.uk
Web: **www.earthscan.co.uk**

22883 Quicksilver Drive, Sterling, VA 20166-2012, USA

Earthscan publishes in association with WWF-UK and the International Institute for
Environment and Development

A catalogue record for this book is available from the British Library

Library of Congress Cataloging-in-Publication Data

The sustainability curriculum : the challenge for higher education / edited by John
Blewitt and Cedric Cullingford.
     p. cm.
  Includes bibliographical references and index.
  ISBN 1-85383-949-3 (pbk.) – ISBN 1-85383-948-5 (hardback)
   1. Environmental education. 2. Sustainability development. 3. Interdisciplinary
approach in education. I. Blewitt, John, 1957– II. Cullingford, Cedric.

  GE70.S875 2004
  333.72–dc22

                                                                        2003021980

Printed on elemental chlorine-free paper

Contents

Part 2

List of Tables, Figures and Boxes

TABLES

FIGURES

BOXES

List of Contributors

Hugh Atkinson is principal lecturer in politics and public policy at South Bank University. He lectures in comparative European politics and public policy at both undergraduate and postgraduate levels. His primary research interest is in British sub-national government. He is co-author of *Local Government from Thatcher to Blair: the Politics of Creative Autonomy* (Polity Press, 2000). He is a former local councillor.

Mark Baimbridge is a senior lecturer in economics at the University of Bradford. His research interests include European integration, the economics profession, higher education and the economics of professional sports. He has published over 50 articles in learned journals and has authored and edited texts such as *The Impact of the Euro* (Palgrave Macmillan, 2000), *Fiscal Federalism and European Economic Integration* (Routledge, 2004) and *Economic and Monetary Union in Europe* (Edward Elgar, 2003).

Colin Bamford is head of the Department of Logistics and Hospitality Management at the University of Huddersfield. He is the author of recent textbooks on economics and of other publications on transport economics, which is his specialist field of interest. He is a fellow of the Institute of Logistics and Transport and a firm believer in the need for a more sustainable transport policy for the UK.

John Blewitt is deputy director of the Department of Lifelong Learning at the University of Exeter. He has been instrumental in producing a regional Education for Sustainability (EFS) Strategy for Yorkshire and the Humber and has worked with the Learning and Skills Development Agency on a number of EFS projects, including Learning to Last. He has published widely on adult learning and EFS.

Jack Bradley and **Joanne Crowther** have an active role in promoting science and engineering at the University of Bradford's School of Engineering, Design and Technology. They have organized an extensive programme of hands-on activities for schools and colleges, giving over 3000 young people a taste of exciting science projects, including designing and building a hovercraft in a day, designing and launching a rocket and an electronics project entitled 'Listen to Kylie through a Cardboard Box'.

Christopher Cowton took up his current appointment as professor of accounting at Huddersfield University Business School in 1996. He was chairman of EBEN-UK (the UK association of the European Business Ethics Network) from 1998 to 2001 and is editor of the journal *Business Ethics: A European Review*. He holds a BA with First Class Honours in accounting and financial management from the University of Sheffield, an MSc in Economics from the University of Wales, an MA (by Special Resolution) from the University of Oxford and a PhD from the University of Sheffield. He is a chartered secretary, Associate of the Chartered Institute of Secretaries (ACIS) and a fellow of the Royal Society of Arts (FRSA).

Cedric Cullingford is the professor of education at the University of Huddersfield. His recent books include *The Best Years of Their Lives? Pupils' Experiences of School* (Kogan Page, 2002), *Prejudice: From Individual Identity to Nationalism in Young People* (Kogan Page, 2000) and *The Causes of Exclusion: Home, School and the Development of Young Criminals* (Kogan Page, 1999).

John Donnelly lectures in the Sociology and Criminology Division at Northumbria University. His research interests centre on development ethics, comparative historical sociology and visual sociology, particular as these connect with issues of moral engagement with global inequality.

Brian Edwards is professor of architecture at ECA/Heriot-Watt University. He was formerly professor of architecture at the University of Huddersfield and served on the Royal Institute of British Architects (RIBA) Energy and Environment Committee from 1995–2000. He is the author of several books on sustainable design, including *Rough Guide to Sustainability* (Riba Publications, 2001) written in collaboration with Paul Hyett.

Robert Garner is reader and head of politics at the University of Leicester. He has published widely on environmental politics, in general, and the politics and philosophy of animal protection, in particular. His books include *Animals, Politics and Morality* (MUP, 1993), *Political Animals* (Macmillan, 1998) and *Environmental Politics* (Macmillan, 2000).

Peter Hopkinson is course leader of the MSc in business strategy and environmental management in the Department of Environmental Science at the University of Bradford.

Meg Huby has a background in environmental biology and is currently a senior lecturer in the Department of Social Policy and Social Work at the University of York. She teaches modules in social and environmental policy and in research methods, and is the author of *Social Policy and the Environment* (Open University Press, 1998).

Peter James is Visiting Professor of Environmental Management at the University of Bradford. He was previously head of Ashridge Management

College Environmental Leadership Programme, and has published and consulted on environmental accounting, benchmarking and performance; measurement, eco-innovation and product development implementing; and environmental strategies and change initiatives.

Phil McManus is a senior lecturer in the School of Geosciences and is partly seconded to be the director of environmental science at the University of Sydney. His research and teaching focus on environmental and urban geography. He wrote the section on sustainable development in the fourth edition of *The Dictionary of Human Geography* (Blackwell, 2000).

Clare Palmer is a senior lecturer in philosophy at the Institute for Environment, Philosophy and Public Policy at Lancaster University. Her research interests include environmental philosophy and she is the author of *Environmental Ethics and Process Thinking* (OUP, 1998). She is also the founding editor of the journal *Worldviews: Environment, Culture, Religion*.

Andrew Parker teaches in the Department of Sociology at the University of Warwick, UK. He is an ex-secondary school teacher and teacher educator whose research interests include the sociology of education, organizational behaviour and gender relations.

Jenneth Parker is co-director of the distance learning postgraduate programme in education for sustainability at London South Bank University. In addition to working in higher education, she has experience in adult and continuing education. She has a background in feminist and environmental movements and has research interests in contemporary ethics and the politics of local and global sustainability, with a focus on social movements. She is currently working on two books derived from her DPhil from the University of Sussex, *Towards an Ecofeminist Ethics: A Critical Realist and Social Movements Approach*.

Matthew Smith lectures in the Sociology and Criminology Division at Northumbria University, and has previously worked for a development education NGO. His research centres on the intersection of development, education and globalization, with a particular interest in the ways development NGOs engage with 'northern' constituencies.

Stephen Sterling is a consultant in environmental and sustainability education working in the academic and NGO fields. He was an architect of the Education for Sustainability Masters programme at London South Bank University, where he is an academic tutor. His key publications include *Education for Sustainability* (Earthscan, 1996), *Education for Sustainable Development in the Schools Sector* (Sustainable Development Education Panel, 1988) and *Sustainable Education – Re-visioning Learning and Change* (Green Books, 2001).

Ros Wade is co-director of the education for sustainability (EFS) programme at London South Bank University. She has been writing and researching for several years in the field of education for global citizenship and helped to develop Oxfam's policy document *A Curriculum for Global Citizenship*. She has recently co-written a study guide on *Perspectives on Environment and Development* for students on the EFS programme.

Karen Warren is professor of philosophy at Macalester College. She has edited or co-edited five anthologies, authored *Ecofeminist Philosophy: A Western Perspective on What It Is and Why It Matters* (Rowman and Littlefield, 2000) and completed a groundbreaking anthology entitled *Gendering Western Philosophy* (Prentice Hall, forthcoming). To learn more about Karen Warren's professional background, interests and accomplishments, please visit her website at www.macalester.edu/~warren.

Adam Van Winsum is the Research Assistant at the University of Bradford working on the Higher Education Funding Council (HEFCE) funded good management practice project Higher Education Environment Performance Improvement (HEEPI).

List of Acronyms and Abbreviations

ARB	Architects Registration Board
ACIS	Associate of the Chartered Institute of Secretaries
AFANet	Thematic Network for Agriculture, Forestry, Aquaculture and the environment
ALERT	Adult Learner's Environmental Training and Resource Project
AUDE	Association of University Directors of Estates
BAT	British American Tobacco
BIE	Business in the Environment
BRE	Building Research Establishment
BSE	bovine spongiform encephalopathy
BT	British Telecom
CfIT	Commission for Integrated Transport
CO_2	carbon dioxide
COPERNICUS	Cooperation Programme in Europe for Research on Nature and Industry through Coordinated University Studies
CPD	continuous professional development
CTC	city technology college
CVCP	Committee of Vice-Chancellors and Principals
DE	development education
DEA	Development Education Association
DfEE	Department for Education and Employment
DfES	Department for Education and Skills
DETR	UK Department of the Environment, Transport and the Regions
DTI	Department of Trade and Industry
EAUC	Environmental Association of Universities and Colleges
EAZ	educational action zone
EBEN	European Business Ethics Network
EC	European Commisson
EE	environmental education
EEE	Electrical and Electronics Equipment Directive
EFS	education for sustainability
ESF	education for a sustainable future

ELV	End of Life of Vehicle Directive
EMS	Estate Management Statistics
EPA	Environmental Protection Agency (US)
EPSRC	Engineering and Physical Sciences Research Council
EPZ	export-processing zone
ESD	education for sustainable development
EU	European Union
EWS	English, Welsh and Scottish Railway
FAO	Food and Agricultural Organization (United Nations)
FE	further education
FE$_2$HE	Further Education to Higher Education
FRSA	Fellow of the Royal Society of Arts
GATS	General Agreement on Trade in Services
GC	global citizenship
GDP	gross domestic product
GIS	geographic information systems
GMO	genetically modified organism
GNP	gross national product
GreenCom	Environmental Education Communication Project of the US Agency for International Development (Academy for Educational Development)
HDI	Human Development Index
HE	higher education
HEEPI	Higher Education Environmental Performance Improvement Initiative
HEFCE	Higher Education Funding Council for England
HEI	higher education institution
ICT	information and computer technology
ILO	International Labour Organization
IPP	integrated product policy
ISEE	International Society for Environmental Ethics
ITK	indigenous technical knowledge
IUCN	International Union for the Conservation of Nature and Natural Resources
JPPSG	Joint Procurement Policy and Strategy Group
LAN	local area network
LCA	life-cycle analysis
LJMU	Liverpool John Moores University
MELA	Mothers of East Los Angeles
MET	material cycle, energy use and toxic emissions
NFER	National Foundation for Education Research
NGO	non-governmental organization
OECD	Organisation for Economic Co-operation and Development

OU	Open University
PAR	participatory action research
PBL	problem-based learning
PFI	private finance initiative
PP4SD	Professional Practice for Sustainable Development Initiative
PPP	public–private partnership
PSHE	personal, social and health education
QCA	Qualification and Curriculum Authority
RAE	research assessment exercise
RIBA	Royal Institute of British Architects
ROHS	Restriction of Certain Substances Directive
SAGES	School of Anthropology, Geography and Environmental Science (University of Melbourne)
SD	sustainable development
SDE	sustainable development education
SEAAR	social and ethical accounting, auditing and reporting
SMT	Senior Management Team
SWOT	Strengths Weaknesses Opportunities Threats
TCPA	Town and Country Planning Association
TNC	transnational corporation
UCL	University College London
UIA	Union of International Architects
UK	United Kingdom
UMIST	University of Manchester Institute of Science and Technology
UN	United Nations
UNCED	United Nations Conference on Environment and Development
UNEP	United Nations Environment Programme
UNESCO	United Nations Educational, Scientific and Cultural Organization
UNICEF	United Nations International Children's Emergency Fund
US	United States
USDA	United States Department of Agriculture
UUK	Universities UK
VSO	Voluntary Service Overseas
WBL	work-based learning
WCED	World Commission on Environment and Development
WESDE	women–environment–sustainable development–education interconnections
WEEE	Waste Electrical and Electronic Equipment Directive

WHO	World Health Organization
WISE	Women into Science and Engineering (University of Bradford)
WSSD	World Summit on Sustainable Development
WTO	World Trade Organization
WWF	World Wide Fund for Nature

Chapter 1

Introduction

John Blewitt

At the Earth Summit in Rio in 1992, education was identified as one of the key forces central to the processes of sustainable development during the 21st century. Some years later, the goal of sustainability and the need for education in all of its forms in order to seriously engage with this imperative remain as significant as ever – possibly more so, as many of us are directly experiencing the risks, uncertainties and pressures of working and living within a global-ized, weightless knowledge economy. As wealth increases for some, global poverty, insecurity and inequality are an obdurate reminder that economic development is far from even and far from fair. Higher education (HE) is implicated in all of this, for it is no longer in the privileged position of simply observing, criticizing and evaluating what goes on beyond the seminar room or campus. It, too, is a global player imbricated in both the production of knowledge and wealth and the maintenance of poverty and insecurity through its growing role as servant to the global economy. Higher education therefore helps to shape the material reality we all experience and the ways in which we attempt to understand, reflect on and, perhaps, even change it.

Sustainable development and the goal of sustainability are slowly permeat-ing the values, policies and practices of government, business and education. For many people this permeation seems to be occurring in geological rather than human time. This book explores just one aspect of HE's engagement with the sustainability agenda, focusing largely on where the sector is currently positioned and how it might, and arguably should, evolve in the future. For good or ill, universities are notoriously conservative creatures despite their apparent liking for internal restructuring. The dominance of disciplinarity remains important in the intellectual organization of teaching, learning (the cultural reproduction of knowledge) and, perhaps, also research funding. As new areas of learning and research emerge, as universities become increasingly 'relevant', disciplinarity remains the locus of attention and the intellectual axis for comprehending contemporary developments. New 'disciplines' such as media studies, informatics or environmental science are emerging as the global tendency (or 'real world' demand) is increasingly towards transdisciplinarity and the social distribution of knowledge and knowledge production. Signifi-cant higher learning, including research, now takes place in private and government think tanks, corporate research laboratories and even in the public media. Knowledge, as opposed to mere information, is becoming increasingly rooted in specific contexts of application that go beyond the rules and perspectives of single subject disciplines. Indeed, universities are increasingly urged by governments to become more effectively involved in knowledge and technology transfer. Gibbons et al (1994) identify four features of this 'Mode 2' transdisciplinary knowledge, which is additionally characterized by its heterogeneity, social accountability and reflexivity. It is not hierarchical or fixed but subject to change and alteration:

1   It develops a distinct but evolving framework to guide problem-solving efforts.
2   Solutions involve movements in many directions, and theoretical and empirical work.
3   The diffusion and dissemination of new knowledge to participants takes place through, rather than after, the process.
4   It is dynamic and constantly evolving.

The skills and experiences that people bring to this enterprise are heterogeneous, and despite all the critical semantic arguments about the conceptual fluidity or vagueness of sustainability and sustainable development, their practical realization will be an aspect of this Mode 2 transdiciplinarity. Sustainability is complex and complicated, with no single discipline definitively addressing either the problems or the solutions: it incorporates technological, philosophical, economic, social, ecological, political and scientific dimensions. This may be illustrated through an examination of real-world issues or projects that are motivated by concerns over sustainability – for example, in Green architecture, eco-design, gender and development; integrated and sustainable transport; global citizenship; and lifelong learning.

Although sustainability and sustainable development certainly require a transdiciplinary or interdisciplinary approach to teaching, learning and research, disciplinarity is still an inviolable fact of university life, particularly in the more research-led traditional institutions in the UK. The disciplines are unlikely to disappear or to lose their significance as ways of comprehending (or not comprehending) the contemporary world. Their apprehension of sustainability issues, processes and imperatives therefore becomes of key significance for many students who study them. The humanities and social sciences enable us to reflect upon our worlds in ways that are not tied to performance criteria, executive summaries, business plans, scientific logic, trade laws or government regulations. The reflective and, indeed, reflexive nature of the disciplines allows the formation of new understandings of self and others and their relationship to the natural world. The recent emergence of eco-criticism within literature studies (Bate, 2000) and counter-intuitive rather than revisionist interpretations of social relationships and new technology in history (Sale, 1996) offer opportunities for all of us to stop to think, see, listen and learn. The collective message from the contributors in this volume is that the co-evolution of the disciplines and sustainability is sometimes uneven, sometimes profound, but always signalling an, as yet, unrealized potential that may in the future herald a radical transformation of learning, knowledge and understanding. The role of disciplinarity is often unrecognized or even summarily dismissed in conversations about education for sustainability. This is a pity, for all of us still have a lot to learn. Interestingly, even students on new programmes focusing specifically on sustainability, such as the BA/BSc in Sustainable Development at the University of Wales at Bangor, offer multidisciplinary and interdisciplinary learning opportunities as well as practice-based educational experience. Reflexivity remains the key to personal growth and social learning and, as such, is a key element, together with de-traditionalization, of our late modern age:

> *The reflexivity of modern social life consists in the fact that social practices are constantly examined and reformed in the light of incoming information about those very practices, thus constitutively altering their character. . . In all cultures, social practices are routinely altered in the light of ongoing discoveries which feed into them. But only in the era of modernity is the revision of convention radicalized to apply (in principle) to all aspects of human life, including technological intervention in the material world.*
> (Giddens, 1990, pp38–39)

Lifelong learners in further, higher and adult education should be, and are, increasingly encouraged to be reflexive and reflective if a more just and sustainable world is to be fashioned.

The current issues of disciplinary change, curriculum development, capacity-building and the nurturing of a critical environmental literacy can only be realized in the process of changing our relationship with time, the natural world and the traditions of our own thinking. As Foster (2001, 2002) says, we need to recapture a view of education as being an end in itself since it is through our learning that we collectively and individually recreate ourselves, our understanding of the world and, in the long run, the world itself. Additionally, without the capacity to make ('deep sustainability') judgements for tomorrow, the social intelligence necessary to create a culturally mature and institutionally sophisticated learning society may not develop. This social intelligence requires the flourishing of the humanities, social sciences and 'meta-scientific modes of understanding'. A learning society, Foster (2002, p39) writes, 'lives by the fullest exploration of experience imaginatively alert to all its complexities'. As a corollary, Stables and Scott's (2002) discussion of critical environmental literacy presents the need to move beyond 'humanism and the discourses of modernity' while avoiding the partial and sometimes incompatible nature of other literacies – scientific, technological, economic and so on. As Bowers (2001) has shown, the language and, particularly, the metaphors we use in our sense-making activities can limit (perhaps even to the point of preventing) the proper development of an ecological understanding of the human–nature relationship. Our language is littered with anthropocentric, industrial, mechanistic and computational metaphors, whereas at the root of a 'deep sustainability' consciousness and conscience, *ecology* should be understood as encompassing the interdependency of social, cultural and biotic activities and relationships. The concepts of restoration, preservation and conservation, Bowers (2001) argues, should be borrowed from the ecological sciences and re-articulated to accommodate social relationships and practices. In this way, the critical environmental literacy that Stables and Scott (1999) advocate could, effectively:

- Restore our amazement at the unknowability and finitude of life, which transcends our own material desires and rationality.
- Provide an understanding of the historically and culturally situated nature of scientific knowledge, technology and creative art.
- Ensure that when we attempt to act sustainably we do so from a belief in its moral value and with a willingness to learn from it.

Sometimes it seems that reason and rationality, whether in scientific guise or not, is the primary enemy of sustainable development. But it should be recalled that just as many people wish to renew humanity's spiritual, affective and intuitive capabilities. Reason remains a key element in the generation of any critical literacy, knowledge, understanding or practice. Universities are places that, hopefully, still offer cultural and intellectual space where critical reason may develop, be discussed and questioned. Reason is possibly a prerequisite for a form of learning that will enable us to better look after ourselves and our environment. As Field (2000, p154) concludes in his analysis of lifelong learning:

> An ever more greedy capitalism needs rational, humanistic and know-ledgeable critics as a prerequisite for human survival. Is the learning society amenable to change?

In some ways HE has been prescient in outlining an agenda for sustainable learning and institutional change. In 1990, under the auspices of President Jean Meyer of Tufts University, 22 presidents, rectors and vice chancellors from universities across the world issued a ten-point action plan to engage HE in the quest for a sustainable future. The first three action points of the Talloires Declaration read:

1 *Increase awareness of environmentally sustainable development*: use every opportunity to raise public, government, industry, foundation and university awareness by openly addressing the urgent need to move towards an environmentally sustainable future.
2 *Create an institutional culture of sustainability*: encourage all universities to engage in education, research, policy formation and information exchange on population, environment and development to move towards global sustainability.
3 *Educate for environmentally responsible citizenship*: establish programmes to produce expertise in environmental management, sustainable economic

development, population and related fields to ensure that all university graduates are environmentally literate and have the awareness and understanding to be ecologically responsible citizens.

Three years later the group of European universities that had formed COPERNICUS (Cooperation Programme in Europe for Research on Nature and Industry through Coordinated University Studies) launched its University Charter for Sustainable Development. The central concerns of COPERNICUS include interdisciplinarity, lifelong learning, sustainable production and consumption, partnerships and networking, teacher education and the creation of virtual learning environments.

At the turn of the millennium, in 2000, following some years of discussion and financial support from the Dutch government, 'the unfinished business of Rio' was finally completed with the publication of the Earth Charter (2000). This charter sets out 16 principles and an ethical framework that falls into four major areas:

1   respect and care for the community of life;
2   ecological integrity;
3   social and economic justice and democracy;
4   non-violence and peace.

The charter aims to foster a more sustainable way of life by persuading educational institutions and learners to transcend our human-centred approach to knowledge, understanding and action. Some progress is already being made in some universities (Clugston, Calder and Corcoran, 2002; Calder and Clugston, 2002); but not all observers are confident that HE is capable of more than piecemeal change. Bosselmann (2001) argues that administrative structures are alien to staff and students alike and are only responsive to instrumental demands to use resources more efficiently. Faculties and disciplines are incapable of interdisciplinary cooperation, while the university, as a whole, 'has no ethos or collective conscience for sustainability'. Progress in the UK during the decade following the *Toyne Report* (Toyne, 1993) adds substance to this pessimistic assessment, as do some contributors to this volume.

Although declarations of principle are important signposts, the everyday reality of educational administration, management, funding, career development, teaching and learning in its various forms offer more than a 'challenge' to champions of education for sustainability (EFS) within the university sector. These champions – leaders at all levels – need to seek methods by which others may adapt themselves, endorse and then promote the required shifts in teaching, learning, curriculum, research, institutional management, policy and practice that will build a more sustainable world. Adaptive leadership – mobilizing people to address new problems through new learning – is, as Heifitz (1994) shows, the most appropriate strategy for effecting major and lasting, if not paradigmatic, change. Although this book does not specifically address issues of educational leadership for sustainability, what is implicit in the Earth Charter (2000), the Talloires Declaration and similar initiatives is the recognition that sustainability is not something that can be imposed from above or secured exclusively by action below – it needs both. The processes of sustainable development require leadership, participation and commitment in all areas of the academy. If one of the principal purposes of universities remains the generation of new knowledge or the re-articulation of existing knowledge, then work within and between the disciplines is of primary significance for all our futures. Universities are no longer the ivory towers of popular imagination; but neither are they (yet) exemplars of good sustainable practice or, as Sterling (2001) has it, 'sustainability education'.

Universities should act as exemplars; but too often progress in this area is dependent upon a relatively few committed and invariably overworked individuals. But then there's nothing wrong with being a pioneer.

STRUCTURE OF THE BOOK

The purpose of this book is to offer some scrutiny of current HE practice by looking at disciplinary study, some developmental projects, lifelong learning and the nature and purpose of HE itself. Not all of the disciplines can be covered in one volume and the sciences have been consciously omitted. A great deal of criticism has been levelled at many aspects of scientific activity (Ho, 2000), and to examine science, sustainability and HE is something that is best explored in a separate volume.

Part 1 starts with Cullingford's overview of the purpose of the university at a time that is characterized by change and threat. Cullingford argues that sustainability should become the centre of debate that engages all of us in a fundamental rethink about the nature of HE and its wider responsibilities. One danger Cullingford perceives is that 'sustainability' could become a cliché devoid of any significant intellectual purchase if universities fail in their moral duty to penetrate the masks and veils of media spin, political rhetoric and its own instrumental rationality. This instrumentality, understood increasingly as supporting the needs of the global economy and developing 'human capital', constricts the possibilities of learning throughout life. In Chapter 3, I argue that both sustainability and lifelong learning are obviously and necessarily complementary. Only if we are able to renew our understanding of what lifelong learning could and should be, will a more sympathetic and holistic policy and practice emerge. In Chapter 4, the meaning of sustainability in the context of education theory and practice is analysed by Sterling who explores the provenance of the term 'education for sustainability' or EFS and outlines the key theoretical and philosophical principles informing its likely realization in the university sector. One way in which lifelong learning and HE, as a whole, can discover a new sense of purpose sympathetic to the holistic goals of sustainability is to nurture learning opportunities that foster global citizenship. In Chapter 5, Parker, Wade and Atkinson review their own achievements at London's South Bank University, which, although significant, also highlight the distance still to be travelled if the larger institutional structures, organization and ethos are to be renewed to support processes of sustainable development. This experience is taken up by Hopkinson, James and Van Winsum, in Chapter 6, in their discussion of the Higher Education Environmental Performance Improvement Initiative (HEEPI). This environmental management initiative aims to reduce the considerable environmental impact of those universities involved in the HEEPI partnership. Although there are 'shining' examples of good practice in individual universities, the problem for the future is how this can transform the learning cultures of the institution and the sector as a whole. In Chapter 7, Bradley and Crowther look at how engineering and eco-design at the University of Bradford has transformed curriculum development and approaches to teaching, learning and recruitment. Product design is one of the most significant, if sometimes unrecognized, aspects of our everyday lives and it is this resonance with the practical and the everyday that is informing Bradford's attempt to captivate the interest of young designers in schools and colleges. Part 1 concludes with Karen Warren's exploration of issues relating to gender, development and sustainability and the importance of eco-feminism for sustainable development and sustainable development education. In Chapter 8, Warren argues that an eco-feminist philosophical perspective 'has the potential to achieve widespread, multidimensional, cross-disciplinary and interdisciplinary goals and results in curricular transformation around sustainable development issues'. This is a challenge to all curriculum managers in the modern university and one that has significant epistemological implications.

Part 2 focuses on the manner in which certain disciplines have responded to the sustainability agenda and the ways in which they might or could develop further. In Chapter 9, Edwards offers a wide-ranging reading of architecture's professional and academic engagement with sustainability and environmental design. The historical perspective he offers enables us to place current developments within their context. The role of professional associations, research, changes to environmental law and examples of important curricular developments add force to Edwards's hope that sustainable design will one day become a cultural movement uniting 'art, science and nature'. In Chapter 10, Bamford follows on with an examination of current transport policy and planning, indicating the shortcomings of both. Indeed, a serious problem lies in the shortage of suitably qualified transport planners and the need for universities to fulfil their role in addressing this 'skills gap'. The problem, as always, is easier to diagnose than cure. Accountancy is not something that regularly figures prominently in books on education or sustainability. Cowton's upbeat contribution, in Chapter 11, shows that in a post-Enron world the education of future accountants needs to build on the work of those committed individuals who do actually make a difference. If the profession viewed sustainability as important, argues Cowton, 'then it seems highly likely that university curricula would soon fall into line'. Baimbridge's discussion of economics in Chapter 12 shows that growth is the dominant principle in the minds of mainstream economists. This is not to deny the importance of those who have challenged the dominant paradigm; but it does suggest that the problem for those who wish to 'mainstream sustainability' is the discipline's defining conceptual orthodoxy and its money-orientated quantitative methodology to which most economists subscribe.

Social policy is the subject of Huby's contribution in Chapter 13. After exploring the nature of social policy as an academic subject, she argues that an understanding of the linkages between social and environmental issues is essential in achieving social justice and political democracy. She writes that 'there is a need to ensure that students in higher and further education are aware of the importance of environmental protection for social welfare'.

In Chapter 14, Smith, Donnelly and Parker explore the various connections of sociology to sustainable development, showing that with the discipline's increasing 'dispersal and diffusion' this task is by no means straightforward. The central part of the chapter is devoted to an examination of a number of key textbooks designed to introduce undergraduates to sociology. Their conclusions are not terribly heartening. The problem lies, perhaps, as much with sociologists and our system of education as with sociology itself.

Another central social science discipline is reviewed by Garner, in Chapter 15, who notes that development, environmental politics, environmental public policy and Green political thought are present in many undergraduate and postgraduate politics programmes. Garner's analysis concludes that 'the future of the politics of sustainable development within academia is now assured'.

Of all the disciplines, geography seems to be well known for continually reinventing itself and is ostensibly closer to sustainability issues than many others. In Chapter 16, McManus starts by stating that geography is an 'ideal discipline' for the academic advancement of sustainable development. His conclusion is that this ideal has yet to be realized. Perhaps this is because critics within the discipline perceive much of the literature about sustainable development as lacking in rigour, and geography itself as essentially divided into the physical and human, which does not allow for connective concepts – such as sustainability – to take root easily. Finally, Part 2 ends with a discussion of philosophy, a key discipline within the humanities and the production of knowledge as a whole. In Chapter 17, Palmer offers a view on the contribution of philosophy to the developing understanding of sustainability and the problems faced by philosophers who seek to secure a place for sustainability in the discipline. Unfortunately, academic philosophers seem to be experiencing a double bind – criticized for being too abstract and conceptual by practitioners and policy-makers and for being insufficiently rigorous by their colleagues, who tend work in more technical or traditional areas. Palmer concludes by noting that 'the idea of sustainability is not sacred, good beyond question'; but neither is it something that can simply be ignored or dismissed.

In Chapter 18, Cullingford concludes by offering a powerful critique of current HE practice. Sustainability, he writes, is 'an inescapable dilemma of our time, a matter of study and reflection, and a challenge to action'. The subject of sustainability and of HE is, or rather should be, about 'the sustainability of the human spirit as well as the environment'. The underlying message of this book is that on both counts our universities could do better.

REFERENCES

Bate, J (2000) *The Song of the Earth*, London, Picador

Bosselmann, K (2001) 'University and Sustainability: Compatible Agendas?', *Educational Philosophy and Theory*, vol 33, no 2, pp167–186

Bowers, C (2001) 'How Language Limits Our Understanding of Environmental Education', *Environmental Education Research*, vol 7, no 2, pp141–151

Calder, W and Clugston, R M (2002) 'US Progress Toward Sustainability in Higher Education', in Dernbach, J C (ed) *Stumbling Toward Sustainability*, Washington, DC, Environmental Law Institute

Clugston, R M, Calder, W and Cocoran, P B (2002) 'Teaching Sustainability with the Earth Charter', in Filho, W L (ed) *Teaching Sustainability at Universities: Towards Curriculum Greening*, Franfurt, Peter Lang

Earth Charter (2000), available at www.earthcharter.org/files/charter/charter.pdf

Field, J (2000) *Lifelong Learning and the New Social Order*, Stoke on Trent, Trentham Books

Foster, J (2001) 'Education as Sustainability', *Environmental Education Research*, vol 7, no 2, pp153–165

Foster, J (2002) 'Sustainability, Higher Education and the Learning Society', *Environmental Education Research*, vol 8, no 1, pp35–41

Gibbons, M, Limoges, C, Nowotny, H, Schwartzman, S, Scott, P and Trow, M (1994) *The New Production of Knowledge: The Dynamics of Science and Research in Contemporary Societies*, London, Sage

Giddens, A (1990) *The Consequences of Modernity*, Cambridge, Polity

Heifitz, R A (1994) *Leadership Without Easy Answers*, Cambridge, Mass, Harvard University Press

Ho, M-W (2000) *Genetic Engineering: Dream or Nightmare*, London, Continuum

Sale, K (1996) *Rebels Against the Future*, London, Quartet Books

Stables, A and Scott, W (1999) 'Environmental Education and the Discourses of Humanist Modernity: Redefining Critical Environmental Literacy', *Educational Philosophy and Theory*, vol 31, no 2, pp145–155

Stables, A and Scott, W (2002) 'The Quest for Holism in Education for Sustainable Development', *Environmental Education Research*, vol 8, no 1, pp53–60

Sterling, S (2001) *Sustainable Education: Revisioning Learning and Change*, Totnes, Green Books

Talloires Declaration, available www.ulsf.org

Toyne, P (1993) *Environmental Responsibility: An agenda for Further and Higher Education (The Toyne Report)*, London, HMSO

Part 1

Chapter 2

Sustainability and Higher Education

Cedric Cullingford

It is a symptom of our time that any suggestion that universities are in a state of crisis is dismissed as absurd. Universities proliferate – new ones are founded and student numbers increase. They are major employers and are seen by governments as not only necessary, but crucial in the competition for wealth creation. There are few articles and fewer books that question the role and purpose of the modern university. Suggestions of doubt are not only discussed, but are significantly and tellingly followed by the question of which university the person who challenges the system is from, carrying the assumption that some kind of vindictive recrimination will follow. Universities are both in competition with each other and subject to external control, which has a profound psychological effect.

There was a time when books with titles such as *The Crisis of the Modern University* were almost commonplace. That was a sign of comparative complacency and certainty that people had time to contemplate and weigh up what place universities have in society as a whole in the notion of culture and civilization. If universities thrive, they are doing so in particular ways. They are, with their science parks and industrial links, a central part of the modern economy. Their students are primed for employment, like an investment; their alumni then give the richer universities even more. In such universities with such outputs, there is little doubt and even less questioning. In an age of presentation of the centrality of marketing, universities play their part. There is no place for any hints of disturbance.

The modern university is part of the ethos of the time. Universities from their earliest foundations have always reflected their wider societies and their purpose has evolved as societies have evolved. The dominating motif of Newman's (1873) 'idea of a university', with its moral ideal of the disinterested pursuit of truth that combines human understanding with knowledge, has long since faded away, like the dominance of the classics. While new subjects have evolved over the years, the presiding concern for universities in the early modern age remained that of scholarship and accumulating wisdom for its own sake. The idea of scholarship has been, in turn, gradually overcome by the idea of research – as exemplified by the PhD, which is at once an initiation into an elite, an original contribution to knowledge and a sign of capacity to undergo more research. For many years British universities resisted the doctorate – a 'continental' invention – on the grounds that it obstructed the core university activities of scholarship and teaching. It is only during the later half of the 20th century that research, particularly in the sciences, has become the defining characteristic of academics.

Research into any subject has all kinds of connotations, especially when it is part of an assessment exercise or dependent on contracts. One reason that the notion was resisted in British universities was that research can either be carried out for its own sake, for furthering the general scholarship and human understanding, or it can be a means to an end, the end being, essentially, financial. There is money in research and this is where the emphasis now lies. Contracts bring income and the research findings can be even more lucrative. Oxford, the home of lost causes, now boasts a significant number of millionaires who have made their money by exploiting their academic research. What is noteworthy about this is the fact that instead of possible criticism, such entrepreneurship is praised. This seems to be what universities are now for. Science parks and industrial links emphasize the commercial base. Those universities that exploit their alumni most lucratively are deemed to be the most successful.

This conception of the modern university – selling products, obsessed with income and responsive to the wishes of government – might be the product of natural development. The question is whether such a style of operation is a result of how universities see themselves or whether it has been foisted onto them. As with other institutions, there is increasing use of external inspection. No longer are universities 'secret gardens'. In matters of accountability and measurable outcomes, they are also put into 'league tables', ranked against each other not only in scholarly esteem but paraded year by year before the general public. Academic superciliousness has always been with us: 'Where did you go to university? Oxford? Ah. . .good and what did you read? Engineering? Oh dear.' Never before, however, has superciliousness become a matter of policy.

The question remains regarding why universities have changed. One argument would be that the expansion of student numbers inevitably changes the ways in which the universities operate. The resource base per capita per student has been deeply eroded. Years ago the vice chancellors of British universities were asked by the government of the time what would happen if there were a 1 per cent cut in their income. All but one replied that it would mean the end of civilization as we know it – days in which the notion of civilization could still be contemplated. The financial cuts since then are well known. Universities continue to operate, albeit differently; but such change to the fame and ethos of universities cannot simply be ascribed to money.

One of the greatest changes to universities is the focus of control. In the Robbins report of 1963, the foundation of the argument rested on the independence of universities from external control, even if they were financed by the state. The report resulted in the University Grants Committee, which was deliberately created in order to isolate universities from political control and interference. The Educational Reform Act of 1988 swept all that away, to be replaced by a 'command structure' of direct control. This control is manifested in ways that are sometimes subtle and pervasive, sometimes contradictory and sometimes immediate. There is a Quality Assurance Agency that inspects all aspects of what is taught, or rather the way in which what *should* be taught is presented, invoking the axiom that 'if it is not written down, it did not take place'. The agency ostensibly enters places that Her Majesty's Inspectors were afraid to tread. Instead of teaching, the lecturers spend their hours justifying what they would have taught had they had the time to do so.

The Quality Assurance Agency is just one of the symbols of external control and is the first step towards a national curriculum for Higher Education (HE). There are many parallels with what has happened to schools. The emphasis on outside control; the league tables; the details of what should be taught and how it should be taught, as in the literacy flows (let alone the constant inspections); the naming and shaming; and the special measure that allows a weak institution to be taken over – all of these could be harbingers of what will happen to universities, whatever the rhetoric of privatization. There are many signals that suggest that universities should be prepared for what is to come. The curriculum for initial teacher education (or 'training' as the government tellingly prefers to call it), which is a part of many universities' portfolios, is already out of university control. The detailed benchmarks illustrate the centralized control. Research assessment exercises merely confirm the acceptance of central rules and the ability to present marketable cases to those in control. The agencies, ostensibly independent of government, are, in fact, no more independent of government than a supplier to a large supermarket.

Against the Robbins report principle, we are confronted with the fact of government control. The principle of the independence of universities has been broken down. If the freedom of the press were challenged, or the independence of the judiciary, there might be an outcry; yet the universities seem pusillanimous in having acquiesced in this. They have accepted their loss of power and the erosion of their status as easily as they have submitted to the decimation of salaries (chief executive apart) compared to other professions.

Contradictions and ambiguities regarding the nature of universities abound. They are presented as public companies, while ostensibly being privatized. They are large local employers, yet produce products for the national stage. They encourage private and personal initiatives and at the same time do so in the name of the collective good. They are at once cajoled into recruiting more students and then punished for doing so. They are, almost simultaneously, vilified for being too elitist and not elitist enough. They are encouraged to be entrepreneurial and independent, acting as a privatized company, and at the same time publicly accountable.

All of these contradictions and many more restrict the possibilities of even thinking about the purpose of universities. That appears to be a luxury long since past, given the 'pressures' of all of the regulatory forces. Their flourishing and their struggle to survive seem to go hand in hand. As long as they do their job and are essentially compliant, they will survive in some form or another. The means of achieving such regulatory submission is not just a matter of manipulating the purse strings, but also manipulating the league tables. If anyone should question this, his or her university is singled out for inspection. League tables can become a weapon with which to single out the awkward as well as the weak. Compliance is the only reward.

This picture of universities, recognized by those from within and taken for granted in the public mind, should be put into context. Universities and their sense of purpose change according to the times in which they are set. This is reflected in the official language of accountability and private enterprise, of competition and efficiency, all reflecting the projected public image of self-assertion and control, whether they represent reality is another matter.

The consequence of these circumstances of the time are rarely considered in the debate about the state of universities. The introduction of direct State control in 1989 and the shock of 11 September 2000 are reminders of some of the profound questions that challenge previous assumptions about universities as private guardians of unchanging standards. Universities in the Western world have had to confront deeper challenges than state control. On the one hand, they continue to thrive in an atmosphere of complacency. The output of students, publications and patents abounds. They are part of multifarious communities, both local and international, and represent networks of scholars and entrepreneurs. Those who know how to use the available systems thrive. On the other hand, they feel themselves beleaguered by outside events and by external control. They cannot be in isolation from world events but expect genuine independence. The question is whether this is what universities are for?

Let us remind ourselves why anyone should have the temerity to raise such an issue. Earlier generations were concerned with answering profound questions. The place of universities was to help deal with the most important issues of the day, those that affected everyone, even if only the educated could properly attend to them. Most of the issues, then, were religious and the answers, to some extent, were prescribed. Any scholarship was essentially there to address the big issues of the time, rather than pursued for its own sake. Currently, there are careers to be made from knowledge, and new knowledge abounds. Instead of being driven by causes, we are being pulled by new forms of communication and the power of new technology. One of the most often employed truisms of the day concerns the speed, as well as the inevitability, of change; but little attention is paid to what change is for or what it might lead to. We are so caught up in the generation and assimilation of knowledge that we have little chance to pause. New techniques continue to surpass and supplant earlier ones until the only means of survival is to limit the amount of knowledge that we are willing to receive. This is called specialism. A university, as the term implies, was once concerned with sharing knowledge, with bringing different disciplines together. Today, the hegemony of subjects appears to be stronger than ever. Specialism is not only based on self-protection but on self-interest. There is no career to be made in crossing subject boundaries. It is important to mark out a particular territory and to create a personal network. The 69 subjects that are entered in the assessment competitions are a result of the judgement of individuals who rely on the networks of their own particular specialism. In these conditions the use of language is as much a way of asserting control over a field as a means of communication. Despite current means of communication, the secret of success is in creating new boundaries of discipline and creating an exclusive area of study. Those disciplines that not only appear to connect to others but have practical outcomes are the least fashionable. Those that try to do good for its own sake, such as education, seem to strike an atavistic fear of upsetting the normal scholarly rules of competition.

In such a scenario the major questions about the purpose of universities remain unanswered. The holocaust of World War II brought out new insights into the bestiality of mankind, even in the most developed of cultures. Like a tragedy, it was divided into parts, with an overriding theme of self-destruction and inescapable inhumanity. However, at the dying of the war, there was certain knowledge that life would, despite the terrors, continue and that there would be another – perhaps more humane – generation to follow.

We cannot rely anymore on the myth of ontological security. We have the means of mass destruction. We are constantly reminded by the media of the organized collective murder in the Middle East, at one moment, in Africa at another, in New York the next. The very means of power creates the possibility of conflagration. One form of power depends upon deliberate political decisions. The other form is more subtle and slowly destroys the shared trust on which normal living depends. Whatever the scientific arguments about the causes of, for example, global warming and the depletion of the ozone layer, as well as the environmental uncertainties of growing genetically modified food, no one doubts the capacity of human beings to manipulate their environment – although this fact has still not been properly imbibed within the public consciousness. The consequences of everyday behaviour on the environment are more subtle – though no less devastating, in the long term – than environmental disasters such as Chernobyl.

The problem with the notion of sustainability is that it has become a cliché. This is one of the reasons why there is so much disagreement in defining the term: it is open enough to give room for intellectual manoeuvre; but it has also become part of a politically correct mannerism in which different groups misuse the term in a way that tends to de-legitimize the resonance of the idea. We live in an age of cliché in which 'spin' – that notion of self-presentation which becomes a goal in itself – replaces reality. Here, everything depends upon how you justify what you would do if you had the time to do it. When phrases such as 'robust, sustainable, lifelong agenda-setting' trip off the political tongue, all kind of legitimate intellectual ideas are contaminated.

At one level, the definition of 'sustainability' is very simple and moral. It means paying attention to the long-term consequences of actions and, by implication, thinking of others who might suffer from the immediacy of one's personal greed. It is usually associated with the environment, but has also been purloined as a term that is supposed to give gravitas to political action – the notion that there is a statesmanlike vision of the future covering up the concern with the immediacy of the next election. All politicians want the world on their side. Definitions are applied with political convenience. It is, to some extent, inevitable that sustainability has become a Humpty Dumpty word.

The problem is that the very significance of the idea – like globalization – has become a victim of verbal dexterity. Profound concepts, in general, have so many resonances that they result in various interpretations. What makes 'sustainability' unusual is not its propensity to generalization, but its careless application within so many contexts. It is a real problem that 'sustainability', as a word, is distasteful to many because it is frequently and clumsily misused. There are many individuals who become weary and tired of those who insist upon the importance of the idea. If every politician continues to use the term freely as a mark of personal vision, but without thought as to its meaning, then they risk devaluing the term.

One of the functions of universities as centres of culture should be to guard against the exploitation of clichés, to expose the fraudulent and to remind us of the real meanings of words and the significance of concepts. This task should not be underestimated. It implies an intellectual rigour and a personal honesty that is counter to the tone of the age in which nothing legitimate is deemed to exist until it is inspected and nothing is inspected until it is made manifest in writing and so more easily accountable. The hidden, the complex, the subtle and the actual have little place in a world of mission statements, measurement and presentation. Recognizing this is not to criticize the age in which we live: it is a fact of life, even if temporary, that has profound consequences. The dangers are that in the distaste for the misuse of particular words, the very notions that they suggest become contaminated with the peculiar unrealities of 'spin'.

Let us take one example of the pervading reliance on grand statements. The sense that we live in a rapidly changing world has become such a cliché that it not only informs but justifies the greater assertions. It is no surprise that every new initiative is presented as a radically different, centrally transforming, earth-shatteringly original proposal, until it is forgotten. The world of education, generally, with its centralized control, is particularly affected by new initiatives and policies, with constant change. There is little time for evaluating initiatives such as transforming the leadership of schools, as Greenhalgh proposes:

> *A radical agenda for education is underway. By 2006, the education landscape will look very different from today. This agenda, which includes setting national standards, developing responsibility, encouraging flexibility in pay and conditions, and promising choice and contestability, requires transformational leadership in our schools.* (Greenhalgh, 2003)

One might wonder if there is anything sustainable about continual, radical transformation; but this kind of rhetoric does not invite serious scrutiny – it positively dislikes it.

We are so busy being bombarded by political preaching in the broadest sense that we have become unused to questioning. Besides, we are not given the opportunity or the time for reflection. In this way, all concepts are reduced to sound bites; since their legitimacy cannot be questioned for lack of time, they become the playthings of politicians. There is always a danger that a universal concern, such as religion, will become an excuse for pathological extremes. 'Sustainability' is subject to such wild interpretations as the immediate end of the world, as we know it, or to a constant problem, such as food production, that mankind always manages to solve with comparative equanimity. It is no wonder, then, that sustainability has been distorted into cliché, especially given the level of debate that surrounds it and the propensity of the media to use exaggerated discourse.

The more important reason for the misuse of the term sustainability lies in its very significance. Environmentally, the world is under threat and the potential disasters very real. Unless there is a more powerful and shared political agenda concerning the minor catastrophes, the larger dangers – starvation, genocide and the threat posed by weapons of mass destruction – will become completely out of hand. The long-term nature of the threat to our environment creates a false sense of complacency, while day-to-day events and the urge for immediate gratification assume huge importance in people's lives: 'We live in a tragic age so we refuse to take it tragically' (Lawrence, 1932).

The global problem will not, however, go away despite the complacency and short-term obsessions of party politics. Just 30 years ago, it was received wisdom that if the rain forests continued to be logged there would be significant climate change with more volatile and extreme conditions. These warnings have been proved correct. Every year we read about the increasing size of deserts and sandstorms – for example, in northern Manclusia – and huge floods – for example, in Bangladesh. The rain that used to fall for weeks now falls in days. We then read in the *Proceedings of the National Academy of Sciences* that mankind's demand for natural resources and land is at least one fifth more than the planet can supply. The fact that resources are being used up faster than they can be regenerated confirms that we are heading towards an environmental disaster. The very repetition of the warnings and the graphic reminders of the consequences of environmental degradation through images reproduced by the media have become part of the routine of modern living. Usually, however, disasters happen elsewhere so that a phrase such as 'global warming' is interpreted as a more pleasant climate. Nevertheless, we cannot go about from day to day bearing the burden of such potential environmental disasters on such a scale. At the same time, we know that the only way to address the issues is collectively, with a sense that everyone needs to be involved in the response to moral responsibility. This is why universities are so important, symbolizing the sharing of intellectual resources and the disinterested pursuit of truth.

Sustainability is a term that arises in response to a potential environmental and human disaster. It can be a knee-jerk reaction or a genuine concern for concentrated and moral intervention. It cannot be separated from that other great concept or word of our time, 'globalization'.

The scale of the problems that face humankind is not just parochial. Although it is tempting to look at the wasting of resources in other countries as a local problem that demonstrates the failure of a particular state or regime – consider countries such as Venezuela or Indonesia that have squandered all of the advantages of their natural resources – in the end, environmental degradation affects us all.

Globalization reminds us that 'sustainability' is a moral as well as an environmental concept. We need to recognize the shared responsibility and the shared opportunities. The context in which we operate contains, after all, many opportunities. Never before have we had the means to address the issues of global poverty and natural resource depletion so effectively. Living standards have, generally, risen greatly. This shows in the increasing life span. The means for action are there and the responsibility that goes with them. The question is whether there is a collective willingness to take on the responsibility when it is easier to withdraw from intervention.

The dilemmas and the choices are real. They demand not just scientific study but detailed intellectual debate. Let us take the internet as an example. Is the worldwide web just an example of the belligerent democracy of capitalism? Is it just a symbol of the worst of Western (particularly American) culture? Or is it, on the other hand, genuine in its role of encouraging cultural interchange – a communication system that is interactive rather than purely commercial? Can it be used to expand healthcare systems to remote areas and can it assist in breaking down the barriers to treating AIDS? Does the internet actually encourage greater democratic participation, enabling disenfranchised individuals to communicate with each other, even to the extent of effecting political change in South Korea? The opportunities presented by the internet create complex dilemmas, and are often wasted. The history of the World Bank is a case in point. The dumping of external expertise on unwilling recipients and the vast generosity extended to greedy dictators suggest a lack of real attention to the consequences of action – the kind of research that any university should undertake. In spite of global interventions, furthermore, the issues of global poverty and disease remain.

The North–South divide is also becoming larger as the disparity between the rich and poor continues to increase. The great issue is that of fairness. Should one put up with the fact that it suits some people to keep others poor, just as too many governments seem to want to keep their people uneducated? If unfairness is the great issue, what can be done about it? When should intervention arise?

The 18th-century notion of the nation state developed into multifarious and virulent nationalism, suggesting that each country is sovereign and can do as it wishes. At what point, then, should nations intervene and is there a case for waging war on global terror? To what extent is the McDonaldization of the world inevitable and is it itself a form of cultural intervention? To what extent, indeed, is any extension of Samuel Smile's prerogative of 'self-help' countermanded by the necessity of state help? Polanyi (2002) argues that there is no profit for anyone in subsistence dependence. Will the rich get richer at an incrementally faster rate than the poor as a result of external aid? On coming across a newly discovered hill tribe in Papua New Guinea, has intervention already inadvertently taken place in the fact of discovery? Should they remain isolated in their past?

These are not theoretical dilemmas; nor are they insoluble, however difficult. They are the subjects that should concern all of those who are engaged in more than making money. Some might argue that anyone with the right to vote should also have the responsibility to think. Others might suggest that only the ability given by a university education confers such awareness. The overall tension is between the immediacy of making money – focusing only on profit – and the consequences of making money: the impact on all people, for good or for bad. Should universities be like businesses or is the role of universities to remind us that there is more to life than making money? Should the prevailing complacency that solutions will present themselves to the world's disparities in wealth be allowed to continue? The purely capitalist stance would suggest that even from the point of view of profit, there is a need for more consumers, for the raising of living standards and for more education.

These complex and worldwide issues should be at the heart of universities' endeavours. The previous role of universities as a civilizing force and the depository of wisdom rested on religious foundations. Since the awareness and knowledge of other religions as a result of information technology, such a basis for universities is no longer possible. There are, however, other shared values that could affect universities, and at a time of international opportunities as well as threats, universities have a choice. Universities can either eschew all moral purpose beyond making money for themselves and for their students – who, if successful will more than pay back their due through alumni associations – or may be engaged in the larger moral issues of the time.

Universities have advantages. They are centres of empirical research. They have the means to make objective analyses of issues without political intervention. They contain a variety of different disciplines and different styles of thought that could continue powerfully. They have the prerogative to apply ethical standards and see beyond financial accounts and statistics. They are, furthermore, concerned with 'culture' in the broad sense as it affects all people.

Above all, universities should be engaged in the two great issues of the time. One is the question of fairness. In the face of great poverty, not only on an international scale, but visible in the slums and suburbs that surround every university, should one turn one's back and say that this is inevitable or that it is of no particular concern? Does a sustainable future involve widening the gap between the rich and poor?

The other great issue for universities is that of the polarization between the masses and the elite. Does 'more' inevitably mean 'worse'? Universities are deeply involved in this debate. The problem is that the same forces that create the 'Balkanization' of institutions find universities divided even within themselves on the theme of separate subjects and approaches. It is as if they consisted of many separate cultures and even more layers of debate. In an ostensibly postmodern world – another term ready for scrutiny – the lack of cross-disciplinary studies verges on the absurd. Universities should focus on studying not just subjects for their own sake, but the central issues of the time. 'Sustainability' and its implications should not merely be defined within a political context but should have resonance within academia and remain at the centre of debate, engaging individuals in deeper realms of thought.

As Auden wrote:

> *The intellect, by revealing to us unsuspected relations between facts of which we have a personal and therefore emotional experience and facts of which we have a secondary awareness, enables us to feel about and therefore to be affected in our actions by the former. It widens the horizons of the heart.* (cited in Mendelson, 2002)

Conclusions

We need to remind ourselves to contemplate those things that we take for granted. When we are deeply immersed in institutions and in global issues, we tend not to look at them freshly or realize that they are part of the fabric of our individual lives. Universities seem to thrive, but are under threat. The environment, both natural and political, is equally under threat as never before.

We live in a time of cultural dissolution, the end of a shared academic culture rooted in recognized values. Our reality is provided by mass media, where we glimpse the lifestyles of a privileged few. The conveniences of communication systems and travel make the grasp on 'real culture' tenuous. In the place of shared understandings we have parochial academic exclusiveness, with separate discourses concerned with 'reflexivity' and 'deconstruction'.

There are many universities, and the number increases year by year; but the idea of what constitutes a university is evaporating. A core academic ideal is replaced by locally managed subjects, with new subjects invented as fast as dialogue between disciplines is lost. The most ephemeral of 'discourses' flourishes in the name of being up to date. The lessons of the past are systematically ignored as if all events were, at best, relative and as if the uncertainties brought in by so many fields of study, from Freud to Schoenberg, and from Auda to Einstein, are all that we are left with. The irony is that in parallel with all of this uncertainty and individualism, there is ever increasing accountability. Trust has not really been replaced by risk but by inspection.

There are big issues for universities to deal with, including the state that they are in. Higher education is fast becoming a commodity rather than a value – yet another eclectic means of knowledge-seeking. Universities are part of a 'knowledge industry', full of parochialism and the personal rejection of shared academic dialogue or a sense of purpose. What has been seemingly lost as unsustainable is the sense of universal humanism, the possibility of transcendentalism and the power of reason. One day, universities might be forced to reconsider what they have to offer in a world of global poverty, environmental degradation and uncivilized behaviour. This is the big issue of our time.

REFERENCES

Greenhalgh, R (2003) *Leading Transformation*, Nottingham, National College for School Leadership, Corporate Plan 2002/2006

Lawrence, D H (1932) *Lady Chatterley's Lover*, London, Heinemann

Mendelson, E (ed) (2002) *WH Auden: Complete Works: Prose*, vol 2, 1939–1948, Princeton, Princeton University Press

Newman, J H (1873) *The Idea of a University Defined*, London, Longman's Green

Polyani, K (2002) *The Great Transformation*, Boston, Beacon Press

Robbins Report (1963) 'Report of the Committee Appointed by the Prime Minister under the Chairmanship of Lord Robbins 1961–1963', London, HMSO, Cmd 2154

Chapter 3

Sustainability and Lifelong Learning

John Blewitt

Involuntary population movements and inter-ethnic conflicts, the failures of international aid and support for vulnerable peoples and nations, and above all the difficulties of environmental degradation and resource depletion all demand responses that transcend boundaries. [They] all – if in different ways – represent important learning challenges. Environmental problems and solutions are a good example, since this is an area in which governments have no answers that are independent of the attitudes and behaviours of individual citizens; nor can we take solutions, ready made, from expert knowledge, as the experts tend to disagree on both the causes and the answers. The knowledge economy, and reflexive individualism, are at the heart of both the problems and the solutions. If lifelong learning has no part to play in this of all areas, we might as well forget it. (Field, 2000)

LIFELONG LEARNING AND THE LEARNING SOCIETY

Lifelong learning has become the defining principle of contemporary education but has lost much of the holistic tone that characterized discussions during the 1970s. In 1972 the United Nations Educational, Scientific and Cultural Organization (UNESCO) report *Learning To Be* argued that lifelong learning cannot be reduced to a fixed content but is a process whereby human beings learn to express themselves, question the world in which they live and help to shape a democratic, safe and equitable future. 'The idea of lifelong learning is the keystone of the learning society'. The report continues:

The lifelong concept covers all aspects of education, embracing everything in it, with the whole being more than the sum of its parts. There is no such thing as a separate 'permanent' part of education which is not lifelong. In other words, lifelong education is not an educational system but the principle in which the overall organization of a system is founded, and which accordingly underlies the development of each of its component parts. (Faure et al, 1972, pp181–182)

Gelpi (1979) argued that lifelong learning should focus on human development, civic participation and empowerment. He believed that lifelong learning
needs to be continuously reviewed, informed by new research and, essentially,
emancipatory. He noted that 'the repressive forces of our society are ready to
increase the time and space given to education, but only on the condition that
it does not bring about reinforcement of the struggle of men [sic] and of peoples
for their autonomy' (Gelpi, 1979, p2). As head of the Lifelong Learning Unit at
UNESCO he feared that governmental and global economic pressures could
lead lifelong learning to marginalize some people at the expense of others,
arguing just two days before his death that the dominance of technical training
would 'kill off education'. Some years later Jacques Delors's *Learning: The
Treasure Within* (Delors, 1996) declared that *learning throughout life* would be
one of the keys to our success and survival in the 21st century. The report
presented as paramount the need to understand other people in the world and
to fashion educational opportunities around four 'pillars':

1   learning to do;
2   learning to know;
3   learning to be;
4   learning to live together.

References to self-awareness; respect for others; the environment; globalization; cultural change; people's social role in the community; and the changing
nature of work underpin the report's analyses and recommendations:

> *While humankind is increasingly aware of the threats facing its natural
> environment, the resources needed to put things right have not yet been
> allocated despite a series of international meetings, such as the United
> Nations Conference on Environment and Development (UNCED), held
> in Rio de Janeiro in 1992, and despite the serious warnings of natural
> disasters or major industrial accidents. The truth is that all-out economic
> growth can no longer be viewed as the ideal way of reconciling material
> progress with equity, respect for the human condition and respect for the
> natural assets that we have a duty to hand on in good condition to future
> generations.*
>
> *We have by no means grasped all the implications of this as regards
> both the ends and means of sustainable development and new forms of
> international cooperation. This issue will constitute one of the major
> intellectual and political challenges of the next century.* (Delors, 1996,
> p13)

Longworth and Davies (1996) identify eight changing parameters for lifelong
learning, including, among other factors: the influence of science and technology; the role of industry; global demographics; changes in the nature of
work; and environmental imperatives. Their understanding of lifelong learning attempts to cover the whole range of human experience but endorses an

individualist and instrumentalist orientation to learning which distances their prospectus from traditions of liberal adult education and collective endeavour and, to an extent, from the thinking of Gelpi and Delors. Accordingly, the individual is viewed as primarily responsible for his or her learning. Longworth and Davies (1996, p22) write that 'lifelong learning is development of human potential through a continuously supportive process which stimulates and empowers individuals to acquire all the knowledge, values, skills and understanding they will require throughout their lifetimes and to apply them with confidence, creativity and enjoyment in all roles, circumstances, and environments'. However, lifelong learning must address the changing nature of our natural environment, and sustainability issues must be kept 'constantly in the forefront of popular consciousness' (Longworth and Davies, 1996, p31). But after half a page of this they have nothing more to say to exemplify the distance between the lifelong learning and education for sustainability (EFS) discourses. Both are complementary; but there has been relatively little dialogue between them until now. Debates and practices on active citizenship, community empowerment, social capital and economic regeneration are enabling EFS to transcend its ghetto of environmental education and lifelong learning to surpass its overriding economistic preoccupations, incorporating as it does formal, non-formal and informal learning (CEC, 2000). However, much informal learning is individualized and quite personal, bound up with social and cultural changes, consumerist fashions, social identities and the consequences of post-Fordist economic restructuring (Field, 2000). It is inextricably linked to our attempts to reflexively make sense of the changes in our everyday lives, our environment and our experience of work.

Medel-Añonuevo, Ohsako and Mauch (2001) suggest the lifelong learner needs to be clearly in tune with this changing world and our place and responsibilities within it. The lifelong learner must be:

- an active and creative explorer of the world;
- a reflexive agent;
- a self-actualizing agent; and
- an integrator of learning.

In an age of super complexity and interconnectedness, much of our learning is action learning and, as such, constitutes an intervention in the world. EFS recognizes that we are no longer able to interpret the world in various ways since we must use our learning to change it and ourselves. Theorists and practitioners may develop new ecological paradigms for lifelong learning and human development; but the innovative thinking and action required to effect this occurs at a time when our education and funding systems prefer to manage pre-specified learning outcomes and 'work ready' students. This context offers a considerable but not impossible challenge to lifelong learning if our future conduct is to become ecologically sound, socially and morally just, politically empowering and economically workable. As Jucker (2002) notes, a bit of nature watching is not enough.

LEARNING TO DO

The dominant rationale of lifelong learning is to raise skill levels and enhance the knowledge base of individuals so that they may operate more effectively in a fluctuating labour market. The argument runs that globalization, rapidly changing technology, increasing financial uncertainty, economic risk and the burgeoning knowledge economy require everyone to engage in continuous work-related learning throughout their working and non-working lives. It is about developing 'human capital' and increasing the performativity and employability of future and existing workers – or, as Usher, Bryant and Johnston (1997) suggest, their *efficacy* (that is, a more advantageous positioning in the marketplace). This approach was reiterated in the UK government's 2003 White Paper *The Future of Higher Education* (DfES, 2003) with vocational Foundation Degrees becoming a major vehicle for achieving the 50 per cent widening participation target for 18 to 30 year olds and reaching groups previously absent from higher education. Critics such as Coffield (1999, 2000), Field (2000) and Cruikshank (2002) maintain that lifelong learning is actually an ideological mask for social control at a time when economic changes are polarizing society. Coffield (1999, p488) writes:

> Lifelong learning is being used to socialize workers to the escalating demands of employers, who use: 'empowerment' to disguise an intensification of workloads via increased delegation; 'employability' to make the historic retreat from the policy of full payment and periodic unemployment between jobs more acceptable; and 'flexibility' to cover a variety of strategies to reduce costs that increase job insecurity.

Furthermore, in the globalizing economy, skills are becoming as ubiquitous as knowledge and skills training may be less about gaining a competitive edge as arresting economic decline. By stressing the need for continuing skills updating, and by making learning more accessible through modularization or the creation of 'bite-size' learning opportunities, lifelong learning contributes to a growing sense of unease and uncertainty. This is worsened by the consequent fragmentation of knowledge and the decontextualization of skills development. In addition, Wolf (2002) contends that there is no simple connection between widening participating in higher education, higher attainment levels and economic growth, although the drive to widen participation in higher education among traditionally disadvantaged groups does contribute to nurturing a more sustainable and socially just society. Lifelong learning must therefore tune into other sustainable development processes that require a more balanced, ecological and holistic focus (Huckle and Sterling, 1996; Sterling, 2001).

Work-based learning (WBL) is currently challenging many universities to find new ways of working. Organizations such as Forum for the Future and initiatives such as the Sigma Project are exploring the ways in which public- and private-sector organizations can develop a management framework of actions and principles that support learning communities which 'embed sustainability into mainstream organization policy, strategy, practice and procedures'. The key principles of sustainability will then inform the continuous professional development (CPD) of business and non-business people, private- and public-sector employers and employees, university vice chancellors, administrators, lecturers and support staff. Working with 14 professional institutions, including building services, accountancy, engineering and architecture, the Professional Practice for Sustainable Development Initiative (PP4SD) has produced course material designed to direct future staff development towards sustainability issues (Martin and Hall, 2002). More generally, WBL shares with EFS many heuristic approaches to learning, including a negotiated curriculum; action and problem-based learning; holistic and generic outcomes; partnership working; mentoring; and ensuring that learning moves beyond the localized and immediate, reflective practice. Unlike in many vocational programmes, it would be inappropriate to pre-specify WBL outcomes because the tasks derived are invariably to search, enquire and discover new ways of doing business. This will develop individual and organizational 'capabilities' that integrate knowledge, skills, personal qualities and understanding to be used effectively in both familiar and 'in response to *new and changing*' circumstances (Stephenson, 2001). Having said this, accredited occupational standards in vocational sectors (for example, manufacturing, heating and ventilating) do specify skills and competencies; but they should, arguably, accommodate key sustainability principles.

The concern with *learning to do* therefore raises issues of ability, capacity and competence. The idea that the behaviour, attitudes and predisposition of learners is to act in a more ecologically sensitive manner has received attention in the Danish *'Folkskole'*. The concept of 'action competence' incorporates conscious intentionality, an awareness of the value-laden nature of action and a focus on root causes rather than on symptoms of issues or problems. The accumulation of action competencies fosters transformative learning experiences, which, over time, will build more sustainable cultures, communities, businesses and universities. As Jensen and Schnack (1994) note, simply getting a school or a business to recycle its waste is not enough. The importance lies in the learning and the future possibilities that are generated by it. The problem is whether skills development and competence is a worthwhile currency in higher education (Bennett, Dunne and Carre, 2000).

LEARNING TO KNOW

The relevance of systems thinking, global responsibility, cultural diversity and biodiversity, intergenerational and species responsibility, participation and democracy to sustainable development means that learning has implications far beyond improving employability or facilitating skill acquisition. Thinking and acting sustainably requires individuals to recognize that they are individuals only at the expense of severing connections with the wider social and natural worlds. It means thinking critically and creatively and more than tweaking established routines or existing patterns of behaviour. It means being able to connect private troubles to public issues transgressing personal, class, ethnic or neighbourhood boundaries. It means that lifelong learning must encourage an ecological literacy where the basis for 'knowing' is rooted in a series of relationships and modes of engaging with the social and natural worlds that include:

- *embodied knowing*: experiential and action orientated depending upon physical presence;
- *symbolic knowing*: mediated by conceptual understandings, including spoken language, images, media and computer-based communications;
- *embedded knowing*: procedures shaped by practical routines and technology;
- *encultured knowing*: shared understandings achieved through social relationships and participation in communities of practice (*sensu* Hamilton, 2002).

For Orr (1992), Earth-centred education nurtures 'a quality of mind that seeks out connections'. He writes:

> *The ecologically literate person has the knowledge necessary to comprehend inter-relatedness, and an attitude of care or stewardship. Such a person would also have the practical competence required to act on the basis of knowledge and feeling. Competence can only be derived from the experience of doing and the mastery of what Alisdair MacIntyre describes as a 'practice'. Knowing, caring and practical competence constitute the basis of ecological literacy.* (Orr, 1992, p92)

EFS must ensure that cognitive, affective and aesthetic dimensions of learning are not compartmentalized. An understanding of signs and symbols, metaphors and stories bind people into networks of understanding that may constitute new relationships between self and others and the natural world. Stables and Bishop (2001) argue for a strong conception of environmental literacy. They distinguish between the functional (facts), cultural (socially significant) and critical (to critique and reconfigure), proposing the environment itself is a text. A critically literate person would engage with sustainability issues holistically, reflexively interrogating their own lived experiences and actions.

An environmental or ecological literacy can be fostered in formal and informal learning environments. Following an experiment in which he found that his planning and design students rated an image of a theme park better than that of a natural wildlife habitat, Burley (2002) developed an approach to encourage (and evaluate) sustainability literacy in a formal course at the University of Michigan. Barton (2002) shows that many literacy practices exist in everyday community-based activities, constituting elements of informal learning that, at key moments, make local democracy a lived reality rather than a set of abstract principles or incomprehensible structures. His discussion of a community's attempt to prevent their local council from selling off allotments to the private sector illustrates that local everyday problems may be recognized as aspects of wider global processes. The literacy practices that inform the community's emerging understandings and actions cannot be reduced to a set of discrete individual skills for they are part of a cultural context, a community achievement and a possible future resource for people's learning. As Barton (2002, p148) writes, 'It is by understanding everyday practice and everyday learning that we can support sustainable activities.'

In his study of sustainable development literacy in Central Appalachia, Flaccavento (2002) also shows the significance of the habitual learning processes of everyday lived experience. The practice of sustainability is rarely a result of a conscious decision to change one's way of life. Rather, it emerges from a reflexive relationship between thinking about priorities and the actual experience of living in the world, of making a living and protecting the prospects of the next generation during a period of change. The informal and non-formal learning emanating from doing things differently shapes our values and 'sense of possibilities'. Flaccavento concludes:

> *Sustainable development and sustainability education are, to a large degree, based upon the sense of possibilities, specifically the possibility of alternative ways of living, working and relating. This sense of possibility must be based, first and foremost, in experience or will quickly degenerate into wishful thinking and naiveté. Sharing in the experience of a diversified organic farm, or the experience of a low-impact horse logging operation, or the experience of a table made from scrap wood and low-value lumber species all engender a sense of possibility.* (Flaccavento, 2002, p198)

People in remote rural areas or deep inside the inner city need to base their understanding of alternatives on the experience of doing, but also on the ability to recognize sound argument from false debate; sense from non-sense; science from scientism; and local knowledge from folklore or mysticism. Equally, EFS must not discard the value that certain disciplines and methods have in enabling us to go beyond our immediate sensory experiences, intuitions and prejudices. Otherwise we may not be able to envision or sense a possibility of sustainable alternatives.

The public understanding of science is an important element of EFS and lifelong learning, particularly when fear and suspicion of genetically modified foods or the power of big corporations increase distrust of science and the probity of scientists. As Wolpert (1993) writes, scientists must ensure that their views are reliable, particularly in socially sensitive areas 'to the point of over cautiousness'; in turn, the public must 'demand the evidence and critically evaluate it' (Wolpert, 1993, p163). This requires both parties to share a critical literacy and a willingness to converse. The growth of interest in popular science writing and television programmes may help to nurture these literate conversations. O'Riordan (1998) takes up the notion of a 'civic science', suggesting that interactive partnerships between scientists, resource managers and citizens is key to effecting social and environmental change. Major areas of concern may focus on natural resource limits, social and environmental justice, intergenerational responsibilities, policy-making and implementation or corporate liability arrangements. The learning that emerges through this process will be new, exploratory, critical, reflexive, and lifelong and 'life-wide'.

Science and the relationship between nature and human responsibility comprise a principle concern of EFS. The Eden Project in Cornwall is a spectacular feat of engineering, innovative design and human enterprise. It is an attempt to marry science, horticulture, sustainability and learning with spectacle, entertainment and commercial viability. Innovative approaches to informal learning aided by environmental art, 3-D installations and actor guides underpin visitors' experiences of the impressive bio-domes, with each plant and section telling a story. A concern for the precariousness of human existence and the profligacy of human culture is pervasive. The performance of the actor guides taps visitors' imaginations and emotions, re-articulating and revitalizing learning experiences in new ways, thereby creating the grounds for dialogue between scientists, horticulturalists, Green activists and themselves. As Smit (2001, pp162–164) wrote:

> *Eden would be dedicated to inspiring people to reflect on the vital role of plants and come to understand the need for a balance between, on the one hand, husbandry – growing them for our use – and, on the other, steward- ship – taking care of them on behalf of all living things.*

To this end:

> *First it is necessary to create awareness of the part we play in the natural world. Exploring the problems and potential solutions comes next. Engaging people's interest in pushing for change is a function of the first two stages, combined with convincing them that their efforts can make a difference either individually or collectively. Apathy is often a by-product of powerlessness. Empowerment can create a tiger.* (Smit, 2001, pp162– 164)

The Eden Project is quickly becoming a symbol of sustainable learning and an icon of popular culture, with an immense potential that few institutions have realized so swiftly. Too often, popular culture reinforces unsustainable habits, values and attitudes. There are exceptions, though. Lifelong educators may use films such as *Erin Brokovich* to develop an understanding of environmental and social justice in working-class and black and ethnic minority communities. Natural history television series such as David Attenborough's *Life of Mammals* inform and entertain; but cultural products may also deceive (Monbiot, 2002) unless people are also critical and ecologically literate lifelong learners.

LEARNING TO BE. . . SUSTAINABLE

Literacy also constitutes the basis for an active citizenship encompassing life skills (Hopson and Scally, 1981), global and development perspectives (Jones and Alexander, 2002) and a predisposition to engage with social, civic and environmental affairs that democratizes everyday life (van Steenbergen, 1994). Citizenship involves a set of social practices; knowledge and understanding; political and ecological literacy; moral obligations; duties; and a commitment to social justice. It is part of the UK's national curriculum, is becoming increasingly significant in post-16 learning and forms a key aspect of learning in neighbourhood renewal and community regeneration. Increasingly, sustainable development is recognized as integral to these areas (Cohen and James, 2002), and citizenship obligations and duties should infuse the whole field of lifelong learning. For example, Adult Learner's Environmental Training and Resource Project (ALERT) is a European Union project created to produce environmental education for adult learners in disadvantaged communities and, as such, helps to develop a predisposition for active citizenship (Shaw, 2002). However, active citizenship cannot develop in an intellectual, social or cultural vacuum.

If private cars are to be used less as a primary mode of transportation or as a way of communicating individual power or status, then other modes of transportation need to be valued more and be available. Using the bicycle or walking to work may certainly be healthier; but is riding a bike cool or, indeed, safe? If the comfort and modern conveniences of the car are to be substituted for the bus, tram or train, then it is important to feel good when travelling by these modes. Given a choice between a bus or tram, people tend to opt for a tram for reasons of status rather than sustainability. Some may calculate the environmental pros and cons of the two; but few people would base their decision on ethical grounds alone. This is a challenge for an ecologically grounded lifelong learning as the values of sustainability should be factored into the decision-making equation without embarrassment. Other things being equal, travelling by tram should become the rational and sustainable thing to do; but policy-makers, planners and politicians will need to learn, think and act sustainably, too, if these alternatives are to be realized. This is a challenge for the CPD requirements of professional associations and the lifelong learning strategies of university departments and partnerships.

Higher education has a responsibility to be a place where new answers can be sought, choices widened and thinking encouraged. This has traditionally distinguished HE from routine forms of vocational training, and the concept and emerging practices of sustainability offer a new and necessary heuristic. Wals and Jickling (2002) state that we do not *know* what a sustainable society will actually look like despite the many vision statements and expressions of principle. An emancipatory relationship needs to develop between HE, lifelong learning and EFS, enabling new understandings to grow and evolve. There are no recipes for this. Mental models need to be transformed, curricula need to be reviewed, problems must be posed, and confidence must be acquired in order to address both normative and practical issues. Lifelong learners need space 'to examine critiques of scientism and technical rationality, and related lifestyles' and to discover alternative ways of thinking, valuing and doing. However, Wals and Jickling (2002, p228) warn:

> *When it [sustainability] becomes an organizing principle or a predetermined end of education, it may well stifle creativity or hinder critical thinking or, worse yet, become un-educational. Focusing on sustainability provides an opportunity for accessing higher learning (epistemic development) and new ways of knowing (the paradigmatic challenge), precisely because the concept is so slippery and open to different interpretations, and so more potentially complex (involving ethical, moral, aesthetic and spiritual issues, as well as the more conventional technical, economic, social and cultural ones).*

This will involve quite a complex learning that does not require precise and predictive outcome statements. Barnett (2000) suggests a new pedagogy for super-complexity needs developing, where students engage directly with uncertainty and new frameworks for understanding. Skills learning and objective- and outcome-setting, he says, must be challenged for both assume a rigidity and a narrowing unsuited to living in a constantly changing world. Indeed, researchers on situated learning argue that many skills are context specific and are only partially transferable. What is needed is an approach to performance and sustainability learning that will enable a person to learn the skills, knowledge and procedures pertinent to other milieus. The process model of curriculum development is of special significance to lifelong learning and EFS. We learn through what we do, the way in which we do it and the environments that we inhabit and shape. Lifelong learning must offer space for creativity and assessments that enable learning to continue when problems seem immense. It must encourage a reflexive disposition, recognizing that intelligence evolves contextually and throughout life. Too great an emphasis on planned learning may squeeze out emergent outcomes that are significant to EFS, and which are, as Hussey and Smith (2002) argue, 'antithetical to good educational practice'. Knight (2001, p378) states:

> *A process curriculum should name the areas in which students will be able to make – and defend – claims [to learning]. It directs attention to, but does not specify, exactly what ought to appear as a result of learning processes applied to worthwhile content in rich learning environments/ communities.*

Lifelong learning and EFS must be integrated within the fabric of everyday life. An organization's Green transport plan, if operating effectively, should change attitudes and behaviour to private car use and buildings designed or refurbished according to high environmental standards; should provide formal and informal learning opportunities; and should have a subtle influence on the life world, life experience and conduct of individuals and groups. Meaningful learning relationships are of the utmost importance, and in the wider learning context, as Bennetts (2001) suggests, mentoring is a most valuable approach for thorough processes of reflexivity and reflection: it promotes learning that 'appears to be self-perpetuating' and deeply rooted. Indeed, the importance of work-place mentors with a keen understanding of sustainability has been recognized by a number of practitioners and is something that could figure more prominently in developing skills and capabilities.

LEARNING TO LIVE TOGETHER. . . SUSTAINABLY

Charities such as Groundwork and organizations such the Community Development Foundation are deeply involved in developing sustainable neighbourhoods and social inclusivity. Local Agenda 21 stimulated a number of community empowerment projects focusing directly on social and environmental sustainability issues (Warburton, 1998). The informal learning opportunities that these initiatives created are profoundly important aspects of much non-formal lifelong learning. When HE institutions are also directly engaged, the skills and understanding fostered among community members may facilitate widening participation. However, Mayo (2000) shows how community-based learning in area regeneration may help to increase social capital through capacity-building. This learning is often problem-focused; cooperative; transformative; invariably transdisciplinary and interconnected; creative; experiential; and 'sustainable'. When learning is long term and holistic, learners become self-directed and collaborative. A local community who sets about reclaiming land for its social or recreational use or organizes a housing project adopts a problem-based learning (PBL) methodology that may foster both active cooperation and independent thought. PBL can also be effective within the seminar room (Faulkner, 2001).

EcoCal is a household environmental assessment technique that requires limited computer skills, enabling students to calculate and evaluate their ecological footprint. Originally developed by the environmental campaigning group Going for Green, it has been widely used by community and voluntary groups. It has also been used by the Open University (OU) in its level one interdisciplinary course Working with Our Environment: Technology for a Sustainable Future. After calculating their environmental impact, students are required to consider ways of reducing it by developing a more sustainable lifestyle. Crompton, Roy and Caird (2002) state that the average OU household has an ecological footprint that needs a 60 to 70 per cent reduction to achieve sustainability. After having undertaken the course, many students changed their thinking, reviewed their personal lifestyles and discussed household environmental issues. Many planned to cut their energy consumption and alter their mode of transportation. The authors concluded that, in many cases, the course 'prompted genuine changes in attitudes and behaviour'.

Other issues central to community regeneration and sustainable development may be readily addressed through appropriate lifelong learning opportunities. The need to resolve personal, social or ethnic conflicts without resort to violence or hatred is a prerequisite for community regeneration and development in both inner city and some rural neighbourhoods. Respect for cultural difference and valuing cultural and biological diversity is a principle aspect of combating racism, xenophobia and the generalized fear of 'otherness' fed by ignorance and the privatized existence that so many of us lead and for which our formal education system prepares us. Too frequently, to be physically safe is to be locked within the compound of your gated community if you can afford it or to feel the need to incarcerate others if you can't. Moral panic focusing on paedophilia, mugging or Frankenstein foods is not confined to those without higher education qualifications or simply a figment of the opportunistic imagination of tabloid editors. It has its roots in lived experience, informal learning, and community and individual action. Facts may be difficult to come by; but the problem often lies in our capacity to make reasonable judgements or to trust others in science, government, business, education ('you are only interested in bums on seats') or even in our own communities. In the place of reasoned judgement comes a gut feeling and behaviour, values and attitudes that ostensibly offer protection and survival. The precautionary principle that informs much of sustainability thinking and practice becomes, in this context, an aversion not to risk-taking but to clear thinking and civilized conduct. Referring to working-class vigilantism on the Paulsgrove Estate in Portsmouth following *News of the World* reports on paedophiles, Thompson (2001, pp19–20) writes:

> *So far as adult learning is concerned the evidence of Paulsgrove speaks of agency and outrage on the part of the protestors – but also of ignorance. It reveals the fine line between people power and 'mob rule'. Education should not seek to cancel outrage but it can confront ignorance. If educators are not prepared to struggle alongside learners to create useful and democratic knowledge, based on reason and emotion, shaped in the context of ethical and political considerations, which link personal troubles to public issues, the local to the bigger picture, and in which everyone of us has something to learn and something to teach – then the field is left clear for the* News of the World *and their like to do their worst.*

Learning to live together involves learning to speak to and with each other. Oakshott (1989) suggests that we inhabit a world of understanding and misunderstanding. 'Doing' presupposes reflective consciousness and 'agency' postulates the capacity to act and recognize that action changes things. We need to envisage alternatives and seek to realize them if we are to be free agents. As Oakshott (1989, p37) says, a person 'is "free" not because his/her situation is alterable by an act of unconstrained "will", but because it is an understood situation and because doing is an intelligent engagement':

> *Perhaps we may think of the components of a culture as voices, each the*
> *expression of a distinct and conditional understanding of the world and a*
> *distinct idiom of human self-understanding, and of the culture itself as*
> *these voices joined. . .in a conversation – an endless unrehearsed adven-*
> *ture in which in imagination we enter into a variety of modes of under-*
> *standing the world and ourselves and are not disconcerted by the differences*
> *or dismayed by the inconclusiveness of it all. And perhaps we may*
> *recognize liberal learning as, above all else, an education in imagination,*
> *an invitation into the art of this conversation in which we learn to*
> *recognize the voices; to distinguish their different modes of utterance; to*
> *acquire the intellectual and moral habits appropriate to this conversational*
> *relationship; and thus to make our debut* dans la vie humane.
> (Oakshott, 1989, pp38–39)

Our understanding and misunderstanding of, for example, crime, community conflict, genetic modification, environmental pollution, democratic renewal, global warming, the future of work, urban regeneration and widening partici-pation are all potential topics for the necessary conversations on lifelong learning and sustainable development.

Informal educators such as Smith (1994) note that conversation is a com-plex political activity involving the possibility of change and a configuration of qualities that must be nurtured throughout the learning process – mutual trust, respect, a willingness to listen, and the risking of cherished opinions and learning that leads to informed committed action. In order to be authentic and sincere, conversations need to be cooperative and substantially open, like good learning in universities. As Wolfe (2001) notes, it is through conversation that we 'turn around our ideas and experiences with each other' and 'entertain the possibilities of future experiences'. Good conversations are essentially 'genera-tive' with logic, reason, emotion and imagination all having roles to play:

> *At our best, through conversation we seem able to free our own particular*
> *ideas and thinking from the existing limits of our current understanding.*
> *In such instances, real, human participants build upon each other's*
> *contributions, acknowledging or refining the part each plays so that they*
> *work together with an increasingly shared resource.* (Wolfe, 2001, p129)

Higher education and lifelong learning must develop a culture in which actual and metaphorical conversations about sustainability take place. This view of education requires a cooperative and collaborative approach to learning that is forward looking and may take place in the classroom, the work place or in the community. It may be delivered on a flexible or distance basis via a creative and critical appropriation of e-learning methods and technologies. Following Collins et al (2002), cooperative learning may be understood as teachers and learners working together towards a common end, whereas collaborative learning involves each participant's views and actions, helping to decide or influence the nature of the learning outcome. Collaborative learning exhibits many aspects of good learning – namely, 'active and interactive participation, intrinsic motivation, rich communication, trusting relationship and the potential to transform thinking and lives' (Collins et al, 2002, p122). Obviously, collaborative learning requires a willingness or disposition to collaborate, which may be reinforced by the process and experience of the learning itself. Collaborative learning involves confronting issues of power and authority, as well as working across differences and boundaries relating to the problem, task or topic at issue:

> *Thus a willingness to collaborate incorporates a readiness for peers to grant and accept authority over each other's work – for example, in terms of peer appraisal. Collaborative learning can also challenge the traditional view of teachers' authority and the way in which that authority is exercised. In this way collaborative learning can be about revitalizing democracy.* (Collins et al, 2002, p112)

Like collaborative learning, EFS is inherently social; but current forms of lifelong learning involve approaches that, as Field (2000) notes, commodify learning – frequently isolating the learner/consumer. Networked communities may emulate aspects of the face-to-face interaction, with computer technology and software offering virtual learning environments that may provide access to unimaginable, but frequently unmanageable, amounts of information and data. Bowers (1995) argues that computers facilitate culturally specific ways of knowing in their design, logic system and language that become privileged, thereby discounting forms of tacit or contextual knowledge that are acquired elsewhere at other times. 'Memory', 'access' and 'intelligence' are the iconic metaphors of computer-mediated learning. He suggests that we are beginning to see ourselves in the same ways as we see computers and that to question computers is to question the very nature of human progress. Indeed, many aspects of lower levels of information and computer technology (ICT) learning aim to overcome resistance to using computers by building technical skills, personal confidence and unquestioning trust in the technology. The ICT culture reinforces a data-based process model of thinking that is rooted within a modernist paradigm, but which, in effect, offers only a partial technological fix to realizing the goals of employability, environmental sustainability and democratic participation.

Computers are valuable learning tools; but the technology constitutes one mode of understanding among many. ICT may enhance learning by creating 'communities of practice' and aspects of social learning that may also, eventually, become distributed communities of learning. Wellman (2001) sees ICT as developing new types of communities that transcend locality and neighbourhood, which being rooted in a 'cognitive homogeneity' offers possibilities of greater diversification than found in 'real life' communities. Green and Keeble (2001) and Liff and Steward (2001) show that ICT can be a focus for social inclusion within a geographical community by embedding aspects of students' everyday experience in the technology itself and basing learning fundamentally on interest, interaction and collaboration. However, as Dabinett (2000) shows, acquiring 'know-what' or 'know-how' skills does not alone empower or develop communities. Empowerment requires the exploitation of technology and information through the ownership and control/regulation of at least part of the networks, linking up with mainstream activities, funding regimes and service delivery. The development and application of a critical literacy is also needed to make sense of social and power relationships, which to some extent resonates with Illich's (1973) discussion of learning relationships, networks and webs:

> *Things are basic resources for learning. The quality of the environment and the relationship of a person to it will determine how much he learns incidentally. Formal learning requires special access to ordinary things, on the one hand, or, on the other, easy and dependable access to special things made for educational purposes.* (Illich, 1973, pp81–82)

Lifelong educators therefore need to be constantly mindful of Illich's question: 'What kinds of things and people might learners want to be in contact with in order to learn?'

LEARNING FOR THE FUTURE

In a world that is rapidly changing and whose ecosystems are in danger of collapse, skills and knowledge rapidly become obsolete. Learners will draw lessons from experience, assimilate new ideas and develop new practices and skills as they pragmatically revise conceptual frameworks. Experience is not simply a given upon which knowledge is based for it can be invested with a plurality of significant meanings. People are enabled through EFS to 'theorize' and reflexively make sense of their experience in order to develop new ways of living, working and thinking. For the present, many experiences that gain credit points or meet performance or funding targets are not necessarily important in achieving sustainability. Future lifelong learners need to fashion generative learning communities to effect sustainable change. The individual cannot be the primary locus: the realization of sustainability principles requires collective endeavour. Gilchrist (2001, p109) states:

> *A sense of community is not simply a sentimental figment of our collective imagination. It emerges from the real experience of being connected into the flow of energy and ideas that characterize robust and vibrant networks. People who are actively engaged in social networks are able, individually and collectively, to learn from experience and to adapt to changing circumstances.*

Education for sustainability should remind lifelong learners of the linkages between the human and natural worlds. Widening participation is one aspect of lifelong learning; but what is learned, how learning is organized and its implications for future conduct are also of crucial importance. Education for sustainability needs to bind emancipatory politics (combating exploitation, injustice, oppression and exclusion) with life politics (genetic modification, health, diet, cloning and the environment) by developing human capabilities, a critical ecological literacy and an ethic of responsibility. It requires us to change our approach to consumption, business and the economy (Korten, 1995) to consider other peoples and species; but if a paradigm change is to occur in lifelong learning, we must first experience it at home and in school. Groundwork's RMC Greenlink scheme shows children waste minimization aspects of local industry. Evaluative research (RMC Greenlink, 2002) indicated a 26 per cent increase in six key elements of a child's environmental learning cycle – awareness, concern, action, knowledge, understanding and responsibility – which corresponds to major strands within the active citizenship elements of the UK's national curriculum. Green schools offer a platform for a new type of learning, including an active engagement with parents and adults in their local communities. Universities committed to lifelong learning must learn from these Green schools and start thinking and acting in similar ways. Some are already doing it; but the dead weight of past generations weighs heavy. One thing is for certain though, as Einstein once said: 'The significant problems we face cannot be solved at the same level of thinking we were at when we created them'. It is salutary to recall that in the past highly educated people have caused a great deal of damage to our planet. We therefore need to redefine lifelong learning and re-articulate what is meant by a *learning society*. Edwards, Ranson and Strain (2002, p533) write:

> *It is the development of reflexivity, the capacity to develop critical awareness of the assumptions that underlie practices, especially the meta-cognitive, interpretative schemata that constitute worlds, which we should see as central to an adequate theory of lifelong learning. . . To develop a critical form of lifelong learning entails the capacity to develop and sustain reflexivity. Such learning should engender the potential for individuals and communities to (en)counter the trajectories of their lives and to enhance their capabilities; not simply to adapt to the (dis)locations of the contemporary condition, but also to engage with them.*

REFERENCES

Barnett, R (2000) 'Reconfiguring the University', in Scott, P (ed) *Higher Education Reformed*, London, Falmer Press

Barton, D (2002) 'Literacy practices in Local Activities: An Ecological Approach', in Hautecoeur, J-P (ed) *Ecological Education in Everyday Life*, Toronto, University of Toronto Press

Bennett, N, Dunne, E and Carre, C (2000) *Skills Development in Higher Education and Employment*, Buckingham, Oxford University Press

Bennetts, C (2001) 'Lifelong learners: in their own words', *International Journal of Lifelong Education*, vol 20, no 4, pp272–288

Bowers, C A (1995) *Educating for an Ecologically Sustainable Culture*, Albany, SUNY

Burley, J B (2002) 'Sustainability Legibility: a Michigan State University Experience', Paper presented to *An International Think Tank on Education for Sustainability*, Earth Centre, Doncaster

CEC (2000) *Memorandum on Lifelong Learning*, Brussels, Commission of the European Communities

Coffield, F (1999) 'Breaking the consensus: lifelong learning as social control', *British Educational Research Journal*, vol 25, no 4, pp479–499

Coffield, F (2000) 'Lifelong learning as a lever on structural change? Evaluation of White Paper: *Learning to Succeed* – a new framework for post-16 learning', *Journal of Education Policy*, vol 15, no 2, pp237–246

Cohen, J and James, S (eds) (2002) *Learning to Last: Skills, Sustainability and Strategy*, London, LSDA

Collins, J, Harkin, J and Nind, M (2002) *Manifesto for Learning*, London, Continuum

Crompton, S, Roy, R and Caird, S (2002) 'Household ecological footprinting for active distance learning and challenge of personal lifestyles', *International Journal of Sustainability in Higher Education*, vol 3, no 4, pp313–323

Cruikshank, J (2002) 'Lifelong learning or re-training for life: Scapegoating the worker', *Studies in the Education of Adults*, vol 34, no 2, pp140–155

Dabinett, G (2000) 'Regenerating communities in the UK: Getting plugged into the information society?', *Community Development Journal*, vol 35, no 2, pp157–166

Delors, J (1996) *Learning: The Treasure Within*, Paris, UNESCO

DfES (2003) *The Future of Higher Education*, HMSO, London

Edwards, R, Ranson, S and Strain, M (2002) 'Reflexivity: towards a theory of lifelong learning', *International Journal of Lifelong Education*, vol 21, no 6, pp525–536

Faulkner, V (2001) 'Making multicultural education "real"', *Teaching in Higher Education*, vol 6, no 4, pp473–485

Faure, E et al (1972) *Learning To Be: The World of Education Today and Tomorrow*, Paris, UNESCO and London, Harrap

Field, J (2000) *Lifelong Learning and the New Social Order*, Stoke on Trent, Trentham Books

Flaccavento, A (2002) 'Sustainable Development Literacy in Central Appalachia', in Hautecoeur, J-P (ed) *Ecological Education in Everyday Life*, Toronto, University of Toronto Press

Gelpi, E (1979) *A Future for Lifelong Learning*, Manchester, Department of Adult and Higher Education

Gilchrist, A (2001) 'Working with Networks and Organisations in the Community', in Richardson, L D and Wolfe, M (eds), *Principles and Practice of Informal Education: Learning through Life*, London, Routledge/Falmer

Green, E and Keeble, L (2001)'The Technology Story of a Woman's Centre: A Feminist Model of User-centred Design', in Keeble, L and Loader, B D (eds), *Community Informatics: Shaping Computer-mediated Social Relations*, London, Routledge

Hamilton, M (2002) 'Sustainable Literacies and the Ecology of Lifelong Learning', in Harrison, R, Reeve, F, Hanson, A and Clarke, J (eds) *Supporting Lifelong Learning: Volume 1, Perspectives on Learning*, London, Routledge

Hopson, B and Scally, M (1981) *Lifeskills Teaching*, Maidenhead, McGraw-Hill

Huckle, J and Sterling, S (eds) (1996) *Education for Sustainability*, London, Earthscan

Hussey, T and Smith, P (2002) 'The Trouble With Learning Outcomes', *Active Learning in Higher Education*, vol 3, no 3, pp220–233

Illich, I (1973) *Deschooling Society*, Harmondsworth, Penguin

Jensen, B and Schnack, K (1994) 'Action Competence as an Educational Challenge', in Jensen, B and Schnack, K (eds) *Action and Action Competences as Key Concepts in Critical Pedagogy*, Copenhagen, Royal Danish School of Educational Studies

Jones, K N and Alexander, T (2002) *The Global Learning Challenge*, London, Development Education Association

Jucker, R (2002) '"Sustainability? Never heard of it!" Some basics we shouldn't ignore when engaging in education for sustainability', *International Journal of Sustainability in Higher Education*, vol 3, no 1, pp8–18

Keeble, L and Loader, B D (eds) (2001) *Community Informatics: Shaping Computer-mediated Social Relations*, London, Routledge

Liff, S and Steward, F (2001) 'Communities and Community e-gateways: Networking for Social Inclusion', in Keeble, L and Loader, B D (eds), *Community Informatics: Shaping Computer-mediated Social Relations*, London, Routledge

Longworth, N and Davies, W K (1996) *Lifelong Learning*, London, Kogan Page

Knight, P T (2001) 'Complexity and curriculum: A process approach to curriculum-making', *Teaching in Higher Education*, vol 6, no 3, pp369–381

Korten, D C (1995) *When Corporations Rule the World*, London, Earthscan

Martin, S and Hall, A (2002) 'Sustainable Development and the Professions', Paper presented to An International Think Tank on Education for Sustainability, Earth Centre, Doncaster

Mayo, M (2000) 'Learning for active citizenship: Training for and learning from participation in area regeneration', *Studies in the Education of Adults*, vol 32, no1, pp22–35

Medel-Añonuevo, C, Ohsako, T and Mauch, W (2001) *Revisiting Lifelong Learning for the 21st Century*, UNESCO

Monbiot, G (2002) 'Planet of the Fakes', *The Guardian*, 17 December 2002

Oakshott, M (1989) 'A Place of Learning', in Fuller, T (ed) *Michael Oakshott on Education*, New Haven, Yale University Press

O'Riordan, T (1998) 'Civic Science and the Sustainability Transition', in Warburton, D (ed) *Community and Sustainable Development*, London, Earthscan

Orr, D W (1992) *Ecological Literacy: Education and the Transition to a Postmodern World*, Albany, SUNY

RMC Greenlink Report (2002) *Education, Industry and Sustainable Development*, available at www.groundwork.org.uk

Shaw, J (2002) Adult learners' Environmental Training and Resources Project: A European Partnership, in Field, J (ed) *Promoting European Dimensions in Lifelong Learning*, Leicester, NIACE

Smit, T (2001) *Eden*, London, Corgi

Smith, M K (1994) *Local Education: Community, Conversation, Praxis*, Buckingham, Open University Press

Stables, A and Bishop, K (2001) 'Weak and strong conceptions of environmental literacy: Implications for environmental education', *Environmental Education Research*, vol 7, no 1, pp89–97

Sterling, S (2001) *Sustainable Education: Re-visioning Learning and Change*, Totnes, Green Books

Thompson, J (2001) *Rerooting Lifelong Learning: Resourcing Neighbourhood Renewal*, Leicester, NIACE

Usher, R, Bryant, I and Johnston, R (1997) *Adult Education and the Postmodern Challenge: Learning Beyond the Limits*, London, Routledge/Falmer

van Steenbergen, B (ed) (1994) *The Condition of Citizenship*, London, Sage

Stephenson, J (2001) 'Ensuring a Holistic Approach to Work Based Learning: The Capability Envelope', in Boud, D and Solomon, N (eds) *Work-based Learning: A New Higher Education?* Buckingham, Oxford University Press

Wals, A E J and Jickling, B (2002) 'Sustainability in higher education: From doublethink and newspeak to critical thinking and meaningful learning', *International Journal of Sustainability in Higher Education*, vol 3, no 3, pp221–232

Warburton, D (ed) (1998) *Community and Sustainable Development*, London, Earthscan

Wellman, B (2001) 'Physical Place and Cyberplace: The Rise of Networked Individualism', in Keeble, L and Loader, B D (eds), *Community Informatics: Shaping Computer-mediated Social Relations*, London, Routledge

Wolf, A (2002) *Does Education Matter? Myths About Education and Economic Growth*, London, Penguin Books

Wolfe, M (2001) 'Conversation', in Richardson, L D and Wolfe, M (eds), *Principles and Practice of Informal Education: Learning through Life*, London, Routledge/Falmer

Wolpert, L (1993) *The Unnatural Nature of Science*, London, Faber

Chapter 4

An Analysis of the Development of Sustainability Education Internationally: Evolution, Interpretation and Transformative Potential

Stephen Sterling

INTRODUCTION

In little more than three decades, sustainability education has emerged and evolved from marginal beginnings to claim the necessity and to indicate the possibility of fundamental change in our collective view of the purposes and nature of education and learning – a change which, if made effective, would be critical to the quality of life of future generations. Yet, it is clear that such profound change is by no means assured. While the progress of environmental and sustainability education over the last three decades has been impressive, it also has been slowed by a degree of incoherence and constrained by a largely uncomprehending and resistant mainstream.

This chapter looks briefly at the evolution of this approach to education, and the discourse surrounding its meaning and significance. It argues that – in order to address current conditions of unsustainable lifestyles, systemic complexity and uncertainty – a change of educational culture is required that builds on and goes beyond the traditions of 'environmental education' and subsequent expressions of sustainability education. This culture may be referred to as 'sustainable education', a broad term that suggests a holistic educational paradigm concerned with the quality of relationships rather than product, with emerging rather than predetermined outcomes. This is associated with an emergent, yet fragile, 'postmodern ecological worldview' that challenges the limits of modernism and transcends deconstructive postmodernism.

Box 4.1 *Use of terms*

This chapter uses the term 'sustainability education' as a catch-all to include environmental education (EE), education for sustainable development (ESD), education for sustainability (EFS) and education for a sustainable future (ESF). Beyond these terms, 'sustainable education' is used to suggest a change of educational paradigm, rather than a modification of, or to, the existing paradigm.

THE EVOLUTION OF SUSTAINABILITY EDUCATION

Many of those involved in the field view education for sustainable development (ESD) or education for sustainability (EFS) as emerging around the time of, and stimulated by, the first Earth Summit in Rio – the 1992 UN Conference on Environment and Development (UNCED). But as with any educational movement, there have been important antecedents, and an understanding of some of the threads that have lead to the current movement helps in understanding the contemporary debate and the tensions within that debate.

The beginnings of environmental education (EE) can be traced back as far as the interested researcher wishes. Some point to the influence of such figures as Locke and Rousseau, who influenced a whole lineage of educational thinkers such as Pestalozzi, Froebel, Montessori, Steiner and Dewey and who put emphasis on the learner and the learning environment, on learning by doing and participation, and on differentiated learning needs and styles. In the UK, some see Sir Patrick Geddes (1854–1933) as the father of modern environmental education. He was, perhaps, the first to make the vital link, fundamental to environmental education, between the quality of the environment and the quality of education.

Whatever the start point, if we look at the history of the movement, it is possible to discern two apparently contrary but simultaneous trends. The first is increasing *inclusivity,* and the second is *fragmentation,* or what might be termed 'coherence' and 'incoherence'. This section begins with the first trend. From the 1940s, in the UK, the main emphases were rural studies and nature studies, and this widened out during the 1950s to environmental studies, which included local history and geography. By the 1960s, interest in environmental science grew. Disinger (1983) suggests that the first use of the term environmental education was at an IUCN (International Union for the Conservation of Nature and Natural Resources) meeting in Paris in 1948. Whatever its provenance, from the late 1960s, the term began to be used increasingly, and this was reinforced in the UK by the establishment of the Council for Environmental Education in England, which first met in 1968. In the US, in 1970, a United Nations Educational, Scientific and Cultural Organization (UNESCO)/ IUCN conference adopted one of the first – and later widely adopted – definitions of EE. Whereas the dominant environmental and rural studies traditions were particularly interested in the natural environment, the new concept of EE began to be interpreted more widely. Specifically, urban studies grew as a movement championed by the Town and Country Planning Association (TCPA) education unit's *Bulletin of Environmental Education* and with it interest in social and political education as a component of the nascent idea of EE. The next critical factor was the uptake of the concept of EE at an international level, and this introduced the global dimension to the field in both conceptual and 'sphere of interest' terms. Very importantly, international endorsement, particularly through IUCN and UN organizations (UNESCO and the United Nations Environment Programme, or UNEP) during the 1970s lent considerable weight to an area that otherwise may have remained in obscurity on the margins of mainstream educational interests.

It is important to see the emergence of environmental education in context. The early 1970s saw the first wave of Western environmentalism. Landmarks here include Rachel Carson's *Silent Spring* (Carson, 1962), eco-philosopher Arne Naess's 1973 paper on deep and shallow ecology, which later gave rise to the Deep Ecology movement (Naess, 1973), and, notably, the launch of the Club of Rome's seminal report on the *Limits to Growth* (Meadows et al, 1972), which was timed to coincide with the first UN Conference on the Human Environment, held in Stockholm in 1972. The Stockholm conference was the first international conference to identify education as an important means of addressing environmental issues (Recommendation 96), and this identified role has been reiterated in various guises at international conferences and in high-level documents on environment and development over the three decades since.

Although environmental education received high-level endorsement, another important incipient movement was finding expression in some Western education systems, spurred on by the involvement of non-governmental organizations (NGOs) and aid agencies in areas such as poverty, human rights and anti-racism. Thus 'development education' arose, emphasizing empowerment, 'conscientization', participation, democratization and social action, summed up in the term 'critical pedagogy'. This movement was given impetus particularly by Freire's work in adult education in Brazil and his subsequent writing (Freire, 1972), and echoed later by writers such as Giroux (1992), who advocated the role of the 'transformative intellectual', and Fals-Borda and Rahman (1991) and Chambers (1997), who emphasized participatory action research (PAR) methodology.

Meanwhile, during the 1970s and 1980s, the boundaries of what was meant by environmental education expanded. By the 1980s, this one term encompassed environmental studies and field studies, environmental science, environmental interpretation, urban studies, heritage education, conservation education and global environmental issues education, and different interests promoted different aspects, often through separate organizations and groups. At the same time, the boundaries of environmental education became less distinct and gradually more permeable. Varying groups interested in aspects of education for change interpreted the transformative role of education differently. Hence, the spectrum of what was sometimes referred to as 'adjectival educations' included such emphases as development education, peace education, human rights education, anti-racist education and futures education, while global education made a bid to represent them all.

Within this apparent fragmentation and incoherence there was, at the same time, some growing – perhaps intuitive – sense of commonality, of parts within a greater whole. While environmental education and development education arose from separate roots and traditions, the growing equation of 'environment' and 'development'– notably first argued in the World Conservation Strategy of 1980 (IUCN, UNEP and the World Wide Fund for Nature, or WWF) – meant that the two parallel educational movements inevitably became more closely associated. This became an important trend during the 1990s as environmental education became increasingly redefined as 'education for sustainable development' and development education as 'education for global citizenship', and both were seen as sister movements. In some developing countries, however, the Western distinction between environmental education and development education was greeted with incomprehension: here, environment and development issues were widely seen as two sides of the same coin; therefore, environmental education was inevitably also development education. Meanwhile, global educators (for example, Greig, Pike and Selby, 1987) suggested that the various contemporaneous 'change educations' pointed towards an underlying common and holistic view of education. At the same time, the Brundtland Report of the World Commission on Environment and Development (WCED, 1987) put the concept of sustainable development firmly into the arena of national and international debate, and subsequently gave rise to the UNCED conference in Rio de Janeiro in 1992, which reviewed progress since the Stockholm conference held 20 years earlier.

The Brundtland Report and the Rio Summit had a profound effect on subsequent debate concerning education for change, and from 1992 the terms education for sustainability (EFS) and education for sustainable development (ESD) emerged strongly internationally. Before examining the meaning and current interpretations of these terms, it will be helpful to review the status and effect of this movement.

In some ways, the growth of interest in, and provision of, environmental and sustainability education – from a standing start somewhere around the mid 1960s – has been very impressive. Since then, there has been a modest explosion of interest in environmental education and training worldwide. Work on, for example, philosophy, research methodologies, pedagogy, curricula, resources, communication and dissemination strategies has multiplied with support from international agencies such as UNESCO-UNEP (through the International Environmental Education Programme) and IUCN (through its Commission on Education and Communication); internationally active NGOs such as WWF; intergovernmental agencies such as the European Commission (EC) and the Organisation for Economic Co-operation and Development (OECD); national government policy and strategies; national NGO programmes; and increasing academic involvement and research networks, both at national and international level.

Yet, the results of all this work and activity are widely regarded as disappointing, both in terms of effects on learners and on educational systems. First, as far as it is possible to tell, it appears that environmental education and training programmes in the formal and non-formal sectors have made some, but not a great deal of, difference to society's views or behaviour in relation to environment or sustainability issues, except to those relatively few people who have experienced excellent programmes. As UNESCO's then director-general commented at the last UNESCO international environmental education conference (held in Thessaloniki), 'Who would deny that too little has been achieved?' (Mayor, 1997, p1). Sauvé (1998, p47) notes that programmes have all too often been based on knowledge acquisition rather than the development of ethical and critically reflective competencies: 'The record is not impressive with regard to the importance of the social, environmental and educational challenges at issue'.

Second, the 'reorientation' of education towards environment and development called for and agreed in the Rio Summit's Agenda 21, Chapter 36, showed few serious signs of progress in the decade that followed. By the time of the World Summit on Sustainable Development (WSSD), held in Johannesburg in 2002, the verdict was much the same. A UNESCO report (UNESCO, 2002, p9) prepared for the WSSD notes that 'much of current education falls far short of what is required', and calls for a 'new vision' (UNESCO, 2002, p10) and 'a deeper, more ambitious way of thinking about education' (UNESCO, 2002, p8).

In the 30-year period from 1972–2002, then, we move from a limited conception of the nature and role of environmental education, through a period of conceptual expansion and logical alliance with parallel 'education for change' movements, to a call for the reorientation of education as a whole in the context of, and in the pursuit of, sustainable development. Here, then, is a paradox: the more conceptually far-reaching that the movement has become, and the more strategically ambitious, the more difficult it is for education as a whole to respond adequately.

Clearly, this difficulty is related, in part, to the daunting quality of the goals that have been associated with sustainability education. For example the UN Intergovernmental Conference on Environmental Education held in Tbilisi in 1977 stated that one of the goals of such education was to 'create new patterns of behaviour of individuals, groups and society as a whole towards the environment' (UNESCO-UNEP, 1978). Furthermore, sustainability education has not been able to make a decisive difference where it has worked from a marginalized status – that is, where the dominant conception of the purpose and goals of education (its broader context) have, as a whole, remained largely either unchanged or oriented towards economic goals. (The proposed UN Decade of Education for Sustainable Development may address this issue, to some extent.) At a deeper level, however, the problems of integrating sustainability within educational policy, theory and practice, or of educational reorientation, may be interpreted as issues of fundamental epistemology and a lack of sufficient clarity about the philosophic challenge posed by sustainability education.

Before exploring this deeper territory, it will be helpful to review, first, the debate that has surrounded the use of terms internationally, which has indicated both the perceptual and conceptual difficulties in, and richness of, the area.

THE TERMS DEBATE: EE, EFS OR ESD?

In 2002, a spontaneous internet discussion quickly sprang to life among international members of the IUCN Education Commission when one member lamented the apparent loss of 'environment' in the new 'education for sustainable development' speak. The speed with which this self-organizing debate took hold is illustrative of the degree of importance and the meaning that people attach to different terms.

There is nothing new in this phenomenon: for example, Goodson (1983) relates the tensions that the term environmental education gave rise to, particularly amongst UK geographers during the 1970s when it was first struggling to win acceptance. More latterly, the main contention has been between the terms environmental education (EE), education for sustainability (EFS) and education for sustainable development (ESD). Other terms include education for a sustainable future (ESF) and sustainability education. With the introduction of the latter four terms since the Rio Earth Summit, varying viewpoints have emerged (see, for example, Jarnet et al, 1998; Hesselink et al, 2000). These views include:

- those who say that EE is synonymous with ESD;
- those who say that ESD is a component of EE;
- those who say that EE is a component of ESD;
- those who wish to do away with ESD altogether; and, conversely,
- those who feel that ESD is a better term than EE and the latter should be dropped.

Others prefer ESF. Still others take a pluralistic approach and state that it is the quality of practice that counts, not what it is called. Before attempting to clarify this picture, let us look at the significance of nomenclature.

The importance of labels is that they carry meaning. This is double edged. While labels serve to simplify and communicate, they can also confuse through implying both more distinctiveness and shared understanding than may, in fact, be the case. Intended connotation and actual interpretation can differ markedly. So the undoubted utility of these names as shorthand in communication is countered by the possibility of misunderstanding between parties, and this danger is increased by the proliferation of similar labels. The IUCN/ Dutch government internet 'ESDebate', held with over 30 international educators during 1999–2000, tried to shed light on the issues arising from the labels problem. While there was some dispute, 'most participants appear to regard ESD as the next evolutionary stage or new generation of EE' (Hesselink et al, 2000, p12).

Part of the issue here concerns which of the terms appears the more encompassing. Historically, the sustainability terms have emerged later than environmental education by some 25 years, echoing a shift of concern and perception in wider society, from 'single-issue environmentalism' towards a more (if not fully) holistic realization of the interdependence of issues and, specifically, economic, social and environmental aspects.

The subtleties of distinctions between these terms, as used by those within the debate, are likely to elude the educators and policy-makers on the outside whom the same debaters and proponents wish to influence. Yet, while the pluralistic approach – 'all these terms roughly indicate a similar orientation, so let's not worry overmuch about labels' – has some merit, the potential for confusion about different labels, particularly amongst 'outsiders', remains.

This dilemma may be clarified by looking at two dimensions: the *horizontal* and the *vertical*. The former concerns the scope of the field, the latter concerns the philosophical base. The latter is important, and this chapter will return to it later. For now, this section notes that, for example, ESD can be interpreted very differently. The term is catching on politically, and some educators are following suit. While there is some strategic advantage to this, there is also some evidence that it is seen as a non-contested form of education supporting a non-contested and mainstream definition of sustainable development, where more radical interpretations and critical thought are squeezed out. With regard to the horizontal dimension, and employing a systemic model of nesting systems, the key terms may, from an evolutionary view, be usefully seen as forming a hierarchy, as presented in Figure 4.1.

This model affirms, as noted in Figure 4.1, that the evolutionary pattern (indicated by the arrow) is one of increasing inclusivity and that the emergence of new terms indicates a recognition of the limits of previous terms, while still respecting their validity. Thus, EE has been traditionally concerned with the quality of the environment, and less concerned with social, economic and political aspects of change. The focus of reports of the seminal UN Belgrade and Tbilisi environmental education conferences of 1975 and 1977, respectively, concentrated on the problems of the environment rather than those of the people.

Partly a product of the confluence of the concerns of environmental education and development education, ESD has sought to encompass the social, economic and environmental dimensions of change and of alternative futures. Here, this chapter also includes education for a sustainable future (ESF) and education for global citizenship. The proponents of EFS have argued that ESD is outer-directed and possibly too instrumentally oriented, and that we need to consider the inner dimensions of valuative psychological and perceptual change. They argue for education 'for being' rather than (just) education 'for becoming'. Lastly, some commentators like myself argue that sustainability indicates both the grounding and possibility of a change of educational paradigm as a whole – hence, 'sustainable education'.

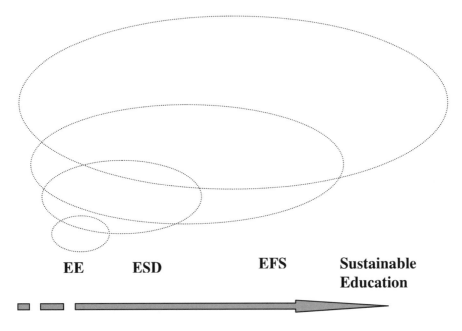

EE **ESD** **EFS** **Sustainable Education**

Direction of evolution

Figure 4.1 *The evolution of key terms*

Note: The dotted circles indicate the need for permeable boundaries and conceptions.

While some might see this tentative model as too simple and definitive, it nevertheless illustrates some key points:

- The practitioners and theorists involved are themselves engaged in a continual (and often difficult) reflexive learning process through which views of the adequacy or wholeness of educational orientations are modified over time.
- Through this process, previous conceptions of this area are subsumed within, rather than negated by, later conceptions.
- The validity of earlier conceptions is not questioned; rather, their claims to sufficiency or adequacy are.

To summarize, this chapter has argued that the whole movement has been characterized by contrary trends of increasing inclusivity and fragmentation, of coherence and incoherence, and that this has led to a lack of substantive progress in influencing policy, theory and practice in the mainstream. To take the argument another step, the following section will look more deeply at interpretation in the field: this is what is referred to as the *vertical dimension*.

INTERPRETATIONS

Any expression of environmental or sustainability education implicitly or explicitly rests on a view both of environment/sustainability and of education. Furthermore, and at a deeper level, these views reflect a worldview, or view of reality. Understanding sustainability education is thus made complex by the existence of a variety of theoretical and practical interpretations, and the fact that at the deeper level of cultural worldview, sustainability education lies partly within and partly without the dominant modernist worldview, which still prevails in education and wider society despite the critique of post-modernist debate. This worldview is often characterized as technocentric, dualistic and reductionist. Thus, paradigmatic tensions characterize the debate because, as Robottom and Hart (1993, p44) state, environmental education is a product of 'both older *and* emerging worldviews' (my italics). This section describes a model that helps to clarify the main paradigmatic stances, and uses this to analyse positions in some of the recent international debate in the field.

I start by looking at the 'environmental responsibility' view of sustainability education, which remains the most influential view in the field despite serious shortcomings. When I began working in environmental education over 30 years ago, first as a teacher and then for the Council for Environmental Education, I shared a fairly simplistic notion of education and change with most of the environmental education community. It was based on the assumption that people were insufficiently aware of the environment and understood little about it. Therefore, we needed to raise awareness and increase understanding; then, we believed, environmental issues were more likely to be addressed and resolved. The notion of paradigmatic positions within environmental education hardly featured in debate, and such critical discourse did not appear in any depth until the early 1990s (Mrazek, 1993).

Since the events that followed the environmental education debate, including the emergence of education for sustainability (EFS) and education for sustainable development (ESD), the idea of remedying environmental ignorance through education has remained strong and influential, even though the argument is often presented in a more sophisticated way than it was decades ago.

In this view, education is seen in instrumental terms as a means to an end. This view is based on a realist and materialist worldview – an instrumentalist and universalist view of education – often giving rise to an instructive, transmissive methodology. The guiding questions are behavioural and may be summarized as: how can education change people's attitude and behaviour towards the environment or sustainability issues? There is a linear and rationalist view of change – an idea that 'education *about* the environment' is sufficient to encourage personal and social change. There is an emphasis on information and communication, and on individual environmental responsibility reflected particularly by government and NGO campaigns concerned with 'getting the message across'. In terms of the sustainable development debate, this rationalist and behaviourist view of education accords with ecological modernization and ecological managerialism.

During the last decade or so, however, a different view of environmental and sustainability education has emerged that rejects the instrumental view of education as a 'destination view' which is 'inherently deterministic and modernistic' (Jickling and Spork, 1998; Jarnet et al, 1998), and this criticism has been extended by some commentators to any mention of education for sustainable development. This critique shifts the historic focus from content and predetermined learning outcomes towards the nature of the learning experience. Thus, many environmental educators are now concerned with the kind of experience that is necessary if we are to nurture personal or social transformation towards sustainability through learning. This is, essentially, an idealist view of the world, and a constructivist view of the learner, which asserts the intrinsic value of education and learning. The emphasis is on the quality of learning and, often, on building the individual's capacity (for example, to think critically, systemically and reflexively), rather than encouraging particular social or environmental outcomes. It recognizes the importance of the learning context and the prior experience, disposition and uniqueness of the learner. The guiding questions are developmental and may be characterized as: how can we facilitate learning, critical thinking and self-development in the context of the sustainability issue? In terms of the sustainable development debate, this constructivist position is logically resonant with capacity-building, self-determination and autonomous development, although the constructivist position is often rather weakly linked to both social critique and critical sustainability discourse.

Hence, this chapter suggests that underlying the international sustainability education debate are two fundamental positions. In terms of worldview and epistemology, this dichotomy reflects the *realism–idealism* tension; in terms of learning theory, it reflects the *behaviourism–constructivism* tension; in terms of methodology, it reflects the *content–process* and *transmission–transformation* tensions.

In simple terms, the first orientation is more interested in the environment or sustainability part of environmental/sustainability education, while the second orientation is more interested in the education part: a difference between what might be termed 'education about and for the environment', on the one hand, and 'education for being', on the other.

Yet, if we look at the environmental and sustainability education literature, the spectrum of paradigmatic positions is commonly represented as a three-part model, particularly during the early 1990s – for example, Robottom and Hart (1993) (positivist, interpretivist and critical); Fien (1993) ('vocational/neo-classical', liberal/progressive, socially critical); Sauvé (1996) (rational, humanistic and inventive). These models still have currency and can be used to interpret positions within the debate. During more recent years, a wider spectrum tends to be acknowledged, reflecting debate in social science. Hence, a range of methodological positions (such as positivist, post-positivist, interpretivist, transformative, post-modern and post-structuralist) are distinguished (see Gough and Reid, 2000; Denzin and Lincoln, 2000).

At a deeper level, however – which might be described as a meta-paradigmatic level – this chapter suggests that the two archetypal positions or tendencies outlined above are operative (see Table 4.1).

It is important to note that these are not two simple 'camps' – the arrow at the base of Table 4.1 indicates that there is a spectrum of possible stances based on these two platforms, and the various three- and six-part models outlined above illustrate and name such stances.

Table 4.1 *Fundamental orientations influencing sustainability education*

Ontology	Realist	Idealist
Epistemology	Objectivist/positivist	Constructivist/interpretivist
Theory of learning	Behaviourist	Constructivist
Function of sustainable education	Remedial	Developmental
Main emphasis	Goals/outcomes	Learning experience
Focus	Knowledge acquisition (and values/skills)	Meaning-making
Seeks	Behavioural change	Capacity-building, self-development
Reflects	Instrumental values	Intrinsic values
Pedagogy	Transmission/instructivist	Transaction/constructivist
Desired change	Integration	Autonomy
Intrinsic problem	Objectivism	Relativism

Notably, this two-part meta-paradigm model does not map *socially critical theory*, which draws upon elements of both fundamental positions shown, and may be said to be reconstructive. Socially critical environmental and sustainability education draws upon the work of such thinkers as Freire (1972) and Habermas and, to this extent, shares some fundamental orientations and concerns about development education. This orientation has been influential in the environmental education debate, particularly in the UK and Australia. It is reflected in PAR methodology, and in terms of sustainable development, relates to movements for self-reliance and alternative development models.

This analysis gives grounding for understanding tensions within the international sustainability education debate. The fundamental tension is between a behaviourist tendency and a constructivist tendency. Those following the former – often driven by a sense of urgency – take a more instrumentalist view of education and seek rapid infusion of sustainability concepts within all aspects of education, focusing particularly on curriculum. Thus, for example, there have emerged several international and internet-based ESD curriculum schemes in recent years. The latter orientation, by contrast, questions the universalism and instrumental rationality inherent in the behaviourist approach, the limited abstract and scientific view of knowledge often promulgated, the top-down methodology employed, and the frequently superficial effect on the learner of content-based approaches. Instead, constructivists emphasize contextualized knowledge; different ways of knowing (in addition to scientific approaches); real-world local issues as a focus for learning; the active role of the learner; and the need for participatory methodology.

With regard to the international debate, it is not overly simple to suggest that much of the rhetoric and international documentation over the last two decades have reflected an instrumentalist orientation, while the professional community of interest – the theorists and practitioners – has increasingly moved towards a constructivist view of sustainability education. At the same time, others have pursued a socially critical, reconstructivist view of education and society.

This analysis helps to account for the relative lack of progress of sustainability education, both in terms of take-up in national systems and at local and institutional level. The behaviourist view tends to provoke an *accommodatory* response from education systems, a tinkering with curriculum content, which may or may not take place to any great depth and level of coherence. The constructivist approach suggests a deeper *reformatory* response, but one which education systems find hard to grasp, or to distinguish from 'good education' that they may claim to already provide. Meanwhile, the reconstructivist approach often suggests a revisioning of education and society too radical or apparently ideological for most educational systems to accept or for which to find starting points.

These problems indicate that a deeper level of enquiry is needed regarding:

- What sorts of education are appropriate to the conditions of the 21st century?
- Does the discourse of sustainability education provide a substantial and coherent base for any necessary revisioning of education?
- How far is our conception of the purpose, nature and role of education still informed by largely unexamined norms of the Western modernist worldview?
- Is this worldview adequate for, and appropriate to, the post-modern conditions of unsustainability, uncertainty and complexity in which we live?

In the laudable efforts to devise sustainability education curriculum packages, strategies for 'delivery' and research agendas, it is this deeper level of critical reflection that, too often, tends to be missing from the debate. We need both a *deeper critique* of where we have come from, and a *broader vision* of where we might be going to in terms of educational philosophy, purposes and practice. There are glimpses of this sense, as Sauvé (1998, p53), writing for the 1998 colloquium on the future of environmental education, indicates:

> *The challenge is to find the basis of an education capable of promoting integral human development, to which environmental education offers an essential contribution. . . [F]rom a reconstructive perspective, it is a search for meaning, for significance in a worthwhile human journey.*

In the sustainability discourse, there have been calls for the *conscious* acceleration of the sustainability transition (Gardner, 2001; Brown, 2001). This implies redefining the meaning of the 'learning society' towards one that begins to understand itself and, if necessary, redirect itself. Parallel to, and helping to enable, such self-realization, we need to give greater attention both to the core beliefs and ideas that influence and limit mainstream educational policy and practice, and to the possibility of a coherent, more whole, more appropriate educational paradigm – echoing UNESCO's call for 'a deeper, more ambitious way of thinking about education' (UNESCO, 2002, p8).

The lack of fundamental progress with the 'reorientation' of education, reviewed above, and the accommodation and containment of sustainability education by the mainstream, underlines the need for articulating an alternative and ecologically grounded educational paradigm, which can inform a change of culture – one that can heal the schism between the realists/ behaviourists and idealists/constructivists and provide a more integrative vision of education. To help meet this challenge, this chapter suggests the concept of *sustainable education*, not as yet another equal term to EFS and ESD, but as the next logical step in the evolution of the field. Suggesting a shift of educational culture, the emphasis here is not on desired outcomes as in 'education for sustainable development', but on the qualities of education itself through which sustainability is manifest as an emergent property.

Sustainable education implies a transformation in educational thinking and practice through which education becomes more transformative. There is, therefore, at least, a double-level learning process involved. This raises the question of the philosophical and educational basis of such change, and this is touched upon in the next section.

TRANSFORMATION

Essentially, sustainability (or, indeed, unsustainability), like justice or health, is an emergent quality arising from sets of relationships in a system, whether viewed at the macro or micro scale. As Bell and Morse (1999) have argued, it is not a 'thing' that can be precisely defined or measured. In people's views of sustainability, there is a tension, they suggest, between the scientism, objectivism and reductionism of the dominant paradigm that attempts such precision, and an emerging paradigm which the authors describe as systemic, holistic and participative. The latter holds that sustainability is more – or less – likely to arise depending upon the degree to which our attention shifts from 'things' to relationships, and from a segregated and dualistic view of the world towards an integrative and participative perspective. This involves more than a simple and dualistic environmentalism, and indicates, instead, the need for 'whole systems thinking' arising from ecologism (Dobson, 1990) and systemic thinking (Flood, 1999), which transcends and subsumes an appropriate mechanism and reductionism. This is why the prospect of sustainable education is, at heart, an epistemological issue.

The grounding for such a shift of view is increasingly well documented. A growing number of commentators and critics have argued for and evidenced the emergence of what might be called a 'post-modern ecological worldview' (Zweers, 2000). This takes us beyond the root metaphor of mechanism that is still at the heart of the modernist project and towards a new 'organicism' based on a 'living systems' (Elgin, 1997; Ho, 2002), 'co-evolutionary' (Norgaard, 1994) or 'participative' (Reason and Bradbury, 2001) view of the world. Such thinking transcends the limits of mechanism, goes beyond the blind alley of relativism that post-modern deconstructionism draws, and moves towards what this chapter calls *'relationalism'*: a systemic or ecological view associated with revisonary post-modernism (Spretnak, 1997) and supported by the implications of complexity theory (Capra, 2002).

In terms of sustainability education, this systemic worldview holds the potential to address many of the issues outlined above. It provides a grounding from which the influence and limits of dominant paradigms may be realized and evaluated, and it promises a coherent philosophy not just for expressions of sustainability education as they have emerged during the last two decades, but for education *as a whole*. This is a daunting but critical point. Any closed definition of sustainability education (assuming it can be achieved to common satisfaction) involves drawing conceptual boundaries. This carries the danger that all other educational policies, theories and practices appear to be outside or beyond these boundaries – and, therefore, actors outside of the boundaries assume or perceive that sustainability education is not their concern.

There is a parallel here with sustainable development: either it is an add-on area of theory and practice (that is, a sectoral interest), or – to a greater or lesser degree – it involves all aspects of social, economic and political organization. So it is with education in the service of sustainable development. This chapter argues that we must avoid sectoralism, and instead suggest, explore and develop 'sustainable education'.

Sustainable education implies four descriptors – educational thinking and practice which is sustaining, tenable, healthy and durable:

- *Sustaining*: it helps to sustain people, communities and ecosystems.
- *Tenable*: it is ethically defensible, working with integrity, justice, respect and inclusiveness.
- *Healthy*: it is an adaptive, viable system, embodying and nurturing healthy relationships and emergence at different system levels.
- *Durable*: it works well enough in practice to be able to keep doing it.

An outline of what such a paradigm implies is provided by Sterling (2001). In essence, it entails an extended and participatory epistemology, a connective ontology and an integrative praxis. Thus, returning to the fundamental epistemological positions summarized in Table 4.1, the new paradigm integrates elements of both positions within a greater whole (see Table 4.2).

Table 4.2 *Towards a sustainable education paradigm: key characteristics*

Ontology	Realist/idealist (relational)
Epistemology	Participatory
Theory of learning	Participative/systemic
Function of education	Remedial/developmental/transformative
Main emphasis	Towards transformative learning experiences
Focus	Meaning-making appropriate to context
Seeks	Wholeness and sustainability
Reflects	Intrinsic and transformative values
Pedagogy	Transformative
Desired change	Contextually appropriate balance between autonomy and integration (ie healthy, sustainable relationships) in and between systemic levels

How a sustainable education paradigm might be achieved in higher education lies beyond the scope of this chapter (but see Sterling, 2004). One indicative example is shown in Table 4.3, which is based on lessons drawn from the European Union (EU) Socrates Thematic Network for Agriculture, Forestry, Aquaculture and the environment (AFANet) project that explored the implications of integrating sustainability within agricultural higher education institutions.

With all such tables, the choice is not between binary opposites, but a change of weighting that moves away from the dominance of the old paradigm, and transforms and conserves some of its characteristics rather than abandoning them in their entirety. What is required is a more adequate and encompassing paradigm that can evolve from where things now stand. This needs to go beyond an accommodatory response by the mainstream.
Thus, sustainable education:

- Implies a fundamental change of purpose or, at very least, an additional key purpose for education.
- Implies embedding, embodying and exploring the nature of sustainability as intrinsic to the learning process. This is education 'as' sustainability –

Table 4.3 *Lessons learned from the AFANet project (1997–2000)*

Integration of sustainability within higher education implies shifts:

From	To
Transmissive learning	Learning through discovery
Teacher-centred approach	Learner-centred approach
Individual learning	Collaborative learning
Learning dominated by theory	Praxis-oriented learning linking theory and experience
Focus on accumulating knowledge and a content orientation	Focus on self-regulative learning and a real issues orientation
Emphasis on cognitive objectives only	Cognitive, affective and skills-related objectives
Institutional, staff-based teaching/learning	Learning with and from outsiders
Low-level cognitive learning	Higher-level cognitive learning

Source: adapted from Van de Bor et al (2000, p309)

nurturing critical, systemic and reflective thinking; creativity; self-organization; and adaptive management – rather than education 'about' sustainability, or education 'for' particular sustainable development outcomes.

- Is not prescriptive, but is indicative and purposeful.
- Affirms liberal humanist traditions in education, but goes beyond them through synergy with systemic and sustainability core values, concepts and methodologies.
- Challenges the limiting effects of characteristics of the dominant mechanistic paradigm, such as top-down control, centralization, managerialism, instrumentalism and the devaluing of humanities and arts.
- Is based on 'systemics' rather than 'systematics' – that is, the emphasis is on *systemic learning* as change, rather than *systematic control* in response to change.

In particular, such a change of educational culture requires a deep learning process by educational actors – policy-makers, managers, theorists, researchers and practitioners. In short, if educational institutions are to play a full and constructive part in the sustainability transition (if they are to provide transformative learning experiences for students), then – as learning organizations – these institutions and their actors need to go through some form of transformative learning experience themselves.

In terms of systemic learning theory, the nature of these deeper levels of learning are well documented and known as double-loop learning (Argyris and Schon, 1996) or second-order change (Ison and Russell, 2000), through which fundamental assumptions are questioned; and beyond this, epistemic learning through which a new paradigm emerges. This simple statement belies the degree of difficulty and resistance often involved. Deep learning can be deeply uncomfortable because it involves a restructuring of basic assumptions caused by the recognition of incoherence between assumptions and experience.

Much of this may sound idealistic, to say the least, given the very real policy, structural and market constraints facing higher education. Yet, there are still choices to be made, both long term and day to day. In essence, how far is any institution a reflective microcosm of a sustainable society, or an unthinking microcosm of an unsustainable society? Whether an institution: audits its curriculum in sustainability terms; reviews its purchasing, investment and local spending with environmental and ethical criteria in mind; audits its ecological footprint; engages in a participative management style; engages its students and their enthusiasms in real-life issues; promotes cooperative and critical inquiry; encourages and facilitates creative, critical and systemic thinking; experiments with inter- and transdisciplinarity; works with staff to develop varied and participative pedagogies; promotes an ethos of caring and inclusion; develops the culture of the learning organization; develops an ethical and responsible research agenda; reviews its fundamental purposes and mission regarding sustainability in higher education – all of this requires the development of a collective intelligence and culture. It requires not a piecemeal or systematic response, but systemic engagement, which may be small scale and gradual at first. The emergence of an appreciable number of national and international websites and networks on sustainability and higher education over the last decade is evidence that significant innovation is occurring, particularly among smaller institutions that are more flexible. Given that there is growing evidence of the sustainability paradigm influencing mainstream thinking, policy and practice in such sectors as economics, politics, agriculture, energy, resource management, transport, health, production, waste, engineering, construction, design, and business and the professions – all areas served by higher education – a corresponding response by higher education is both necessary and timely.

In brief, this chapter argues that those involved in the sustainability discourse have been, and still are, involved in a deep learning process – evidenced in the international debate over the last decade – about the sort of educational philosophy, theory and practice that is appropriate to the precarious and volatile world we now inhabit. Secondly, this movement needs to help catalyse and accelerate a much more widespread parallel learning process in the wider educational community.

With the trend towards the marketization and commodification of education internationally, and the prospect of this diminution and control of education being taken further through the General Agreement on Trade in Services (GATS), the challenge to the sustainability education community is great, indeed. Essentially, we must help to lead educational policy and practice away from a basis in fragmentation, mechanism, objectivism and reductionism, and towards an integrated and holistic ecologism and understanding of systems appropriate to the post-modern world.

CONCLUSION

In little more than three decades of evolution, sustainability education has achieved much. Despite a degree of fragmentation and dispute over nomenclature, it is recognized internationally as a critically important approach in education. The UN has resolved to make the period of 2005–2010 the Decade of Education of Sustainable Development, and this is very much to be welcomed as a significant step forward. Yet, the unsustainability clock is ticking, and there remains a real danger that a 'safe' and neutered form of ESD will be accommodated within the mainstream, which otherwise remains largely unaffected. To counter this, sustainability education needs to mount a deeper critique of the culture of mechanism, modernism and instrumentalism that largely still informs most educational policy. At the same time, it must achieve greater coherence and persuasion through embracing the profound educational potential in the emerging ecological and systemic paradigm that is already influencing sustainability discourse and practice in the wider society that higher education serves.

REFERENCES

Argyris, C and Schon, D (1996) *Organisational Learning II*, New York, Addison Wesley

Bell, S and Morse, S (1999) *Sustainability Indicators – Measuring the Immeasurable?* London, Earthscan

Brown, L (2001) *Eco-Economy – Building an Economy for the Earth,* London, Earth Policy Institute and Earthscan

Capra, F (2002) *The Hidden Connections,* London, HarperCollins

Carson, R (1962) *Silent Spring*, London, Hamish Hamilton

Chambers, R (1997) *Whose Reality Counts? Putting the First Last,* London, Intermediate Technology Publications

Denzin, N and Lincoln, Y (2000) *Handbook of Qualitative Research,* 2nd edition, Thousand Oaks, California, Sage Publications

Disinger, J (1983) 'Environmental Education's Definitional Problem', *ERIC Information Bulletin,* no 2, Ohio, ERIC

Dobson, A (1990) *Green Political Thought: An Introduction,* London, Unwin Hyman

Elgin, D (1997) *Global Consciousness Change: Indicators of an Emerging Paradigm,* California, Millennium Project

Fals-Borda, O and Rahman, M A (eds) (1991) *Action and Knowledge – Breaking the Monopoly with Participatory Action-Research,* London, Intermediate Technology Publications

Fien, J (1993) *Education for the Environment,* Geelong, Deakin University

Flood, R (1999) *Rethinking the Fifth Discipline – Learning within the Unknowable,* London, Routledge

Freire, P (1972) *Pedagogy of the Oppressed,* Harmondsworth, Penguin

Gardner, G (2001)'Accelerating the Shift to Sustainability', in Brown, L (ed), *State of the World: Worldwatch Institute Report on Progress Towards a Sustainable Society,* London, Earthscan

Giroux, H A (1992) *Border Crossings: Cultural Workers and the Politics of Education,* London, Routledge

Goodson, I (1983) *School Subjects and Curriculum Change – Case Studies in Curriculum History,* London, Croom Helm

Gough, S and Reid, A (2000) 'Environmental Education Research as Profession, as Science, as Art and as Craft: Implications for guidelines in qualitative research', *Environmental Education Research,* Special Issue: Qualitative Methods of Inquiry, vol 6, no 1, Abingdon, Carfax Publishing

Greig, S, Pike, G and Selby, D (1987) *Earthrights – Education as if the Earth Mattered,* Godalming, WWF-UK

Hesselink, F, van Kempen, P and Wals, A (2000) *ESDebate: International Debate on Education for Sustainable Development,* Gland, IUCN

Ho, M W (2002) 'To Science with Love', in Cohen, J, James, S and Blewitt, J (eds) *Learning to Last: Skills, Sustainability and Strategy,* London, Learning and Skills Development Agency

Ison, R and Russell, D (2000) *Agricultural Extension and Rural Development – Breaking out of Traditions: A Second-Order Systems Perspective,* Cambridge, Cambridge University Press

IUCN, UNEP and WWF (1980) *The World Conservation Strategy,* Gland, IUCN, UNEP and WWF

IUCN, UNEP and WWF (1991) *Caring for the Earth – A Strategy for Sustainable Living,* Gland, IUCN, UNEP and WWF

Jarnet, A et al (eds) (1998) *A Colloquium On the Future of Environmental Education in a Postmodern World?, Canadian Journal of Environmental Education,* Whitehorse, Yukon

Jickling, B and Spork, H (1998) 'Education for the environment: a critique', *Environmental Education Research,* vol 4, no3, pp309–327

Mayor, F (1997) 'Preface by the Director-General of UNESCO', in UNESCO (1997) *Educating for a Sustainable Future,* UNESCO, Paris

McKeown, R and Hopkins, C (2003) 'EE=/=ESD: Defusing the worry', *Environmental Education Research,* vol 9, no 1, Abingdon, Carfax/Taylor and Francis

Meadows, D H, Meadows, D L, Randers J and Behrens III, W W (1972) *The Limits to Growth: A Report for the Club of Rome's Project on the Predicament of Mankind,* New York, Universe

Mrazek, R (ed) (1993) *Alternative Paradigms in Environmental Education,* Troy, Ohio, North American Association for Environmental Education

Naess, A (1973) 'The Shallow and the Deep: Long-Range Ecology Movements – A Summary', *Inquiry,* Oslo, vol 16, p95–100

Norgaard, R (1994) *Development Betrayed – The End of Progress and a Co-evolutionary Revisioning of the Future,* London, Routledge

Reason, P and Bradbury, H (2001) 'Introduction: Inquiry and Participation in a Search of a World Worthy of Human Aspiration', in Reason, P and Bradbury, H (eds) *Handbook of Action Research – Participative Practice and Enquiry,* London, Sage Publications

Robottom, I and Hart, P (1993) *Research in Environmental Education,* Geelong, Deakin University

Sauvé, L (1996) 'Environmental Education and Sustainable Development: Further Appraisal', *Canadian Journal of Environmental Education,* vol 1, Whitehorse, Yukon

Sauvé, L (1998) 'Environmental Education Between Modernity and Postmodernity: Searching for an Integrating Educational Framework', in Jarnet, A et al (eds) *A Colloquium On the Future of Environmental Education in a Postmodern World? Canadian Journal of Environmental Education,* Whitehorse, Yukon

Spretnak, C (1997) *The Resurgence of the Real,* Reading, Mass, Addison-Wesley

Sterling, S (2001) *Sustainable Education: Revisioning Learning and Change*, Totnes, Green Books

Sterling, S (2004/in press) 'Higher Education, Sustainability and the Role of Systemic Learning', in Corcoran P B and Arjen, E J W (eds) *Higher Education and the Challenge of Sustainability: Contestation, Critique, Practice, and Promise*, Dordrecht, Kluwer Academic

UNESCO-UNEP (1978) *Intergovernmental Conference on Environmental Education, Tbilisi, USSR, 14–26 October 1977: Final Report*, Paris, UNESCO

UNESCO (2002) *Education for Sustainability – From Rio to Johannesburg: Lessons Learnt from a Decade of Commitment*, Paris, UNESCO

Van de Bor, W, Holen, P, Wals, A and Filho, W (2000) *Integrating Concepts of Sustainability Into Education for Agriculture and Rural Development*, Frankfurt, Peter Lang

WCED (1987) *Our Common Future*, Oxford, World Commission on Environment and Development and Oxford University Press

Zweers, W (2000) *Participation with Nature – Outline for an Ecologisation of our Worldview*, Utrecht, International Books

Chapter 5

Citizenship and Community from Local to Global: Implications for Higher Education of a Global Citizenship Approach

Jenneth Parker, Ros Wade and Hugh Atkinson

INTRODUCTION

Concepts of global citizenship (GC) can also include notions of local and national ecological citizenship, although this is currently underemphasized. This chapter briefly considers this issue in relation to education for a sustainable future (EFS) and situates the debate in this context. In considering issues of community and citizenship, we could say that environmental education (EE) has been concerned with human membership of the community of life and our duties towards that community. Development education (DE) has been more concerned with the community of humans and their mutual well-being. Particularly in the UK, the development of EFS has involved the synergy between EE and DE. This chapter considers some of the possible tensions and overlaps between these educations in relation to the local and global.

EDUCATION FOR SUSTAINABILITY: LOCAL AND GLOBAL

With respect to globalization, EE and DE can be seen as having rather different starting points. Environmental education is concerned with the developing understanding of material relationships between local, regional and global ecosystems (Tudge, 1991), which have always existed, and human impacts upon them, which are increasing. DE concentrates more on the social, political, economic and *historical* phenomenon of globalization as a process of social, economic and ethical relations, driven by human actions (see, for example, Alexander, 1996).

Environmental education concerns include:

- ecological interdependency (linking of life systems and materials cycles);

- relationships between social and ecological systems;
- site-specific issues of local ecology in relation to global-scale environment problems;
- local knowledge and specific knowledge of particular ecological systems; and
- implicit valuing of life and diversity.

Development education concerns include:

- economic interdependency and trade relations;
- social and political structures (political freedoms and human rights);
- inequalities in economic relations and debt;
- political power relations (local, national, regional and global);
- cultural rights (attitudes and values);
- value commitments (for example, justice and equality).

There are numerous interesting tensions that arise between these two orientations, which a critical and innovative higher education (HE) curriculum is well placed to explore. Clearly, important issues arise when considering ecological global citizenship in relation to more exclusively humanistic concepts of GC; however, this chapter cannot explore the full extent of the implications of bringing ecological citizenship into current global citizenship agendas. Indeed, we hope that this topic will form part of a continuing dialogue between EE and DE orientations in the UK and elsewhere.

IDENTITY, COMMUNITY AND CITIZENSHIP

Citizenship in the UK

Citizenship must be seen as a politically contested concept, ranging from notions of the well-behaved citizen characteristic of modern state discourse to the call by social movements for citizens to act for a better world. Currently, the model of citizenship that has largely found favour with UK politicians is an uneasy mixture of two elements. First, a state approach recommends limited participation in representative (rather than participatory) democratic institutions and attention to the duties of the citizen to obey state law. This approach tends to lead to a curriculum involving an uncritical education about state political institutions. Second, a communitarian/Christian approach emphasizes membership of family and community and the importance of related duties (Etzioni, 1988). Given that market liberalism encourages the pursuit of individual interests and versions of the good life, this attempt to inject some 'values' can only be a sticking-plaster approach, as Poole has powerfully demonstrated in his *Morality and Modernity* (Poole, 1991). On this basis, state-sanctioned citizenship approaches are likely to encourage children and young people to take part in community-based caring activities and charitable work. In this respect, the UK administration is happy to enshrine the individualistic profit motive more deeply in our social and political institutions, but seeks a moral fig leaf in the more 'private' realm of family and community in order to claim value commitments.

At their best, citizenship school curricula in the West can support the development of participatory democratic forms, involving children in running schools. But, generally, UK government citizenship ignores the fact that the most active citizens include those participating in movements and non-governmental organizations (NGOs), which governments often find inconvenient and challenging. For example, in the UK there are more members of environmental NGOs than there are of political parties. This citizenship curriculum does not touch on crucial issues of the limits of rights under global capitalism or the ways in which globalizing capitalist economic and social relations often destabilize communities and relations of care – especially in the globalizing economy (O'Neill, 1994). This absence of a rights perspective is illustrated by the UK Qualification and Curriculum Authority (QCA) guidelines on citizenship education (QCA, 2000), although there is acknowledgement about the need to tackle issues of racism. In this uneasy mix of the discourses of state and community, there is a distinct separation between the concepts of 'citizen' and 'community'. This chapter argues that the tensions and relations between these concepts represent an important practical and intellectual challenge, reflecting key aspects of the debates around localization and globalization, linking these to issues of identity in our complex world. These issues are elaborated upon below.

The complexity of community, citizenship and identity in today's multi-layered and multicultural society is also largely ignored or glossed over in the formal curriculum guidance. Evidence from young people indicates that their perception of their identities and, therefore, their duties and relationship to wider communities is complex and changing. For example, Lovejit Dhaliwal (2002), writing in the *Observer*, described the complexities of being gay and Muslim. The article quotes Azeem Ahmed, who says:

> *I have a few identities – you can tell by the music I listen to, the colour of my skin, the food that I eat. I'm also British – the way I was brought up, my schooling, the people I mix with. I also pay my taxes! I contribute to the society as much as I can. I'm also Muslim, which is a very important part of spirituality; nobody can take that away from me. I'm also gay – something I can't change. I'm proud to be gay in the same way I'm proud to be British and Asian and Muslim.* (Dhaliwal, 2002, p4)

Azeem outlines a number of communities of which he is a part and which he negotiates as a part of daily life. Along with a huge number of people today, both young and old, he is able to relate at different levels and in different ways to a range of groups and situations. Azeem and most of his contemporaries are way ahead in recognizing that they have rights, as well as duties, in relation to these different communities.

This example points up the hidden issue in most UK government approaches to citizenship: national identity is but one aspect of Azeem's identity and to unpack this aspect further would demonstrate other complexities. Most members of black and ethnic minorities living in England would not use the term 'English' to describe themselves but 'British'. Identities in the UK are complicated by the inclusion of the countries of England, Wales and Scotland, and the principality of Northern Ireland; these areas reflect both historical/cultural and political elements. Equally, even within England, many white families would align themselves more closely with a local region, such as the north-west or north-east, than with England, which to many is associated too closely with the south-east and home counties. Yet, some parts of the south-east are among the most heterogeneous areas of the country. National identity has been recognized as being problematic in a postcolonial state such as the UK, where patriotism has, at times, become closely associated with far-right, racist groups, such as the National Front. Arguably, when it comes to issues of community, national identity is problematic in relation to the modern state. Some have argued that national identities are imaginary constructs that are deployed by states in various ways. These processes are most clearly seen in times of war and conflict.

Multiple identities and communities: issues of fundamentalism

It is relevant to consider religious fundamentalism in this debate, as this undermines state-centred concepts of citizenship, with their strong counter-assertion of the central moral importance of the community of believers. As contemporary fundamentalism employs modern state structures of law and surveillance without the democratic benefits of citizenship, it is prone to terrorize its subjects and is open to attempted censorship and control. Furthermore, key issues of identity and moral relativism can be seen as running across contemporary fundamentalist forms. Castells (1997) has claimed that some contemporary fundamentalism is a response to the issues of identity raised by globalization. For example, his analysis of right-wing Christian fundamentalism in America points to the perceived need of social actors for clear identities and behavioural guidelines in a world of rapid social and environmental change. In this way, identities are seen as bound up with social behaviours and roles that can be sanctioned by higher (religious) authority, thus removing ethical uncertainties and the threat of relativism. Other critics stress the falling-back on superstition as a response to the hyper-changing and insecure globalizing world. The new (or recycled) fundamentalism in the wider society can also be seen as a process of constructing or reinforcing identities in opposition to social and cultural dollar imperialism and American military might. Consideration of fundamentalism in relation to communities of believers also raises the issue of power relations within communities. Frazer and Lacey (1993) have produced an excellent deconstruction of uncritical notions of 'community' in *The Politics of Community*. These debates should feed into any consideration of community and citizenship.

Many have argued that in promoting capitalist forms of economic globalization, the West simply displays its own dominant economic fundamentalism (Parker, 2002). It is important to note that some commentators on globalization also argue that this economic fundamentalism undermines social democratic state citizenship, as the strictures of the global economy come increasingly to dictate domestic state policies (Woods, 1994). There is abundant evidence that fundamentalist identities and certainties are bought at a high price, especially for women. The enforcement of Western capitalist dogmas has also resulted in a high price being paid by many of the poorest people in the world. Can HE in the West critically address Western forms of fundamentalism in globalization? Can more nuanced and developing forms of moral understanding and practice result from the mutual engagement of global citizens without falling into moral relativism? Furthermore, can our local and global identities be seen as an interactive relationship without imploding under the pressures of our insecure local and global 'worlds'? Here is a rich seam of transdisciplinary debate and investigation of great contemporary relevance with which HE could fruitfully engage – especially with regard to contested concepts of citizenship and community.

Global citizenship approaches: can they offer a way forward?

We have argued that there are unrecognized tensions between concepts of 'community' and 'citizenship' in the UK citizenship debate. Global citizenship (GC) approaches depend upon, and argue for, a recognition of the membership of the global community as morally important and can be seen as arguing for the recognition of rights and duties that fall upon community members. In this way, these approaches include notions of solidarity of international labour and imperatives of global ecological sustainability. They also draw upon ethical beliefs of worldwide faith communities. By way of contrast to the national emphasis on 'duties' in both the US and the UK, global citizenship discourses have emphasized global human rights and have encouraged action to secure these rights. As there is, as yet, no global 'state' to politically underwrite a notion of GC, the tension between state approaches and community membership does not arise in the same way. Some argue that there is, in fact, a developing world system that defines its 'citizens' as consumers. Given the current attempts to impose global trade rules, it can be plausibly argued that this 'system' is attempting to abrogate to itself the status of national states as having legitimate rights for using force and coercion, but at the global level. Attempts to construct the 'global consumer' under these rules are being variously resisted, often in the name of the 'global community' or 'global civil society'. This resistance is sometimes seen as a countervailing power, expressing some elements of a possible future global democracy.

The UK government's initial review of the teaching of citizenship in schools illustrated a national view of citizenship and a related resistance to the notion of global citizenship. This resistance was based on the argument that there could be no such concept without the requisite political institutions of global governance. However, it now seems to be more generally recognized that notions such as global citizenship can properly be aspirational and ethical in a way that must go beyond current political realities. Again, at the global level, this legalistic model of citizenship underlines the fact that national governments generally fail to acknowledge the legitimacy of global movements or 'global civil society'. This has been significantly redressed at the level of the United Nations (UN), where civil organizations are recognized actors at UN events such as the recent World Summit on Sustainable Development (WSSD). Many argue for these good beginnings to be extended in order to democratize the UN more fully. In the UK, the acknowledgement of the concept of global citizenship in the geography subject orders in England (the 2000 curriculum) is perhaps some recognition of the need for civil counterpart to the growing power of such institutions as the World Trade Organization (WTO). Nonetheless (and in a similar fashion to socially uncritical approaches at the UK level), there is a danger that global citizenship in a Western context could simply be a call to the privileged to take on charitable or moral responsibilities for the poverty-stricken 'others' of the world if political education about current world economic, social and political systems is excluded. In this context, the GC concept could become just a sticking plaster on global inequality, ignoring systems and structures of power. Sticking plasters can sometimes be a short-term palliative; but this chapter proposes an interpretation of GC in the context of a developing EFS that can provide a more adequate and holistic starting point for HE.

Oxfam's curriculum for global citizenship

Oxfam's UK curriculum for global citizenship (Oxfam, 1997) was an attempt to build upon the work of environmental and development educators in drawing together a set of principles that could form the basis of lobbying the UK government for an entitlement curriculum for schools. We propose that one way of addressing the issues outlined above is to adapt this approach for HE . Oxfam identified a global citizen as someone who:

- is aware of the wider world and has a sense of his or her own role as a world citizen;
- respects and values diversity;
- has an understanding of how the world works economically, politically, socially, culturally, technologically and environmentally;
- is outraged by social injustice;
- participates in and contributes to the community at a range of levels, from the local to the global;
- is willing to act to make the world a more equitable and sustainable place; and
- takes responsibility for his or her actions.

Oxfam went on to identify a core set of facts, skills and values to underpin this and outlined a broad framework for education. The three broad headings for these are as follows:

1   *Knowledge and understanding*:
    - social justice and equity;
    - diversity;
    - globalization and interdependence;
    - sustainable development;
    - peace and conflict;
2   *Skills*:
    - critical thinking;
    - ability to argue effectively;
    - ability to challenge injustice and inequalities;
    - respect for people and things;
    - cooperation and conflict resolution;
3   *Values and attitudes*:
    - sense of identity and self-esteem;
    - commitment to social justice and equity;
    - value and respect for diversity;
    - concern for the environment and commitment to sustainable development;
    - belief that people can make a difference (Oxfam, 1997, p2).

Oxfam sees this approach as providing 'both a clear goal and outcome as well as a framework which can embrace other "educations", including anti-racist, multicultural, intercultural, human rights, environmental education, world studies, world citizenship and equal opportunities' (Oxfam, 1997, p8). While the starting point for Oxfam is the agenda of poverty eradication, there is a clear attempt to build upon a range of educational movements and, in particular, to bring into prominence the importance of issues concerning sustainability and Agenda 21, which is extensively quoted. This particular conceptualization of GC also highlights the notion of the role of all citizens as local and global actors, as appropriate to the context. It further challenges the marketing of education as a commodity, and warns of the inherent dangers of further impositions of knowledge, which in the current global paradigm implies neo-liberal ideology. This danger is illustrated by the fact that education is now included in General Agreement on Trade in Services (GATS) discussions proposed by the WTO, where education is increasingly seen as a business within today's market economy. If agreed by the WTO, developing countries could be forced to accept Western education companies taking over the running of their education systems. In business terms, UK HE providers would be in a strong position to compete for some of the HE side of this business, and thus become implicated in a new form of cultural colonialism that is unsustainable. A global citizenship approach, such as Oxfam suggests, could provide us with the framework with which to challenge this. At the same time, it could help to develop the knowledge, skills and values that many employers are actually looking for, such as critical thinking and self-esteem.

Meeting the needs of today's learners

We argue that it is crucial for HE to respond to the situation of today's learners and to their concerns. Azeem (cited in Dhaliwal, 2002, p4) framed his identity quite comfortably within the personal (gay), local (school, music) and global (Muslim) communities, and in doing so reflects the complexity of issues that face us all in the world today. This does not necessarily mean that he has the power, confidence or ability to take decisive action on all of these levels; but it does indicate that he is aware of them. Increasingly, young people are opting out of mainstream politics; but this does not necessarily mean that they are not interested in political issues, as is illustrated by the growing number of young people involved in social action (for example, the protests by young people against the war in Iraq). Furthermore, the presence of a number of young people's organizations at the WSSD indicates that issues of sustainable development are very important to them. The presence of many representatives from HE also indicates that HE's responsibility in informing debates and developing values and skills appropriate to a sustainable world is starting to be recognized. WSSD reaffirmed the principles of Agenda 21, which committed governments to integrating 'environment and development as crosscutting issues into education at all levels' (UNCED, 1992, p222) and to ensuring that:

> *A thorough review of curricula should be undertaken to ensure. . .a multidisciplinary approach, with environment and development issues and their socio and demographic aspects and linkages. Due respect should be given to community-defined needs and diverse knowledge systems, including science, social and cultural sensitivities.* (UNCED, 1992, p223)

It is open to question whether the Oxfam approach fully recognizes the complexity of issues of identity, community and citizenship outlined above. However, we recognize the Oxfam framework as a positive initial framework, and expand upon this to include the following key issues for HE – specifically, the need to:

- Take account of complex multiple identities of people today.
- Develop curricula that develop understanding of complex local and global issues.
- Develop skills, competencies and understanding in order to become actors in a complex world at local, national and global levels (within ourselves, as well as our students).
- Acknowledge the interrelatedness and connectedness of knowledge and to develop transdisciplinary ways of working.

- Question the validity of current dominant forms of knowledge that have contributed to the present unsustainable world.
- Engage with different forms of knowledge (for example, local and indigenous knowledge).

IMPLICATIONS FOR HIGHER EDUCATION OF THE PROPOSED GLOBAL CITIZENSHIP MODEL

This section considers implications for HE in terms of curriculum and of HE institutions and programmes as both local and global actors.

New Labour, GC and HE

Universities do not exist in isolation and are part of an iterative cycle of policy change and implementation. Implications for changes in government policy are implicit in the GC approach; but a powerful HE network committed to GC and EFS would have undoubted influence in terms of advocacy for policy change. During the 1990s, although subject to increasing government interference and control, as HE is now, local government managed to find the space and 'creative autonomy' (Atkinson and Wilks-Heeg, 2000) to take a lead in promoting the goals of the first World Summit and led the way internationally in terms of Local Agenda 21. Local government achieved this in the face of a central government, which at one time threatened the very existence of local government (Atkinson and Wilks-Heeg, 2000). By contrast, New Labour wants to see HE expand. Not withstanding resource problems, HE has an opportunity to take on board the modernization agenda of New Labour and to shape it to suit its own purpose. The strategy for HE is, at first sight, hugely instrumental, with a clear emphasis on equipping students with the necessary skills to compete effectively in the knowledge economy. However, its stated aims of widening participation and improving access, though instrumental in their intent, present HE with a host of opportunities to promote GC. Offering more flexible and varied forms of learning, pushing forward the equal opportunities agenda with flair and imagination, working with and in the community are all central elements of any successful strategy to widen HE opportunities.

Some HE providers have already made efforts in the area of sustainable practice and there are, undoubtedly, some who are already pursuing elements of a GC approach, without describing it thus. However, the long-term aim has to be to change the whole ethos and organizational structures of each institution in order to extend GC across the whole university. Research by the National Foundation for Education Research (NFER) (Morris and Schagen, 1995) on attitudinal active change indicates that there are certain triggers to change, such as the existence of motivated and committed champions within the staff force and support from senior management; but without institutional change and a supportive ethos, this can be very superficial.

In recent years, a project by the Development Education Association (DEA) in partnership with London South Bank, Middlesex, Bournemouth and Leeds universities has looked at some of the opportunities and implications for HE of adopting a GC approach (Mackenzie, 2000). The Oxfam framework was used as a starting point and adapted for trial use by HE project partners. This expanded framework has involved several different universities in a range of projects. In one, the chaplaincy has played a leading role in bringing together key players; in another, a core group of interested lecturers took the lead. Bournemouth University, which had had a historical connection with Dorset Development Education Centre, used a GC approach to inform its new vision and ethos for the university.

Academic policy and practice

In the UK, HE has sometimes been guilty of hiding behind the notions of academic freedom and privilege, and, for example, has not had a very strong track record in addressing issues of racism and sexism – both key components of global citizenship – within HE. For example, in 2002, of 130 universities there was not one single member of a minority ethnic group at Vice Chancellor or Pro-Vice Chancellor level (Bhattacharyya and Gulam, 2002). Social exclusion and poverty are also factors that many universities have not seriously addressed except in the form of academic research. When it comes to examining HE policies and practice in relation to these issues, there is little evidence of progress – for example, the overall percentage of students from working-class backgrounds remains the same as 20 years ago. Research in these areas tends to be externally funded and focused, and the very structure of departments, schools or faculties frequently mitigates against joined-up thinking and approaches. In addition, the culture of competition and subject specialism does not encourage the holistic approach that would be necessary to ensure that complex local and global issues could be explored or addressed. Departments rarely talk to other departments; subject specialists usually only relate to other subject specialists.

Developing GC approaches in HE

Nevertheless, although academic freedom may have been an inhibitor, it can still provide the space to develop a GC approach before the entrepreneurial instrumentalism of New Labour makes further inroads into HE. Despite the difficulties of funding and the drive to increase student numbers, the lack of a centrally controlled curriculum gives HE far greater scope to challenge and innovate, as the Strengths Weaknesses Opportunities Threats (SWOT) analysis in Table 5.1 demonstrates. In addition, Higher Education Funding Council for England (HEFCE) is now talking about providing money for widening participation and 'third-stream activities', and there seems to be an opportunity to open up a space for creative change.

Table 5.1 *SWOT analysis: developing GC approaches in HE*

Strengths	Weaknesses
Wide resource of academic expertise and knowledge of complex global and local issues	Competitiveness within the HE sector
	Marketing knowledge
	Narrow focus on subject specialism
Experience of working in partnership with other HE institutions	Lack of sharing ideas and collaboration across departments, schools and faculties
Not constrained by centrally set curricula	Top-down approaches by management in some institutions
Independence of the HE sector	
Democratic and participatory structures within some (primarily traditional) universities	
Strong subject associations in areas such as politics and social science	

Opportunities	Threats
Provide a lead role for the development of more sustainable communities, locally and globally	Academic elitism
	Marketing education, including GATS
Build upon expertise in the sector	Lack of funding puts pressure on fund-led research and course development
Create more inclusive and democratic institutions	Some HE staff lack awareness of complex global and local issues
Draw upon the diversity and richness of the wider community	Some resistance to change
Challenge the marketing of education	Government interference (eg top-up fees)
Improve the image of HE in the wider community	Drive to increase student numbers
Raise awareness across HE sectors of complex local and global issues	
Unlock synergy within institutions and across HE sectors	
Start to break down academic 'snobbery' and elitism	
Encourage more collaborative work across departments, schools and faculties	
Learn from international experience (eg Ball State University)	
Develop further research opportunities	
Support students in developing the knowledge, skills and values for a more just and sustainable world	
HEFCE money for widening participation	
Potential spill-over effects through cross-university networks	

Local and global actions

The DEA projects indicate that there will be different entry and starting points for different institutions depending upon their contexts and the interest and commitment of staff. Looking at the example of London South Bank university, we have analysed the contribution of our postgraduate programme in Education for Sustainability to a global citizenship approach. The context of this was our work in relation to preparing for the WSSD in 2002. Our programme was set up just after the first Rio Earth Summit in 1992, bringing together and developing environmental and development education within the emerging concept of EFS. It thus has the advantage of being constructed in a multi-disciplinary way, with key concerns about sustainability at its core. It is common in that it was developed by a consortium of NGOs and was brought into the university, rather than growing organically within South Bank. This has resulted in both strengths and weaknesses. It is also unusual in that it is, primarily, a distance-learning programme (with students in a wide range of global regions), with a small full-time cohort. In Figure 5.1 we have tried to identify the local, national and global actions and the connections between the programme's activities in relation to the 2002 WSSD. As it indicates, there are frequent links and overlaps between the local, national and global.

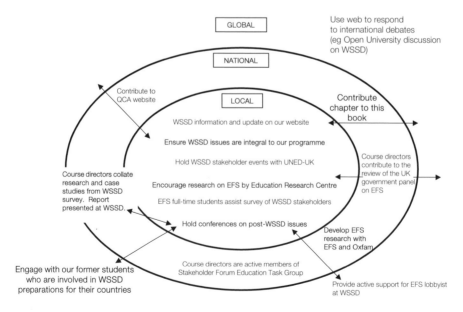

Figure 5.1 *EFS programme: London South Bank University's contribution to the WSSD*

Blocks to change

As is apparent in Figure 5.1, we have managed to contribute in terms of local, national and global actions. However, the achievements at the local level have primarily focused upon our programme and division. When we examine how we have affected the university more widely, either structurally, organizationally or in its ethos, our achievements have been very limited. For example, we have, as yet, been unable to revive the environmental committee or to set up a new EFS committee. In relation to our programme, we have not been able to convince staff who produce our materials that, in order to ensure our credibility in EFS, we need to use recycled paper. Figure 5.1 aptly illustrates the points mentioned earlier about the outward but narrow focus of many within HE.

In analysing the reasons for this, we have identified a number of structural and psychological blocks that represent a series of walls. These are presented in Table 5.2.

Table 5.2 *Blocks to change*

Psychological	Physical/Structural
Our own focus on our area of subject expertise	Compartmentalization of faculties and divisions Lack of opportunities for staff to meet or work together at university level
Close sense of team cooperation with our own tutors and divisional staff	Few staff recreational facilities where meetings can take place informally
Perception that we are too small to influence	Need to fight for recognition and development of our programme
Strong sense of EFS community outside the university, where we feel comfortable	Bureaucratic blocks within university
Difficult to relate to colleagues who do not share our ethos and aspirations	Culture and ethos of some sections of the university

Interestingly, many of the blocks actually seem to come from within ourselves and our own attitudes. We have a strong sense of an academic and NGO community who resides outside of the university, not within; hence, there are mental barriers. There is a tendency, therefore, to relate more strongly and seek support from outside rather than from within. As a result, some change needs to come from our own perceptions and focus. However, we feel that opportunities are opening up, with new university commitments to inclusion, participation, synergy and diversity. Moments of potential change are there when we choose to identify them and spaces for dialogue can be found. That is not to minimize the difficulties in institutional change; but – as has been shown by the DEA projects – opportunities can be created.

CONCLUSION AND RECOMMENDATIONS

What, therefore, are the implications of these issues and debates for higher education? How can HE start to address some of the current imperatives? This final section describes some of our own conclusions for discussion and debate. We have divided them into three areas – namely, institutional organization, curriculum and research – while realizing that these are interconnected and should be seen as overlapping.

In organizational and structural terms, there is a need for:

- champion(s) for GC/EFS at Senior Management Team (SMT) level;
- internal audits of sustainable practices within HE institutions, leading to revised practices that reflect a commitment to sustainable development (for example, energy efficiency and ethical banking);
- a curriculum audit to identify where a GC approach is already happening and where opportunities exist;
- staff involvement in developing a vision and ethos that reflect GC;
- staff development opportunities in GC and EFS;
- structures that encourage and facilitate cross-departmental working and synergy;
- incentives for staff to take on GC approaches within their areas;
- incentives for staff to develop relationships with relevant NGOs/other organizations who can provide partnerships for GC/EFS;
- a strong commitment to inclusion within the recruitment of students and staff so that GC and EFS are a formal part of induction and training for new staff at all levels;
- flexible structures to support the development of a variety of mixed modes for learning, including distance and e-learning, as well as face-to-face contact;
- policies that promote inclusion and access for all, especially those from sectors which have been disadvantaged.

Within the curriculum, there is a need to:

- develop skills, competencies and understanding in order to become actors in a complex world at local, national and global levels (within ourselves, as well as our students);
- take account of the complex multiple identities of people today;
- produce curricula that develop an understanding of complex local and global issues and encourage a community of enquiry;
- identify key areas for debate, research and scholarship in GC approaches (for example, citizenship and community issues, and local and global interactions);
- acknowledge the interrelation of knowledge and develop transdisciplinary ways of working;

- question the validity of current dominant forms of knowledge that have contributed to the present unsustainable world.

In conducting research, there is a need to:

- engage with different forms of knowledge (for example, local and indigenous);
- actively seek out research opportunities that reflect or develop GC/EFS;
- develop transdisciplinary research communities.

HE must adapt in order to be part of the solution and not part of the problem. The challenge for those in HE is to build upon our strengths and opportunities, and to find ways of minimizing threats and weaknesses. We believe that the time is ripe for further UK initiatives in EFS in the higher education sector, linked to international exchange of information and networking with HE providers around the world.

REFERENCES

Alexander, T (1996) *Unravelling Global Apartheid: An Overview of World Politics*, Cambridge, Polity Press

Atkinson, H and Wilks-Heeg, S (2000) *Local Government from Thatcher to Blair: The Politics of Creative Autonomy*, Cambridge, Polity Press

Bhattacharyya, G and Gulam, B (2002) Research seminar on 'Combating Institutional Racism in Higher Education and Further Education' at Anti-Racism Conference, Manchester, October 2002

Byrom A, Kent, N and Speed M (1998) *Children's Knowledge of Global Issues: A Research Study of 11–16 Year Olds*, Development Education Association, London, MORI, January–February 1998

Castells, M (1997) *The Power of Identity: Volume 2 of The Information Age – Economy, Society and Culture*, Oxford, Blackwell

Dhaliwal, L (2002) 'Across the Last Gay Frontier', *The Observer*, 29 September

Etzioni, A (1988) *The Moral Dimension: Towards a New Economics*, New York, Free Press

Frazer, E and Lacey, N (1993) *The Politics of Community: A Feminist Critique of the Liberal–Communitarian Debate*, London, Harvester Wheatsheaf

Mackenzie, A (2000) *DEA Global perspectives in HE project*, Unpublished report

Morris, M and Schagen, I (1995) *Green Attitudes or Learned Responses?* Berkshire, NFER

O'Neill, J (1994) 'Should Communitarians be Nationalists?', *Journal of Applied Philosophy*, vol 11, no 2, pp135–144

Oxfam (1997) *A Curriculum for Global Citizenship*, Oxford, Oxfam

Parker, J (2002) 'Positivist Methodology and Economic Fundamentalism: The Case of the World Bank', Paper given to the Cambridge Realist Workshop, 11 February 2002

Poole, R (1991) *Morality and Modernity*, London, Routledge

QCA (2000) *Guidelines on Citizenship Education*, London, QCA

Tudge, C (1991) *Global Ecology*, London, Natural History Museum Publications

UNCED (1992) *Earth Summit 1992: Agenda 21*, New York, UNCED

Woods, E (1994) *Capitalism against Democracy*, Cambridge, Cambridge University Press

Chapter 6

Learning by Doing: Environmental Performance Improvement in UK Higher Education

Peter Hopkinson, Peter James and Adam Van Winsum

INTRODUCTION

Higher education (HE) has three main forms of environmental impacts:

1   the direct impacts of its activities, such as use of energy and water in buildings or staff and student travel to and from their places of learning and teaching;
2   the indirect impacts on students' knowledge about, and behaviour with regard to, environmental issues;
3   the indirect impacts of research about environmental issues.

Other chapters in this book address the indirect impacts of HE; this chapter focuses on initiatives to minimize the environmental impacts of higher education in the UK. It is based on the experience, and results of, an action learning project known as the Higher Education Environmental Performance Improvement Initiative (HEEPI). This project is driving bottom-up improvement through a 'twin-track' strategy of developing better data about the environmental impacts of participating higher education institutions (HEIs), and by introducing processes – such as interactive workshops – that allow practitioners such as estates and procurement staff to discuss the implications with their peers.

The chapter is organized as follows. The first section summarizes the direct environmental impacts of UK (and, by extension, all) HE bodies. The second section describes various environmental performance initiatives that have occurred in HE in the UK, and how the HEEPI project relates to them. The third section provides more information on the HEEPI project itself, while the fourth, fifth and sixth sections describe three examples of data-driven learning, at Derby and Liverpool John Moores universities, and the University of Manchester Institute of Science and Technology (UMIST). The final section offers some conclusions.

Direct Environmental Impacts of Higher Education

The main direct environmental impacts of higher education include:

- consumption of energy, water and other resources;
- creation of substantial amounts of waste; and
- generation of large numbers of trips by staff, students and other employees travelling to, from and for work.

Energy

The UK HE sector consumes approximately UK£150 million per annum's worth of energy. This is primarily used to heat, light, ventilate and cool buildings. The importance – and cost of – energy is likely to rise in the future as a result of:

- new building regulations, which require sufficient metering in new (and, in practice, refurbished) buildings to enable at least 90 per cent of the estimated annual energy consumption to be accounted for (as well as other stipulations that also require better information);
- the European Energy Performance of Buildings Directive, which sets minimum requirements for the energy performance of all new and large renovated buildings, and requires their certification and – in the case of public buildings – the display of accurate information about their energy consumption and carbon dioxide emissions;
- forecast increases in the price of electricity, gas and water, which many experts believe have been unduly low in recent years.

Waste

UK higher education produces large quantities of solid waste. No one knows how much because very few universities or colleges collect data. But they will need to know more about their total waste volumes and the individual fractions (such as recyclable paper) within it as a result of:

- rising costs: disposal of trade waste is becoming more expensive because of higher operating standards and increases in landfill tax, while it is likely that removal of domestic waste from student residences will also be charged separately in the future (rather than being indirectly funded by council tax payments);
- general social – and, therefore, political – concern about waste disposal, resulting in demands to minimize waste generation and increase levels of recycling to reduce requirements for landfill and to conserve resources.

Water

UK higher education pays water/sewerage bills of over UK £35 million per annum. In some cases this means that water bills are almost as great as heating bills. Despite this, many HEIs do not actively manage and conserve water.

Transport

A life-cycle assessment of higher education environmental impacts by the Open University found that transport to and from places of learning accounts for a greater level of energy consumption than on-site activities (Roy et al, 2002). However, no accurate information is available on the total number of trips made, and therefore their environmental impacts, in the UK.

PREVIOUS INITIATIVES TO IMPROVE ENVIRONMENTAL PERFORMANCE

There have been a number of such initiatives, which have taken two main forms: high-level actions by working groups and external organizations, and actions by the main UK funding body, the Higher Education Funding Council for England (HEFCE).

The 1993 Toyne report was one of the earliest sector-wide initiatives that attempted to focus attention on the link between higher (and further) education and sustainable development, including the environment. It followed the 1992 Rio Earth Summit and received widespread promotion and publicity. It made a series of recommendations, with the most relevant to environmental performance being that 'after consultation with its staff and students, every HE and FE [further education] institution should formally adopt and publicize by the beginning of 1994/1995 a comprehensive environmental policy, together with an action plan for its implementation' (Toyne, 1993).

However, a 1996 review of progress found that out of the 756 HE and FE institutions, only 114 had or were implementing an environmental policy, and those that were making progress were mainly driven by financial savings (Ali Khan, 1996). The review concluded that the majority of institutions and organizations that participated in the 1993 report demonstrated 'considerable indifference' to its recommendations.

Partly in response to these findings, in 1997 a UK non-governmental organization (NGO), Forum for the Future, received funding for an HE 21 project. Its aim was to identify good practice and to demonstrate the opportunities for progress in selected areas of sustainable development. Around 20 HEIs participated. A follow-on project, the Higher Education Partnership for Sustainability – involving a collaboration between Forum for the Future and 18 HEIs – began in 2000, with a focus on implementation. In the case of environmental performance, this has involved promoting good practice and providing tool kits and guidance on selected areas such as waste and one on procurement (see www.forumforthefuture.org.uk).

Another externally led initiative is that of 2001 Business in the Environment (BIE). This organization has developed an Index of Corporate Environmental Engagement, initially to assess leading UK companies. This identifies a number of performance-related elements (for example, the existence of an environmental policy) that are scored by BIE on the basis of information returned in a questionnaire. The results are then published in the form of quartiles. The BIE index has been applied to HEIs in the Yorkshire and Humberside area for some years and is now being rolled out nationally. However, while the final league tables created by the BIE index have been successful in attracting the attention of senior management, the fact that it measures organizational processes rather than actual environment perform-ance means that it is only an indirect stimulus to practical changes on the ground.

In contrast with the external initiatives – which have been primarily driven by environmental and/or sustainability goals – the environment-related work of HEFCE has been more financially driven, with a focus on opportunities for more efficient use of energy and water. At the same time as the Toyne review was being conducted, HEFCE initiated a major review of energy management in the sector, leading to a series of publications and recommendations for more effective practices (HEFCE, 1996). As an example, one recommendation was that a HEI should have a full-time energy manager (or equivalent) for every UK£1 million of expenditure on electricity and fuel. The review also published benchmarks for the energy performance of different types of buildings, such as residential, academic teaching, research and catering . The impact of this energy management review is currently being assessed by HEFCE.

Several studies, and much anecdotal evidence, suggest that the impact of these initiatives on environmental performance has been patchy. While some institutions have very good records on energy and water efficiency (see examples below), many do not. And very few have come to terms with the issues of transport or waste. The most thorough review was conducted on HE energy performance by the Science Policy Review Unit of Sussex University as a part of a European research project (Sorrell, 2000). This identified a large number of barriers to improved energy efficiency and reduced wastage, including lack of policies and resources to implement extant policies, lack of incentives and the existence of disincentives to alter practices.

Existing initiatives, therefore, have a mixed record of success in stimulating environmental improvement; in some cases they have been failures. Anecdotal evidence suggests that one reason for this has been their 'top-down' or 'externally driven' nature. While these approaches can have the advantage of engaging senior management and/or bringing new ideas into the sector, they can – and anecdotal evidence suggests that they often do – appear as idealistic and impractical to the people who are charged with their implementation (typically, professionals in the estates and other operational functions).

THE HEEPI PROJECT

The HEEPI project was established in order to support bottom-up and practitioner-led approaches to supplement, and to help overcome, some of the barriers to top-down approaches (see www.heepi.org.uk for more information). Its origin lay in a series of projects on opportunities for greater energy efficiency and water efficiency within the University of Bradford by students on its MSc course in Business Strategy and Environmental Management. These demonstrated the opportunities for improvement, but also the barriers to their achievement. Investigation showed that Bradford was not the only university in this situation and sparked the idea of a collaborative initiative to take things forward.

The HEEPI project is funded under HEFCE's Good Management Practice initiative and is project-managed by the University of Bradford. It involves a core partnership of Bradford and three other HEIs: Leeds Metropolitan University, the University of Gloucestershire and UMIST, together with the Joint Procurement Policy and Strategy Group (JPPSG) and Yorkshire universities. It also has representatives of the Association of University Directors of Estates (AUDE) and the Environmental Association of Universities and Colleges (EAUC) on its management group. The project began in September 2001 and will run until March 2005.

HEEPI's core aims are to develop:

- better and more comparable data on HE environmental performance to stimulate environmental benchmarking, for example by collecting energy and water data for individual buildings; and
- the capacity of staff with environment-related responsibilities to achieve positive environmental change within their institutions.

In both cases, it builds on the experience of, and works closely with, the experience of practitioner networking bodies such as AUDE, EAUC and ShareFair (supported by the Building Research Establishment). The two former bodies are also represented on the project's management board.

HEEPI's main areas of work comprise the following:

- examination of ways in which existing data collected for the annual Estate Management Statistics (EMS) exercise can be utilized for environmental improvement;
- definition, and preliminary collection, of building-level utilities data;
- actions to gather data, develop indicators and stimulate improvement in procurement, transport and waste;
- in-house improvement actions by the four partner bodies;
- case studies of environmental performance improvement in HEIs.

Use of existing EMS data

One distinctive, if not unique, feature of UK higher education is the collection by HEFCE of a large amount of data on estates management: the EMS. The objective of this is to achieve more efficient use of resources by encouraging benchmarking. As the EMS exercise collects data on energy and water consumption, it is potentially of great value to environmental performance improvement. The potential for this was examined in detail during the early stages of HEEPI through a practitioner workshop and other means. The conclusion was that (although the data has many uses) it is – because it is presented at HEI level only – too aggregated for most environmental benchmarking activities. This is best accomplished by building-level data, which subsequently became the main focus of the project's benchmarking work (see the following section).

However, the EMS data is very useful for broad-brush comparison and awareness-raising purposes. The project has therefore produced data for energy and water consumption per student and per square metre, adjusted to reflect differences in HEIs' subject mix. This reveals major differences in performance. It also suggests that if each HEI in the three lowest quartiles raised their performance to the average of the quartile above them, there would be scope for savings of tens of millions of pounds.

Development of building-level energy and water benchmarking

Much of HEEPI's work during its first two years has focused on developing a benchmarking database of energy and water consumption in individual HEI buildings. This has been achieved through a workshop process to draw in practitioners and allow them to debate key issues and reach conclusions. The process has been enabled by the collection of data on buildings – initially in crude form, and then more refined as common definitions were introduced and other measures were taken to achieve greater standardization and usefulness. The first three workshops focused on these topics; but subsequent ones have examined different types of building (for example, biosciences or engineering) in considerable detail. A number of participating HEIs have already benefited from these detailed comparisons. At one institution, for example, the comparison revealed anomalously high heating in one building, which was subsequently traced to someone manually overriding the pre-set controls. Putting this right should save thousands of pounds a year.

Data, indicators and improvement for procurement, transport and waste

Similar action-learning workshops have been held to identify opportunities for better data, and actions for improvement, in each of these areas. As an example, the four HEEPI core partners agreed to collect detailed information on waste disposal in their institutions. The subsequent discussion of their findings revealed that the costs were generally higher than they previously assumed, and that there were opportunities for improvement which had previously not been noticed.

In-house improvement actions by the four partner bodies

As the lead partner, the University of Bradford has felt a responsibility to take the lead on this topic. As a direct result of the HEEPI project, the university has therefore decided to appoint a full-time environmental manager and to install additional energy metering. It is expected that the costs of these will be recouped in energy and other savings within a three- to five-year period. The other partners have also made a number of improvements.

Case studies of environmental performance improvement in HEIs

The project has also collected examples of good practice – and especially those which have involved a process of developing better information and then using this to drive change – and disseminated these through the medium of case studies. The structure of these cases is designed to appeal to three target audiences: a senior manager; a general audience of estates officers, academics and students; and a technical audience seeking more detail on specifics. The following sections summarize three of these cases.

ENERGY AND WATER EFFICIENCY AT UMIST

In 1997, UMIST appointed a new energy manager, Chris Cunningham, with a brief of reducing energy costs by 10 per cent over three years. Following an initial audit, the university adopted a two-track strategy:

1   Use the existing data and infrastructure to identify 'quick wins' (ie cost-effective improvement opportunities that can be introduced immediately).
2   Plan and implement an investment programme for more numerous and sophisticated meters that can be read by telephone or network connection to enable more improvement opportunities to be identified in the future.

The initial audit revealed that:

- There were considerable variations in the consumption of similar buildings, both with regard to each other and the HEFCE building energy benchmarks.
- There were large variations in usage that could not be identified through monthly or even weekly meter readings.

Only one quarter of water inputs could be related to specific areas of consumption due to a limited number of internal meters. Some meters, furthermore, were not operating properly, or were being read at irregular intervals, so that their data was unreliable.

The immediate responses were, therefore, to repair or replace defective meters, and to undertake a more detailed analysis of buildings that appeared to have excessive consumption. Daily meter readings were taken at 8.00 am and 4.00 pm Monday to Friday over several weeks. This enabled daily, night-time and weekend consumption profiles to be established. The exercise suggested that over half of total electricity consumption (which then accounted for half of UMIST's energy costs) occurred outside normal operating hours, Monday to Friday, 7.00 am until 6.00 pm.

One immediate application of the enhanced information was to follow an example set by Cambridge University and to perform a detailed check of whether the amount of energy-related value-added tax (VAT) being reclaimed was accurate. In fact, it wasn't, and UMIST received UK£80,000 of overpaid tax.

Between 1997 and 2002, UMIST also invested in:

- upgrading of almost all existing meters to those capable of being read remotely, typically at half-hour intervals (code 5-pulsed meters);
- installation of many new sub-meters in order to allow key consumption areas to be measured;
- development of a telemetry infrastructure to enable remote reading, involving data loggers at the meter; power supply; cabling to transmit the information and a telephone or local area network (LAN) link; and, in the case of gas meters, electrical isolation;
- acquisition of sophisticated energy-management software to make more effective use of the additional data.

To some degree, a strategic decision was made to invest in this infrastructure rather than higher expenditure on energy-efficient equipment itself.

The sophisticated infrastructure that now exists enables very detailed analysis of the energy consumption of buildings. A rolling programme is in place in which all access to a selected building is blocked at weekends. Everything possible is then switched off to establish base-load consumption. Over the weekend, blocks of lighting and equipment are switched back on in sequence so that their consumption can be measured. This enables better prioritization of measures, and makes it easier to quantify potential savings from new investment in lighting or other areas.

This investment has been accompanied by the creation of a network of approximately 30 'energy champions' throughout the university's departments. These volunteers liaise with the energy manager on a number of issues, such as purchases of new equipment or pre-notification of utility-intensive experiments. They are also the first point of contact for investigating excessive consumption.

Momentum is also maintained through annual energy budgeting, which set targets for reductions in cost compared with the previous year. During 2001/2002, for example, costs were reduced by UK£200,000 compared to the original estimate. While much of this resulted from milder weather and a drop in utility prices, a good proportion of the reduction was also related to better information.

Some examples of how these benefits have been achieved are listed below.

Trade effluent payments

The costs of discharging wastewater vary according to whether it is trade effluent (which must be specifically licensed and is, generally, fairly cheap because historic prices are charged) or general effluent. In 1998 a North-West Water analysis suggested that UMIST's trade effluent allowance should be reduced, creating an additional cost to UMIST of around UK£6000 per annum. The supplier's calculations were partly based on the level of water consumption; so the concurrent installation of a number of water sub-meters enabled more accurate figures to be obtained on this and, therefore, estimates of effluent discharges. As a result North-West Water withdrew the change. UMIST therefore gained, in addition to other benefits, an immediate UK£6000 a year of benefit from the UK£15,000 that the meters cost.

Unnecessary running of equipment

A detailed analysis of electricity and steam consumption in two chemistry buildings revealed that many activities were carrying on 24 hours a day, even though the buildings were not used at night. An investigation then found that someone had inadvertently switched over an override switch in both buildings, which should have turned the equipment off at night. This had not been picked up by routine testing of the time controls in the buildings. In another building, new pulsed meters identified high out-of-hours water consumption. The main use of water in the building was to cool equipment; but a detailed investigation found that much of the input was returned to waste only marginally cooler than it was received. The implication – which proved justified – was that the water was being simply left to run rather than being matched with the actual cooling needs. As a result, an automated cooling system has been put in place, with the UK£150,000 of investment expected be paid back in reduced water charges in under three years.

Evaluation of energy efficiency measures

Many energy efficiency measures require changes in behaviour and operating practices if their full potential is to be realized. UMIST's sophisticated metering infrastructure now makes it much easier to evaluate the actual impact of new measures so that adjustments can be made and – if necessary – investment plans can be changed. For example, a detailed analysis of electricity use in one building that was being refurbished concluded that there was great scope to reduce consumption for lighting. In the summer of 2002, over 500 T5 luminaries with sophisticated time controls were installed (cheaper alternatives are available; but it was felt that better control would result in greater savings). An evaluation of their first few months of operation showed that this was the case, so that it is now much more likely that similar actions will be taken with future refurbishments. Information of this kind also helps to persuade internal decision-makers that further investment in metering is worthwhile.

A final benefit of improved information is that it enables internal users to make better purchasing decisions – for example, by forcing them to consider long-term utilities consumption – and to have a better understanding of the implications of actions by contractors and other supplier.

The UMIST example therefore shows that:

- It is vital to plan for quick wins from any investment in metering in order to justify the initiative and build support for further progress.
- Utility suppliers can be very helpful in providing information from their own meters and – on occasion – by installing higher-quality meters than normal.
- A network of internal champions can be very helpful in improving information availability and flows, and building support for action.
- It is important to anticipate future requirements for more and better-quality data when installing new meters; they should be capable of being remotely polled by monitoring and targeting software.
- A rolling programme of detailed analysis of consumption patterns in specific buildings can pay real dividends.

WATER EFFICIENCY AT LIVERPOOL JOHN MOORES UNIVERSITY

Like most universities during the 1990s, Liverpool John Moores University (LJMU) had no detailed information on water consumption and simply paid the provider's invoice when it was received. However, in 1998 it was noticeable that water costs were approaching those for gas. In order to investigate what was expected as excessive consumption, LJMU worked with its water supplier to conduct a detailed audit. The first phase was to check the profile of three years' of invoices, which revealed that many invoices were based on estimates rather than actual meter readings, that the university was being billed for some sites that it did not own (and not billed for others which it did) and that some meters were inaccurate and/or leaking at the meter point. The exercise also revealed a major leak at the James Parsons Building, Bryom Street site. This site is situated on sand, and leaks were therefore not physically apparent. They were also not picked up from invoices because these were estimated. The university later calculated that 147,518 cubic meters of water had been wasted over a period of 31 months up to May 1999. The fractured pipe work was repaired immediately, reducing consumption at this site to approximately 1300 cubic meters per month. The previous month before, the repairs registered 3800 cubic meters of water consumed.

The generation of this detailed information eventually resulted in the university receiving a repayment of over UK£80,000 from the supplier. It also stimulated water meter rationalization and supply network downsizing. By having more than one incoming supply, the university was incurring more than one standing charge, which could now be avoided. The information that the new meters have provided highlighted opportunities for (and soon resulted in the implementation of) water efficiency measures, many with paybacks of two to three years or less. These included dams in cisterns; urinal controls; percussion taps; inline restrictors; and replacement showerheads.

The net result of these measures was a reduction of consumption from 268,168 cubic meters in early 1998 to 72,053 cubic meters in early 2001, with a fall in annual costs over the same period from UK£257,288 to UK£95,842. These benefits were gained with an investment of UK£75,000.

In conjunction with the metering and financial improvements, water reduction methods were introduced across the site. The showerhead restrictors alone cut down consumption drastically. Across the LJMU site, the average water flow was 22 litres per minute. All showers in halls of residence, sports facilities and staff changing facilities were updated. This resulted in a reduced water flow of 6.5 litres per minute per showerhead across the campus.

During the three-year improvement programme, the following savings were able to be realized:

- water consumption reduction by 73 per cent;
- water cost reductions by 63 per cent;
- consumption reduced by 383,164 cubic meters, saving UK£298,000.

The total cost for the water efficiency programme was UK£75,000 over the three years. This included:

- repair to underground leaks;
- disconnection of redundant supplies;
- replacement of meters;
- downsizing supply meters;
- condensing supplies to a common source;
- urinal controls, WC dams, push control taps, inline restrictors and replacement showerheads;
- team energy accounting software programme;
- new pulsed meters;
- interfacing with the company TREND BEMS.

The case shows that:

- Water costs are a growing proportion of utilities expenditure; but most people are unaware of their size – hence, building awareness is necessary to achieve action.
- Because water has been neglected in most HEIs, there are great savings opportunities from simple efficiency measures.
- The starting point is a thorough audit of consumption, followed by a metering strategy to build a more detailed picture of consumption.
- The greatest gains are likely to be achieved by a continuous improvement programme, rather than occasional one-off measures.

WASTE MINIMIZATION AT DERBY

Several universities – including the University of Derby – have introduced new 'pay-by-weight' contracts with disposal companies that require accurate measurement of the waste which is collected. This is achieved by combined electronic identification of individual waste containers with an automatic weighing system on each collection vehicle. Doing this enables universities to pay only for waste collected, unlike previously when universities would have paid per skip, irrespective of how full skips were. There is also a greater incentive for HEIs to undertake two win–win actions:

1   Install on-site compactors (which reduce costs associated with transport and disposal that are based on volume rather than weight, and also save landfill space).
2   Separate out recyclable materials.

The data collected means that collection can be better matched with actual generation of waste, allowing savings to be made by reducing the number of bins and/or the frequency of lifts. It also allocates the costs of waste disposal to the departments that are responsible for generating the waste in the first place, thereby giving them a financial incentive to minimizes waste production.

By using the information provided by its new contract, the University of Derby reduced the average number of bin empties per week from 65 to 48 between 1999 and 2002, and the average number of bins on campus from 136 to 118. This equates to a reduction of over 10 per cent in its total waste disposal bill. Several other universities have since followed Derby's lead, including Bradford and Leeds Metropolitan universities.

The process of moving to, and managing, the new waste system was also important. In order to ensure that all interests were involved, the University of Derby set up a tendering team, consisting of the:

- environmental/energy officer;
- waste officer;

- purchasing officer;
- operations officer;
- residential representative;
- cleaning supervisor.

The university also holds regular three-monthly partnership meetings with all of their main contractors, including their waste contractor. These meetings give both sides an opportunity to discuss any concerns that they have with the contract, as well as its successes. As Derby has several sites, key staff from all campuses are invited to the meetings. The value of this approach is illustrated by one site, which disposes of ash from a boiler house. This caused problems in the past as the bins are sometimes too hot to be emptied, leading to a build-up of waste. The discussion identified a solution, which was a change to the site's operating procedures and an increase in bin lifts. The meeting has also helped the contractor to better understand the characteristics of waste generation in higher education, such as the types of waste produced and the monthly variances in the amount of waste to be disposed of.

The case shows that:

- It is feasible to have detailed data on waste generation – whatever contractors may say; it is also highly desirable because it can generate significant economic and environmental benefits.
- Partnering with other HEIs to create joint tenders – and a larger volume of business for suppliers – can help to create incentives for contractors to bear the initial costs of setting up a waste monitoring system.
- A single point of contact – and regular meetings between a university and its waste contractor – can allow quick responses to problems, provide learning opportunities for both sides and highlight improvement opportunities.
- It may take 6 to 12 months to get new systems working; the greatest benefit is likely to occur after several years, when there is a good run of data on waste-generation patterns.
- Using the data to charge departments for waste generated specifically by them can be a powerful driver for waste minimization.
- Contracts need to be flexible in order to take account of variations in waste generation, particularly the difference between term time and other periods.
- Improvements like this can be more easily achieved if key decision-makers are aware of the upward trend in waste disposal costs.

CONCLUSIONS

The previous examples show how environmental performance improvement in HE requires a combination of better data and the ability to learn from it so that it encourages improvement. A key aspect of the latter is the need for individual 'champions' who are supported and encouraged by internal and external networks. The HEEPI project has sought to enable these activities by providing not only better data, but also action learning-based events to strengthen practitioners' networks and to change skills. Experience shows that this can result in an improved understanding of their situation and opportunities, and a greater level of motivation and competence to achieve results.

Environmental performance improvement also has other connections with the learning themes presented in this book. One important aspect of HE education is the credibility of its providers – a concept that can be measured in various ways, but which includes such elements as 'practising what they preach' or 'demonstrating general competence in the way that they conduct themselves'. Any failure to address internal environmental issues can be potentially very damaging to the credibility of courses and other forms of learning that have an obvious environmental component. Since environmental management is often seen as a sign of whether organizations are good at management, in general, there is also a risk that poor environmental performance will create more generic negative impacts upon a provider's reputation.

As this chapter has shown, energy, waste and water management, or transport impacts, can also be very useful areas for student research, particularly when they are studying relevant topics (for example, architecture and environmental management). They typically learn a great deal not only about the technicalities of the topic, but also about how what happens in practice is influenced by organizational and personal factors (for example, the division of responsibilities and the commitment of individuals).

Finally, environmental performance improvement can also provide a means of breaking down the apartheid between 'learning' (for both staff and students) and the 'non-learning' (estates and other operational staff) in higher education. The two sides are often invisible to each other – except on the occasions when things go wrong – and exist in mutual incomprehension. But, as the HEEPI project and other environmental initiatives show, it is possible for both sides to participate in a dialogue that can provide benefits not only for themselves, but for the natural environment as well.

REFERENCES

Ali Khan, S (1996) *Environmental Responsibility: A Review of the 1993 Toyne Report*, London, HMSO

HEFCE (1996) *Energy Management Study in the Higher Education Sector: Management Review Guide*, Reference M 16/96, May, Bristol, HEFCE

Roy, R, Potter, S, Smith, M and Yarrow, K (2002) *Towards Sustainable Higher Education: Environmental Impacts of Conventional Campus*, Print-based and electronic distance/open learning systems, Report DIG-07, Design Innovation Group, The Open University, May

Sorrell, S (2000) *Barriers to Energy Efficiency in the UK Higher Education Sector*, Sussex, Science Policy Review Unit, University of Sussex

Toyne, P (1993) *Environmental Responsibility*, London, HMSO

Chapter 7

Eco-design

Jack Bradley and Joanne Crowther

INTRODUCTION

This chapter argues that there is a need to raise awareness about sustainability issues (specifically, eco-design) among higher education (HE) and tertiary-level students. It suggests that higher education institutions (HEIs) need to address this growing area of interest effectively in order to train the next generation of product designers to develop new and innovative products that are not detrimental to the environment. This new approach will require stakeholders from schools, HE, government and industry to work together in an interdisciplinary manner in order to achieve eco-focused educational programmes. Bradford University's School of Engineering, Design and Technology Eco-Design workshops provide a case study of what can be achieved when stakeholders work together.

DEFINITION

Eco-design is a relatively new way of looking at product development. It aims to assess the entire life cycle of the product. Brezet (1997, p37) defined eco-design as:

> [d]eveloping products where the environment becomes a co-pilot in product development. In this process the environment is given the same status as more traditional industrial values such as profit, functionality, aesthetics, ergonomics, image and overall quality. In some cases the environment can even enhance traditional business values.

A simple working definition of eco-design for our use can be a method of systematically integrating environmental considerations into the design of products, processes and services throughout their lifetime. It can be argued that eco-design goes beyond simply seeking to minimize waste and pollution effects. Instead, it seeks to look at the entire process over the complete life cycle, beginning with choice of raw materials, extraction and processing, production use and end of life.

If performed correctly, eco-design should develop new products that are better and superior to non-eco-friendly products and should open up exciting new markets.

THE IMPORTANCE OF ECO-DESIGN PRODUCTS

Why focus on products? It is claimed that 93 per cent of production material is never used on the final product and 80 per cent of products are discarded after a single use. Scope for improving the environment by utilizing eco-design principles on all new products is vast simply because there are so many produced. Eco-design offers the environmentally astute designer many opportunities for improvement – for example, improving processing and manufacture by incremental innovation; designing products for longer life; being selective in the choice of material and adopting a minimalist approach to the use of raw material. The manufacturing process can be designed to use minimal energy and water and the end product can be designed for low energy consumption. The goal of minimizing pollution throughout the entire life cycle is, of course, the main objective.

THE IMPORTANCE OF TEACHING ECO-DESIGN TO UNDERGRADUATES

Traditional business ideology dictates that companies compete on quality, price and delivery. Customers want a product or service that will satisfy their needs at the lowest price. This thinking gives no consideration to the wider issues that will ensure the long-term sustainability of both the company and the environment.

Brimacombe (2001) argues that the key elements of eco-design are to produce functional products that are lightweight and durable, re-usable, recyclable and non-polluting; these functional products must simultaneously be eco-/bio-friendly, resource and energy efficient and create minimal emissions and waste. Brimacombe further argues that companies which practice eco-design operate from a triple bottom line of being environmentally sound, commercially viable and cost-effective, and socially responsible.

By pursuing the philosophy of eco-design, this will allow the needs of the present generation to be met without compromising the ability of future generations to meet their own consumable needs. This will involve making products/profit responsibly and paying attention to the idea of the triple bottom line:

- Profit: it would be unrealistic not to acknowledge profit as being a major driving factor in a capitalist society; however, it can be argued that short-term gains are at the expense of long-term sustainable profit.

- Environment: the true cost of producing products takes the environment into consideration. Traditional design thinking has been preoccupied with two main areas: production and use. Eco-designers need to be trained to take into consideration wider aspects, such as raw materials, production, use and, most importantly, end of life, including full disposal costs.
- People: progressive companies have for a long time realized that people are the most important resource. Eco-design thinking fully recognizes the important contribution that staff can make and the increased feel-good factor that staff members derive from being part of an environmentally friendly organization.

THE DRIVERS

The drivers for eco-design are well known – that is to say, current legislation and, more importantly, future European directives on product design and manufacture, which include the Waste Electrical and Electronic Equipment Directive (WEEE), the Restriction of Certain Substances Directive (ROHS), packaging regulations, the End of Life of Vehicle Directive (ELV) and the Electrical and Electronics Equipment Directive (EEE). Increasing disposal costs, increasing land fill taxes and all waste products have to be paid for, and the current thinking is that the polluter pays the costs for all of the environmental damage throughout the entire life cycle of the product. Some of these problems can be resolved by adopting simple good housekeeping measures; other more complex problems need a more systematic life-cycle thinking approach.

Customer pressure and policies

The rise of the Green consumer is impacting upon the need for designers to meet what has, in the past, been a niche market. However, with growing public awareness, this market is one of the most rapidly expanding. Large manufacturing companies, acting under consumer pressure or legislation, are forcing Green policies down the supply chain and insisting upon detailed life-cycle analysis of supplier products and associated policies in integrated product policy (IPP).

Taking into consideration the drivers that have already been outlined to improve the environmental impact on product manufacture over the next decade, it is imperative that a new kind of product designer is created. The traditional approach of most designers, design teaching and training is simply to concentrate on the production and use of products without giving much thought to earlier stages of raw material extraction, processing and end-of-life considerations. The main objective has traditionally been short-term profit maximization at the expense of environmental impact. With this in mind, we have considered how the wider context of engineering education may be utilized effectively to address sustainability issues.

In August 2002, the School of Engineering at the University of Bradford underwent a major restructuring and was renamed the School of Engineering, Design and Technology. The rationale behind the move was to reflect the change from a traditional engineering department to a broader school, encompassing not only engineering but also major aspects of design and technology. The new school aims to embrace and meet the aspirational needs of students who wish to enter careers in traditional engineering, together with students who wish to follow career paths in product design and advanced technology. The school has developed from the five previous departments (the Department of Civil Engineering; the Department of Chemical Engineering; the Department of Industrial Technology; the Department of Electrical Engineering; and the Department of Mechanical and Medical Engineering) and concentrates upon six main programme areas (design; civil engineering; mechanical and automotive engineering; electrical and telecommunications; technology management; medical technologies), including a foundation year in order to supplement additional mathematics skills that may be lacking in certain students.

The new school has a firm commitment to teach design as a multidisciplinary subject across all disciplines. However, in 2001 a new optional module in eco-design was offered to the second-year students and eco-design principles were incorporated within the final-year Product Design and Innovation module. The outline syllabus covered the following areas: drivers for eco-design, including current and future legislation; supply chains; innovation; design methods; eco-design tools; and increasing efficiency. Undergraduate students analyse disposal costs, transportation costs, taxation policies and consumer pressure, and take into account provision for the growing number of Green consumers and environmentally friendly supply chains.

Other aspects covered in the module include product life-cycle analysis; product concept and design for sustainable development; resources; material and energy processing; cost-effective use of recyclate; waste reduction; minimized packaging; and distribution. The module also offers best practice industrial case studies and students undertake projects on a variety of topics, including product usage, maintenance repair and reuse, product recycling, recovery and disposal. Finally, students are taught about creative thinking and are introduced to the concept of 'thinking outside the box' in order to problem solve.

In September 2003, a new undergraduate BSc degree course in eco-design was launched at the University of Bradford. This degree course seeks to meet the interests of students, while addressing the needs of industry in light of current and future legislation in eco-design.

Eco-design tools

There are several eco-design tools on the market that were used by the students at the University of Bradford. It was felt that by introducing students to computer-based life-cycle analysis (LCA) tools, this would side-track the students into concentrating on familiarizing themselves with the software, thereby missing out on the key learning objectives.

Computer- based systems have been used by Matthew Simon at Sheffield Hallam University with a measure of success. Simon does, however, state that 'The distinctive features of LCA, with a large database, unfamiliar units and substances and yet considerable uncertainty in data values, lead engineering students to misconceptions and errors in their LCA analyses' (Simon, 2002, p303). He goes on to argue that:

> [i]ndustrial designers, or product designers, are divergent thinkers. They are much more comfortable with a holistic view of a problem and a lateral approach to a solution than engineering designers. In the UK, industrial design students are encouraged to be individualists, not team workers, and not to worry excessively about numbers. So accommodating the concepts of sustainability and life-cycle thinking is not a problem for them. (Simon, 2002)

We have avoided the use of computer based eco-design tools, opting instead for more conventional methods. The tools which the students were initially introduced to were the MET (material cycle, energy use and toxic emissions) Matrix (Visser, 1995, p341). This is a simple tool that easily breaks down a product's manufacturing outputs into the three key areas listed in the title.

The eco-design check list is another useful tool that asks a series of questions concerning the functioning of a product as a whole. This useful checklist assists the students into life-cycle thinking mode and can be used to complement the MET Matrix. Other tools, such as the Eco-Design Improvements Options Chart (Visser, 1995, p341), enable students to list possible improvements to the product under analysis. Finally, the Priority Matrix permits students to systematically prioritize the improvements made using the previous tool. These tools can be found in the 'Eco-Design Promising Guide to Production and Consumption' worksheets (Brezet and Hemel, 1997).Tools that identify the internal and external drivers for eco-design are also useful and have been used at Bradford as a teaching tool.

Students taking the eco-design second-year module were assessed by means of a group life-cycle assessment project. A typical project involved the assessment of a 1980s-style telephone. The students were asked to produce a Gantt chart to monitor progress with the project. The following elements were then incorporated within the project.

In January 2002, the group began their project by attending specific lectures on the subject of eco-design, which also included videos and specialist training.

The next stage involved an introduction to eco-design, tools and methods. The group scheduled a deconstruction exercise into their programme for February 2002; a telephone was used as the product and was disassembled and analysed. The results of this exercise were written up by the group on completion of the deconstruction of the item and upon the group's findings.

The group conducted research into eco-design at the university's J B Priestley Library and via the internet. Areas investigated included the following:

- background and history of eco-design;
- materials used in the manufacture of the telephone;
- other products to investigate;
- external drivers for eco-design;
- the history and background of the telephone.

The results of the group's findings following their research were typed up under the following headings:

- material used in manufacture;
- background of eco-design;
- eco-portfolio matrix;
- MET Matrix;
- history and background of the telephone;
- internal drivers;
- external drivers.

A product life-cycle analysis diagram was produced, together with a design abacus which the group used as a problem-solving tool and as an aid to creative thinking and to generate new ideas. The group also considered the product's packaging in April 2002, and their recommendations were arrived at in May 2002.

The importance of teaching eco-design at tertiary level

Eco-design is not currently included in the national curriculum in any formal context. However, it is clearly important to raise awareness of environmental issues; one way of doing this is to introduce eco-design to students at tertiary-level education, thus giving them a foundation and background in this crucial area.

Surveys from the National Statistics Department for Environment, Food and Rural Affairs were carried out in early 2001 in its fifth survey of public attitudes to the environment in England (DEFRA, 2001). The following findings were reported:

- People were generally most worried about pollution issues.
- People were least worried about local environmental issues.
- Almost two-thirds said that they were 'very worried' about hazardous waste.
- More than half were 'very worried' about pollution in rivers and in bathing waters.
- 59 per cent were 'very worried' about the effects of livestock methods (including BSE).
- Only 22 per cent were 'very worried' about noise.

BRADFORD MODEL FOR TEACHING ECO-DESIGN: EXAMPLE AND CASE STUDIES

During National Science Week in 2002, the School of Engineering at the University of Bradford held a series of workshops for school pupils in year 12. One of these workshops featured the theme of eco-design and was organized in conjunction with Shot in the Dark, Environmental Education Communicators, based in Brighouse, West Yorkshire.

In order to introduce a fun element to the workshop, a creativity and brainstorming challenge was set for the students (the Wheelie Bin Challenge). The group was subdivided into teams of six students and sanitized refuse was presented to each team. The teams were tasked with creating something from the refuse, using their practical skills and imagination. The exercise was created in order to encourage creativity among the students. A small child with a healthy imagination can happily entertain him or herself with the simplest of 'toys' – for example, a cardboard box can become a miniature home. Using invention and creativity, the child is happily engrossed with a simple toy/tool.

This activity gave participants the chance to revert to simple, yet creative, thinking and activity. The concept was actively promoted to the students in order to encourage uninhibited creative thinking. Equally, during the brainstorming sessions of the workshops, students were encouraged to give free reign to their imaginations – and to present ideas randomly and without reservation. No suggestions were rejected. This method of 100 per cent acceptance of ideas enhances the students' confidence to contribute ideas to the group discussions and guaranteed that all suggestions/ideas would be considered.

Feedback from the pupils who took part in the eco-design workshops indicated that there was a clear interest in environmental issues. Students stated that they had learned a lot about the experience. The teaching material was at the appropriate level, and what is of most significant interest is that 70 per cent of the students taking part in the workshops made a clear statement that the workshops would change their lives and attitudes. We believe that it is this life-changing element of the workshops which will have the most profound and long-lasting impact on society.

The participants also felt that the valuable experience they had received during the eco-design workshops should be available to all keystage 4 and year 12/13 students.

Teaching life-cycle thinking

At the core of all eco-design thinking is an understanding of the basic concept of LCA, which is traditionally used for identifying the environmental strengths and weaknesses of a product, comparing products, environmentally benchmarking products and identifying areas of product improvement. There are three key stages involved, starting with identifying and quantifying the environmental aspects involved (for example, how much energy and raw material is used and how much waste is generated and released into the air, water and land). Assessing the environmental impacts of products will require finding empirical evidence and quantifiable detail on all of the aspects listed above. The third stage involves critically analysing the data and identifying opportunities for environmental improvements. This may seem a relatively simple procedure; however, a typical life cycle involves many hundreds of processes, as well as material extraction and chemical production, and each one will have its own particular supply chain with corresponding processes.

Those involved in the design of environmentally friendly products will be aware of the difficulties of using LCA as an environmental decision-making tool. There are several computer-based LCA tools; however, these can be difficult to use and still need considerable research and input of technical data. Understanding an LCA is a specialist task. The general feedback from the International Conference on Engineering Education in Sustainable Development, held in Delft in October 2002, concluded that LCA analysis is a difficult concept for first- and second-year undergraduate students to grasp. The Wheelie Bin Challenge left the workshop design team with the challenge of teaching a complex, high-level subject to year 11 and year 12 students. At this stage, Shot in the Dark was able to offer a suitable teaching tool to overcome this problem. This involved the use of the Ideas Integrated Design Abacus.

Unlike the detail of LCA, the Ideas Integrated Design Abacus takes a broad-brush approach, using scales of magnitude and not precise measures. These scales provide an indication of how far or how close the ideas are from the design goal.

From 21–26 July 2002, the University of Bradford's School of Engineering held a Further Education to Higher Education Summer School (FE$_2$HE). The FE$_2$HE summer school was a pilot scheme in which six UK universities ran summer schools to raise the aspirations of students at further education (FE) colleges and to increase the number of those students applying to study at HE institutions. The scheme was funded by the Department for Education and Skills (DfES) and the Sutton Trust. Fifty participants participated in the summer school at the University of Bradford and the eco-design workshop was included in the programme of events and activities.

The disassembly task

Students were given everyday household items, such as telephones, toasters, hairdryers, back massagers and torches, and were issued with a deconstruction assessment form to complete during the exercise. First, the students identified the product and the product function/service. Students learned that the function of a product could be further subdivided into its primary function (what it does – for example, a kettle heats water), its secondary and supportive functions (for example, in the case of a kettle, cut off heat and indicate when water is boiling), and its discretionary functions (enhancement of product appeal/attractiveness, which makes the product desirable and marketable).

In the second stage the groups dismantled the products and were asked to assess how easy this exercise was and to give reasons for their answer (for example, the product may have been difficult to dismantle due to glue, rivets, etc).

The groups looked at individual components used in the products' construction and were asked to list each one. The next step involved looking at the different materials used to make up the products and, again, students were asked to list these individually.

Once the materials had been identified, the students were asked if any of the materials were hazardous and, again if so, to list these. The students were asked if the materials were easy to identify (for example, types of plastic and metals).

The groups were asked if any of the components or modules could be re-used and, if so, to list those that they felt could be re-used. Again, the groups were asked if any of the materials could be recycled and to list those which they felt could be recycled.

The groups were asked to consider if their products could be easily repaired and to comment on this, as well as on the durability of the products and to look at and comment on any weaknesses that could shorten product life. The groups gave a measured evaluation regarding energy consumption during manufacture and use.

One of the main components of the disassembly exercise involved looking at product packaging. Students were asked if the packaging was reusable and if it could be recycled or composted. Students looked at the material from which the packaging was constructed and were asked to assess if it was made from a singular material or from several materials. Finally, the students were asked if they felt that the product was 'over-packaged'.

Towards the end of the disassembly activity the groups were asked if they could determine any obvious design improvements and to describe these. They were then asked to reflect upon their suggested design changes and assess if they would have a positive or negative impact on the following:

- cost;
- marketing;
- health and safety;
- the environment;
- manufacture;
- the function or service of the product.

Students were informed of current legislation regarding packaging, including the following:

- use of non-hazardous materials;
- reducing the number of containers;
- secondary uses for packaging;
- packaging and litter;

- use of biodegradable material;
- use of recycled materials;
- returnable, refillable systems.

The group was also informed about the ingenuity and inventiveness over the last few years of packaging designers who have helped manufacturers to deliver convenience and freshness to customers, and to find new ways of 'adding value' to the product through aesthetic or practical benefits. The way in which a product is packaged is often one of the major influences on whether people notice it and buy it, particularly in markets such as perfume and cosmetics, where image and branding play a crucial role. It was pointed out to the students that the cost of packaging can often be more than the cost of the product inside.

To compliment the eco-design workshop, the FE_2HE participants were taken on an industrial visit to Interface Fabrics at its Mirfield administrative headquarters in west Yorkshire. Interface Fabrics is a global manufacturing company that produces fabrics and carpet tiles for offices and commercial use. The company has a strong commitment to environmental awareness; indeed, its aspirational goal is to achieve a zero waste level in its manufacturing processes.

The US chairman of Interface Fabrics, Ray Anderson, is fully committed to ensuring that his company's manufacturing operation is as environmentally friendly as possible. The visit to Interface in July 2002 commenced with a lecture on environmental issues by one of the senior designers at Interface. Students watched a video on the effects of global warming and sustainable development. Examples of some of the company's products were shown to the group, including an office chair made from 100 per cent recycled material and other items manufactured from recycled and reprocessed fabric/material, including nettles and glass bottles. The students were shown further illustrations of the company's products and given examples of some of their customer bases, including the Odeon Cinema in Leicester Square. This example presented the group with a case study that they could relate well to and helped students to consider the use of recycled, environmentally friendly products and manufacture in a relevant context.

In addition to the FE_2HE summer school, the School of Engineering, Design and Technology at the University of Bradford also runs the Royal Academy of Engineering Headstart residential course each summer. From 14–18 July 2002, 30 year-12 Headstart participants took part in the course at Bradford.

One of the hands-on projects in the 2002 programme challenged the participants to design a house, taking into account various environmental factors. Participants were divided into teams and each team was given various coloured Lego bricks; each Lego brick represented a particular U-value. The teams were also given a choice of single-, double- or triple-glazed windows, choice of flooring materials and level of roof insulation.

The challenge was to design the most cost-effective, environmentally friendly house with the constraints of a 15-year mortgage at an 8 per cent interest rate. Feedback from the participants indicated that the mathematical modelling of the house proved to be highly challenging. In general, students relate well to issues regarding the environment and are able to apply the mathematical tools in an environmental context, helping them to achieve results.

Evaluation

A simple evaluation of the teaching of eco-design at the University of Bradford has resulted in the following observations, based on feedback from student questionnaires:

- Students at all levels appear to be interested in environmental issues.
- Students expressed an ignorance of environmental issues, coupled with a desire to learn the facts.
- An integrated approach to the teaching of eco-design was well received by the students.
- The teaching material of a highly complex subject was easily simplified to the required level for year-11 and year-12 students.
- Undergraduate students found the subject particularly interesting and have expressed a desire to take their new-found skills and expertise into industry upon graduation.

CONCLUSIONS

The authors recommend a multilevelled student approach, of introducing students to statistical data regarding the environment in order to give a good global perspective for environmental issues. This global view should be linked to practical, hands-on eco-design workshops, which include the disassembly of products and the use of the Design Abacus as a decision-making tool that also provides a simplified life-cycle analysis. This, coupled with the challenge of using sanitized waste products in the Wheelie Bin Challenge, inspires creativity among the participants. However, it is the industrial visit that has the effect of putting into context the theoretical and practical aspects of eco-design. We recommend that, wherever possible, all three learning tools should be incorporated within any environmental teaching programme.

REFERENCES

Brezet, H (1997) *Eco Design: A Promising Approach to Sustainable Production and Consumption*, United Nations Environment Programme

Brezet, H and van Hemel, C (1997) *A Promising Approach to Sustainable Production and Consumption*, Delft, Delft University of Technology (available from Delft University of Technology, Jaffalaan 9, 2628 BX Delft, The Netherlands)

Brimacombe, L (2001) *(Eco) Design for Profit – Achieving Commercial Success,* International Conference, 23–25 April 2001, Sheffield

DEFRA (2001) *Survey of Public Attitudes to Quality of Life and to the Environment: 2001* available at www.defra.gov.uk/environment/statistics/pubatt/content.htm

Simon, M (2002) *Life Cycle Thinking and LCA in Engineering Design Education 81,* Engineering Education in Sustainable Development, TU Delft, 24–25 October 2002

Chapter 8

Sustainable Development and Sustainable Development Education: An Eco-feminist Philosophical Perspective on the Importance of Gender

Karen Warren

INTRODUCTION

Sustainable development education (SDE) involves three basic issues. The first concerns the definition of sustainable development (SD). Its simplest and most well-known meaning was given in 1987 in *Our Common Future* (or the Bruntland Report): '[Sustainable development is] development that meets the needs of the present without compromising the ability of future generations to meet their own needs' (WCED, 1987). The second issue concerns the definition of SDE. A broad but flexible definition is that 'sustainable development education integrates the learning agenda with that of securing a sustainable future' (Parkin and Howard, 2002). The third issue concerns the rationale for SDE. Probably the most widely known and accepted rationale is given in Chapter 36 of Agenda 21, the 40-chapter agreement reached at the UN Conference on Environment and Development (UNCED) held in Rio de Janeiro in 1992, also known as the Earth Summit:

> *Education is critical for promoting sustainable development and improving the capacity of the people to address environment and development issues. While basic education provides the underpinning of any environmental and development education, the latter needs to be incorporated as an essential part of learning. Both formal and non-formal education are indispensable to changing people's attitudes so that they have the capacity to assess and address their sustainable development concerns. It is also critical for achieving environmental and ethical awareness, values and attitudes, skills and behaviour consistent with sustainable development and for effective public participation in decision-making.* (cited in Blewitt, 2002, p3)

While there is dispute about these three issues, this chapter assumes that these three position statements are reasonably accurate. The chapter argues that an eco-feminist philosophical perspective offers an important viewpoint on the interconnections among women, the environment, sustainable development and sustainable development education — what I call women–environment–sustainable development–education (WESDE) interconnections – that are crucial to any adequate understanding and implementation of SD and SDE practices, programmes or policies.

The chapter is organized into three main sections. The first section provides definitions of the key terms used throughout the chapter. The second section gives empirical data that shows the nature and importance of WESDE inter-connections. The third section draws on the preceding two sections to show eight curricular transformation projects that an eco-feminist philosophical perspective helps to illuminate. The chapter ends with a brief conclusion.

CONCEPTS OF GENDER, OTHERNESS, ECO-FEMINISM AND ECO-FEMINIST PHILOSOPHY

Gender and otherness

A minimal-condition conception of 'gender' is that it is a social construction (for example, of identity, roles and analyses) organized around conceptions of biological sex. Typically, the concept of gender is used (though not without controversy) to distinguish biological sex (male, female) from socially con-structed concepts of men and masculinity, and women and femininity. One of the earliest and most famous claims about gender is given by Simone de Beauvoir in 1949 when she wrote, 'One is not born, but rather becomes a woman' (Simons, 1995, p257). Beauvoir's view (and the one presumed in this chapter) is that there is no genetically determined trait or property that all women have by virtue of which they are women; what it means to be a woman means different things in different historical, material and social contexts.

A gender analysis is one that uses gender – typically, being a woman or a man – as the *lens* through which one makes visible, names, describes, observes, evaluates or theorizes about women and men. When a gender analysis is about women, its focus is on the ways in which women have been marginalized, excluded, exploited, subordinated, dominated or oppressed by those beliefs, attitudes, assumptions, roles, policies, systems and institutions that 'justify' the power and privilege of men over women. Gender analysis is also intimately linked with analyses of other marginalized, excluded, exploited, subordinated, dominated or oppressed groups – other 'Others'. The term 'Others' refers to those who are, or have been, marginalized, excluded, exploited, subordinated, dominated or oppressed, whether they are 'human Others' (such as women, people of colour, children and the poor) or 'Earth Others' (such as non-human flora and fauna).

Eco-feminism

Eco-feminism is a feminism that uses gender analysis to describe, analyse and resolve the varieties of ways in which the unjustified domination of women and other human Others has historically been interconnected with the unjustified domination of Earth Others (the non-human environment). These interconnections may be historical; empirical; socio-economic; conceptual; linguistic; symbolic and literary; spiritual and religious/theological; epistemological; political; ethical and theoretical (Warren, 2000, pp21–42). Because eco-feminism grows out of and reflects different feminist perspectives on these (alleged) interconnections, it is not surprising that there is not one meaning of 'eco-feminism'. Rather, eco-feminism is an umbrella term for a social movement and theory that claims that environmental problems are intimately interconnected with, and mutually reinforced by, unjustified systems of human domination ('isms of domination'). Despite differences among eco-feminists, all eco-feminists agree that it is not possible to seriously address most environmental issues without also addressing the gender, race/ethnic, socio-economic, geographic and colonial issues. For eco-feminists, environmental issues, such as gender issues, are issues of social justice.

An eco-feminist analysis is unique in that it is the only gender or feminist analysis that explicitly includes non-human animals and nature in its analysis of women and 'women's issues'. Eco-feminists begin with claims about women, not because women's oppression is more important than other forms of oppression (it is not), but because a focus on women reveals important features of interconnected systems of human domination that may or may not be reached from other starting points. In the context of a gender analysis of SD and SDE, eco-feminism focuses on women of different races/ethnicities, socio-economic status, geographic locations and historical locations in order to reveal specific features of gender domination that bear on issues concerning the non-human environment, development and education.

Characterization of eco-feminist philosophy

Eco-feminist philosophy is an eco-feminism that draws on feminism, philosophy and ecology in its gendered analyses of 'isms of domination'.[1] As a *feminism*, eco-feminist philosophy uses gender analysis as the starting point for critiquing interconnected 'isms of domination.' As an *ecological* position, eco-feminist philosophy incorporates ecological and environmental insights about the non-human world ('nature') and human–nature interactions into its theory and practice. As a *philosophy*, eco-feminist philosophy provides *conceptual analysis* (for example, what is meant by 'eco-feminism'?) and argumentative proof or *justification* (for example, what are the arguments in support of eco-feminist claims?) concerning issues that are *basic* and *general*. As such, eco-feminist philosophy is inherently prescriptive. It involves the advancement of positions, practices, policies and solutions for eliminating unjustified 'isms of domination' and for replacing them with genuinely liberating, life-affirming, life-sustaining, democratic, intentional and sustainable communities, systems and practices.

For the purposes of this chapter, eco-feminist philosophy is characterized in terms of four key claims:

1   There are important interconnections among the unjustified dominations of women, other human Others, non-human animals and nature.
2   Understanding these interconnections is crucial to an adequate understanding of, and solution to, unjustified 'isms of domination'.
3   Environmentalism, feminism, development and sustainability projects should include eco-feminist insights concerning the interconnections among unjustified 'isms of domination' in their practices, policies and programmes.
4   A failure to include these eco-feminist insights will result in an inadequate understanding and implementation of SD and SDE practices, projects and policies.

Since eco-feminist philosophy is a philosophy, there is no more basic place to start in showing the significance of eco-feminist philosophy to SD and SDE than with a gendered analysis of patriarchal (and other) oppressive conceptual frameworks, practices and institutions that have functioned historically to maintain, perpetuate, and 'justify' the dominations of women, other subordinated humans, non-human animals and nature.

Oppressive conceptual frameworks, practices and institutions

A *conceptual framework* is a set of basic beliefs, values, attitudes and assumptions that shape and reflect how one views oneself and one's world (Warren, 2000, p46). As a socially constructed lens through which one perceives reality, a conceptual framework is affected and shaped by such factors as gender, race/ethnicity, class, age, emotional orientation, marital status, religion, nationality, colonial influences and culture.

Some conceptual frameworks are *oppressive*. An oppressive conceptual framework is one that functions to explain, maintain and 'justify' relationships of unjustified domination, exploitation, subordination, oppression, marginalization or exclusion. When an oppressive conceptual framework is *patriarchal*, it functions to maintain, perpetuate and sanction the power and privilege of men over women. When it is *white racist*, it functions to maintain, perpetuate and sanction the power and privilege of whites over people of colour (similar descriptions apply to conceptual frameworks that are *class-based, colonialist* or *ethnocentric*).

There are five common features of oppressive conceptual framework and the behaviours, policies and institutions that they sanction (Warren, 2000, pp46–48). First, they involve *value-hierarchical thinking*: up–down thinking that attributes greater value (status, prestige, power, privilege) to what is higher (or 'up') than to what is lower (or 'down'). By attributing greater value to what is up, the up–down organization of reality serves to legitimate inequality, 'when, in fact, prior to the metaphor of up–down one would have said only that there existed diversity' (Gray, 1981, p20).

Second, oppressive conceptual frameworks, behaviours, policies and institutions involve *oppositional value dualisms:* disjunctive ('either-or') pairs that are exclusive (rather than inclusive), oppositional (rather than complementary) and that place higher value (status, prestige) on one disjunct than the other. Value dualisms ascribe higher status to what has historically been identified as 'male,' 'white' or 'Northern' (from the Northern hemisphere), or 'North', than to what has historically been identified as 'female,' 'of colour,' 'nature' or 'Southern' (from the Southern hemisphere), or 'South'.

The third and fourth characteristics of oppressive conceptual frameworks, behaviours, policies and institutions are that *power* and *privilege* are conceived, exercised and institutionalized as the (justified) power and privilege of 'ups' over 'downs'. The unjustified and institutionalized power and privilege of men over women, whites over people of colour, or the needs of the North over the needs of the South, reinforce the power and privilege of 'ups' over 'downs' in ways that keep 'downs' unjustifiably subordinated, dominated, marginalized, exploited or oppressed.

The fifth and philosophically most important characteristic of oppressive conceptual frameworks, behaviours, policies and institutions is that they sanction a *logic of domination* – that is, a logical structure of argumentation that 'justifies' domination and subordination, marginalization and exclusion, exploitation and oppression. A logic of domination is the moral stamp of approval for unjustified subordination since, if accepted, it provides a justification for keeping the 'downs' down. Typically, this justification takes the form that 'ups' have some characteristic (minds, reason or rationality, education, wealth, knowledge) that the 'downs' lack and by virtue of which the domination, subordination, marginalization, exclusion, exploitation or oppression of 'downs' by 'ups' is justified.

The importance of the logic of domination cannot be overstated. It is the moral premise that ethically 'justifies' the subordination of 'downs' by 'ups' in up–down relationships of domination and subordination. It involves a substantive value system according to which *superiority justifies subordination* (or, whatever is up is justified in being up and in dominating whatever is down). It is a process whereby others are constructed as inferior – that is, as Others. As Gruen (1996, p442) claims, in white patriarchal culture, the logic of domination 'constructs inferior others and uses this inferiority to justify their oppression'. And, the logic of domination links the dominations of women, other human Others, non-human animals and nature.

EMPIRICAL DATA ON WOMEN–ENVIRONMENT–SUSTAINABLE DEVELOPMENT–EDUCATION (WESDE) INTERCONNECTIONS

With the relevant definitions in place, consider now empirical data relevant to SD and SDE that illustrates WESDE interconnections. From an eco-feminist philosophical perspective, if SD and SDE are to become social realities, patriarchal (and other) oppressive conceptual frameworks, and the behaviours, policies and institutions that they sanction, will have to be overcome.

Women and trees, forests and forestry

Trees and forests have been central to the evolution of both ecological systems and human culture. But when British rule commercialized forestry in India, for example, the access to forests by rural Indians was restricted, and management practices that aimed at maximizing timber output for a cash economy were introduced. This led to widespread Gandhian *satyagrahas* – campaigns of non-violent civil disobedience by local Indian men and women. One such movement was the Chipko movement. In 1974, 27 women of Reni in northern India took simple but effective action to stop tree felling. They threatened to hug the trees if the lumberjacks attempted to cut them down. The women's successful protest saved 12,000 square kilometres of sensitive watershed. But the Chipko movement also gave visibility to two basic complaints of local people: commercial felling by contractors damages a large number of other trees, and the teak and eucalyptus monoculture plantations are replacing valuable indigenous forests.

Forests in much of the South are inextricably connected to rural and household subsistence economies governed by women. Where women are the primary managers of forests, tree shortages pose significant problems for women. The invisibility of women as forest managers by Western developers has significantly affected women's abilities to maintain domestic economies that are dependent upon trees. This is especially the case where First World development projects have implemented solutions to the problem of tree shortages by replacing indigenous, multi-species forests with monoculture tree plantations (such as teak and eucalyptus).

An eco-feminist philosophical perspective can show why this is so. First, trees provide five essential elements in these household economies: food, fuel, fodder, products for the home (including building materials, household utensils, gardens, dyes and medicines) and income-generating activities. As trees become scarce and men increasingly seek employment in the cities, women must carry out their own and men's former jobs, walk longer distances to collect firewood, and create forest products on degraded soils. As new technologies and development projects targeted at cash economies are introduced, it is women who have decreased opportunities to use trees to maintain previously sustainable domestic economies or to use wood as a source of income (for example, by making objects that can be sold at market).

Second, women face restrictive customs, taboos, and legal and time constraints that men do not face. Where men and women in the South have different access to credit, community-based organizations, land and training, women are disproportionately less likely to gain access to credit and the sort of institutional support needed to participate in and control local development.

Third, key assumptions of Western commercial forestry and development projects work to women's disadvantage. These assumptions are part of a Western patriarchal conceptual framework that reflects, reinforces and perpetuates gender bias in forest development projects in the South. One such assumption is that *the outsider knows best* – that the First World forester has the requisite technical expertise to solve the problems of deforestation and tree shortages in the South. But this assumption is often false or problematic (see Warren, 2002, p5). Sometimes it is 'the insider' – the local people, such as the Chipko women of India – who are the experts and who have the indigenous technical knowledge (ITK), or what is sometimes called 'epistemic privilege'. This privileged knowledge about forestry production is based on women's day-to-day, hands-on involvement with forests. This ITK goes far beyond that of many professionally trained foresters (Fortmann and Fairfax, 1988, p105).

A second assumption of Western forestry and reforestation projects is that activities that fall outside the boundaries of commercial fiber production are less important. Yet, these activities are precisely those that women engage in on a daily basis. The 'invisibility' or devaluation of what women do can result in reforestation development projects and management decisions that fail to see that trees have different uses – that trees provide not just food, fuel and fodder but also materials for basketry, dyes, medicines, decorations, shade and community meeting places (Fortmann and Fairfax, 1988, p106).

A third assumption of Western forestry and development projects concerns efficiency. When an economic decision or development project assumes that it is more efficient to have large-scale production using a small number of species of trees than small-scale, community-based forestry using a wide variety of species, women are disproportionately harmed. This is because small-scale production reflects local priorities, involves multiple uses of many species of trees, and is responsive to the social reality of women's importance in agriculture and forest production. To threaten small-scale production is to threaten the livelihood and well-being of women.

Through an uncovering of these three assumptions of Western forestry, an eco-feminist philosophical perspective can explain why Western-imposed forestry projects contribute to the inability of women to maintain their sustainable style of living and disproportionately harm local women, even relative to local men. In addition, as many local or indigenous peoples will say, preservation of forests is not simply about planting trees. It is also about preservation of sustainable communities, diverse cultures and community bonding, as well as the preservation of ecological diversity.

For native peoples in the North, forestry issues are often about sovereignty, the survival of native communities and cultures, and the health of native peoples and their land. Winona LaDuke, Anishinabe activist and vice-presidential candidate of the Green party in the 1996 and 2000 presidential elections in the US, argues that forests have cultural significance for native peoples that often conflicts with mainstream Western economic interests (LaDuke, 1993, 1999, 2002). La Duke describes the work of Leroy Jackson, a Diné (Navaho) who, with a Diné grassroots environmental group, confronted logging interests in the Chuska Mountains in the US. They hoped 'to turn the Navajo Forest Products Industry towards more sustainable forestry practices, particularly in sacred and cultural areas such as the Chuskas' (LaDuke, 2002, pp89–90). LaDuke writes:

> *Jackson's death [in autumn 1993] brings many Native forestry issues to light, particularly the internal battle within many reservations between economic pressures and traditional cultural practices and values. On the Diné reservations, as elsewhere in North America, these struggles will play out with growing intensity as the value of Indian timber in a shrinking supply market adds new pressures to the ecology and cultural fabric of Indian country. . . This is a battle – make no mistake. It is about deforestation and cultural transformation. Throughout Indian country, lines will be drawn and ecosystems may be transformed. And tribal sovereignty will play centrally in the conflict – as tribes decide to exercise their rights to cut their trees. . .or [as] Native Nations may decide to utilize their tribal sovereignty and build a sustainable forestry programme based on whole cultural and ecosystem management. The choices are clearly ours.* (LaDuke, 2002, pp90–91)

Given LaDuke's carefully documented evidence of widespread and disproportionate environmental degradation of native forests, water and food supplies on native lands, especially (LaDuke, 1999), it is no wonder that LaDuke (2002, p97) writes: 'There are sustainable forest models, and they are Native'.

Women and water

Water pollution is an environmental problem that affects people globally and disproportionately. Approximately 1.2 billion people currently lack safe drinking water (Brown et al, 1992, p4). In more than half of the developing countries, less than 50 per cent of the population have a source of potable water or facilities for sewage disposal. The World Health Organization (WHO) estimates that approximately 85 per cent of all sicknesses and diseases in developing countries, including diarrhoea, trachoma, parasitic worms and malaria, are attributable to inadequate potable water or sanitation. It also estimates that as many as 25 million deaths a year are due to water-related illnesses. The United Nations International Children's Emergency Fund (UNICEF) estimates that 15 million children die every year before they are five;

half of them could be saved if they had access to safe drinking water (Warren, 2000, pp6–7).

Water scarcity is of special concern for women and children. Not only are the majority of countries in Africa and many countries of Asia and Latin America considered water-scarcity countries by the UN; in these countries, women and children perform most of the water collection work. Small-scale studies in Africa and Asia indicate that women and girls spend up to 43 hours per week collecting and carrying water (United Nations, 1995, pp49–50). Drinking water is often drawn from public bathing and laundering places, and the same water is frequently used as a public toilet. Lack of sanitary water is of special concern for women and children since – as the primary collectors, processors and distributors of household water – they experience dispropor- tionately higher health risks in the presence of unsanitary water. In addition, development projects that target men for training in water uses, irrigation systems and new water technologies fail to understand the gendered roles women in many parts of the world have for water collection, processing and distribution.

Women, farming and agriculture

It is estimated that women farmers grow at least half of the world's food. In 1985, the UN Food and Agricultural Organization (FAO) estimated that women were responsible for 80 per cent of the world's agricultural production (Buckingham-Hatfield, 2000, p74, citing Dankleman and Davidson, 1988). In fact:

> *Subsistence agriculture is almost exclusively a woman's task and without this work her family would not eat; however, women have title to only 1 per cent of the world's land. Intensive agriculture relying on pesticides and hybrid seeds is claiming land previously used for subsistence (and fre- quently degrading it in the process through erosion and desertification), which displaces subsistence agriculture to less fertile areas. Subsistence farmers (the majority of whom are women) have to travel further to get to land and must work harder to try to restore it.* (Buckingham-Hatfield, 2000, p74)

Mayra Buvinic and Sally Yudelman add that women farmers are poorer than men farmers:

> *As a rule, women farmers work longer hours, have fewer assets and lower incomes than men farmers do, and have almost as many dependents to support. The disparity is not due to lack of education or competence. Women farmers are poorer because their access to credit is limited. Without credit they cannot acquire productive assets, such as cattle, fertilizer or improved seeds, to improve the productivity of their labor.* (Buvinic and Yudelman, 1989, p24)

The so-called feminization of agriculture refers to the increasing proportion of women in the agricultural labour force. A failure to realize the extent of women's contribution to agriculture by First World development policies and practices has contributed historically to the invisibility of women in all aspects of agricultural work: in ploughing, planting, caring for farm animals, harvesting, weeding, processing, and the storing of crops. It also contributes to the inability to 'see' what women know, based on their felt, lived, daily experiences of all aspects of food production and agriculture. As the world's major food producers, women have epistemic privilege concerning those aspects of food production and agriculture that are based on their gendered roles cross-culturally. As Buckhingham-Hatfield (2000, p75) claims:

> *Traditionally, women have been the repository of much knowledge concerning seeds and soils because of their roles in subsistence agriculture. As development agencies move into Third World countries, this knowledge is frequently ignored by development workers who directly approach men to negotiate the uptake of new agricultural practices, such as cash-cropping of high-value goods. . . Alternatively, the knowledge is 'bought' by and patented by the agro-chemical industry which makes it illegal for women (or anyone else besides the patent holders) to continue to use the full diversity of seeds once at their disposal. This has significant impacts on their ability to farm effectively.*

Appeal to an eco-feminist philosophical analysis can explain the failure of development workers to access what women realize: their patriarchal conceptual frameworks prevent them from seeing or acknowledging what women know.

Women and poverty

No matter how poverty is measured, the poor population is largely and increasingly comprised of women and children. Cross-culturally, women are paid less than men, and women in most regions spend as much or more time working than men when unpaid housework is taken into account (United Nations, 1995, p82). Women everywhere control fewer resources and reap a lesser share of the world's wealth than men. Women do more than one half of the world's work, but receive only 10 per cent of the world's income and own only 1 per cent of the world's property. Women-headed households are a growing worldwide phenomenon, with between 80 and 90 per cent of poor families headed by women (Seager, 1997, pp120–121). According to the UN report *The World's Women* (United Nations, 1995), women in poor rural regions are overwhelmingly disadvantaged in dealing with their environment.

There are at least four reasons for this. First, women have less education and training than urban women or rural men, and they are excluded from both traditional rural development programmes that might provide such training and from the credit and other institutional support needed for rural development. The need for gender-inclusive SDE is clear:

> *In rural areas, women's roles are those of the poorest-paid labourers –*
> *weeding, hoeing and carrying water and wood, combined with the tradi-*
> *tional family roles of cooking, child care, healthcare and reproduction –*
> *without even the pay that a labourer expects. While consciousness of these*
> *traditional roles has fostered the idea that women are in some sense natural*
> *custodians of the environment in rural areas, there is no evidence of this*
> *notion and women in rural areas are largely ill-equipped for it. They are*
> *without training, status, access to community-based organizations and*
> *co-operatives, land and property rights, capital, or environmental institu-*
> *tions that make up the dense fabric of rural life and control its develop-*
> *ment.* (United Nations, 1995, p48)

Second, in order to attain sustainable development, the poverty of the 'downs' in up–down systems of unequal and inequitable distributions of wealth must be addressed. As Goodland (1995, p207) states:

> *The welfare of the poor is needed for environmental sustainability. Social*
> *stability provides the social scaffolding of people's organizations that*
> *empower self-control and self-policing in people's management of natural*
> *resources. Social stability of this sort is impossible in the context of*
> *enormous gaps between the rich and poor, because in that context poor*
> *people are often too desperate to practice self-restraint. Thus, environ-*
> *mental sustainability requires social stability, which requires income*
> *redistribution to ameliorate the current status of apartheid practices.*

'Environmental sustainability requires social stability,' social stability 'requires income redistribution', and both environmental sustainability and social stability require social and environmental justice. Where the goals of SDE include the development of 'a new set of values based on social responsibility and global citizenship, equity, justice and inclusiveness' (Parkin and Howard, 2002), the plight of the poor cannot be ignored.

A related third reason is that the so-called 'feminization of poverty' has resulted in unsustainable development and new forms of poverty for women in much of the South. Shiva's distinction between two kinds of poverty, 'subsistence poverty' and 'material poverty,' is helpful here. 'Subsistence poverty' is based on prudent self-provisioning economies (subsistence and sustainable living) that do not participate, primarily, in the market economy. 'Material poverty' is a lack of cash income that results from dispossession and deprivation (Shiva, 1988, p10). Subsistence poverty and sustainable living need not be real material poverty: 'subsistence economies which satisfy basic needs through self-provisioning are not poor in the sense of being deprived. . . [even if] the ideology of development declares them so' since they do not participate overwhelmingly in or consume commodities produced by the market economy of commodity production (Shiva, 1988, p10).

Lastly, even so-called 'natural disasters' such as droughts and floods are only properly understood if one sees their connection to women and poverty.

According to Wijkman and Timberlake (1988), economic or class interests head the list of human-induced factors that affect the occurrences and locations of such 'natural disasters'. They poignantly express the relationship between poverty and those who experience 'natural disasters' when they claim that 'no wealthy person ever died in a drought', 'no relief worker has starved to death during a drought' and 'no journalist has died of hunger while covering a drought' (Wijkman and Timberlake, 1988, p49). 'Natural disasters' are socio-economic environmental issues that disproportionately affect poor people.

Women and development

Mies and Shiva (1993) argue that global economic development that is based on a Western industrial model of progress and development is really 'mal-development', which has caused the impoverishment of women, children and the environment. Where development is capital accumulation and the development of the economy is for the generation of 'surplus' and profits, the result is the reproduction of a particular form of growth (capital growth) and wealth (monetary wealth) based on the commercialization of resource use for commodity production (Shiva, 1988, pp1–2). Western development models and projects that replicate economic development based on commercialization of resource use for commodity production in so-called 'developing countries' have reduced development:

> . . .to a continuation of the process of colonization; it became an extension of the process of wealth creation in modern Western patriarchy's economic vision, which was based on the exploitation or exclusion of women (of the West and non-West), on the exploitation and degradation of nature, and on the exploitation and erosion of other cultures. 'Development' could not but entail destruction for women, nature and subjugated cultures, which is why, throughout the Third World, women, peasants and tribals are struggling for liberation from 'development' just as they earlier struggled for liberation from colonialism. . . Development exclusivity and dispossession aggravated and deepened the colonial processes of ecological destruction and the loss of political control over nature's sustenance base. (Shiva, 1988, p2)

Shiva's main point is that Western-style development has disproportionately displaced women (particularly poor women of colour) from productive activity; eroded their traditional land-use rights (by the privatization of land for revenue generation); undermined women's food production (through the expansion of cash crops); often left women with meager resources to feed and care for children, the aged and the infirm (when men migrated, were conscripted or hired into factory labour by the developers); and appropriated or destroyed the natural resource base for the production of sustenance and survival (by removing land, water and forests from their management and control, as well as by destroying the soil, water and vegetation systems so that nature's productivity and renewability were impaired) (Shiva, 1988, pp2–3).

According to Shiva, the Western development paradigm went wrong for *four* reasons:

1 It focused exclusively on a Western industrial model of progress that necessitated colonialism as a condition for capitalist industrial growth.
2 Its focus on such financial indicators as gross national product (GNP) ignored the costs of environmental destruction and the creation of poverty. Such financial indicators as GNP ignore non-market based, productive natural resource activities.
3 It cannot account for poverty as subsistence living based on prudent self-provisioning economies that do not primarily participate in the market economy.
4 It only perceives of poverty as deprivation (lack of cash incomes).

On this view, the failure of traditional Western development models is traceable to patriarchal Western and colonial conceptual frameworks and the behaviors that they maintain, reinforce and perpetuate (against the 'downs'). An eco-feminist philosophical analysis demonstrates clearly how and why this is so.

Women, native people and environmental justice

In 1987 the United Church of Christ Commission for Racial Justice in the US published a now classic and stunning report entitled *Toxic Waste and Race in the United States* (Commission for Racial Justice, 1987). Using sophisticated statistical analysis, the report indicated that race (not class) is the primary factor in locating hazardous waste in the US. Three out of every five African and Hispanic Americans (more than 15 million of the nation's 26 million African Americans, and over 8 million of the 15 million Hispanics), and over half of all Asian Pacific Islanders and American Indians live in communities with one or more uncontrolled toxic waste sites. The nation's largest hazardous waste landfill, receiving toxins from 45 states, is in Emelle, Alabama, which is 79.9 per cent African American. Probably the greatest concentration of hazardous waste sites in the US is on the predominately African American and Hispanic south side of Chicago. In Houston, Texas, six of eight municipal incinerators, and all five city landfills, are located in predominately African American neighbourhoods (Commission for Racial Justice, 1987).

The health of native Americans is disproportionately harmed by the government's mining of uranium, nuclear-testing and hazardous waste disposal. The Shoshone people suffer the most:

> *Shoshone groups are adamant that any additional radiation risk to their community is unacceptable. The Shoshone Nation – site of the US Nevada nuclear-testing facility – is already the most bombed nation on Earth. The*

Shoshone suffer from widespread cancer, leukaemia and other diseases because of fallout from more than 600 atomic explosions in their territory. To add to this risk is outlandish injustice. (LaDuke, 2002, p27)

LaDuke challenges non-native North Americans to take seriously the empirical data that ties together environmental issues of toxins, forests, land and health with the sovereignty and survival of culturally diverse native communities. She writes:

Within the context of Native thinking, the survival of Native communities, and the issues of sovereignty and control over natural resources, become central to North American resource politics and the challenge for North Americans of conscience. Consider these facts:

- *Over 50 million indigenous peoples inhabit the world's remaining rain forests.*
- *Over 1 million indigenous people will be relocated to allow for the development of hydroelectric dam projects in the next decade.*
- *The United States has detonated all its nuclear weapons in the lands of indigenous people, over 600 of those tests within property belonging to the Shoshone people.*
- *Two-thirds of all resources within the borders of the United States lie under Native reservations – in 1975, Indians produced 10 per cent of all federally controlled uranium.*
- *One third of all low-sulphur coal in the western United States is on Indian land, with four of the largest ten coal strip mines in the same areas.*
- *Fifteen of the current 18 recipients of nuclear waste research grants, so-called monitored, retrievable nuclear storage sites, are Indian communities.*
- *The largest hydroelectric project on the continent, the James Bay Project, is on Cree and Inuit lands in Northern Canada.*
  (LaDuke, 1993, pp98–99)

Women, especially poor women of colour, are organizing throughout the world to fight environmental contaminations of all kinds in their communities. Women often play a primary role in community environmental activism because environmental ills touch their lives in direct, immediate ways. As Hamilton (1991, p43) writes:

Women often play a primary role in community action because it is about things they know best. They also tend to use organizing strategies and methods that are the antithesis of those of the traditional environmental movement. Minority women in several urban areas [of the US] have found themselves part of a new radical core of environmental activists, motivated by the irrationalities of capital-intensive growth. These individuals are responding not to 'nature' in the abstract but to their homes and the health of their children. . . Women are more likely to take on these issues than men precisely because the home has been defined as a woman's domain.

Whether it is toxins, nuclear-testing, uranium radiation, hazardous waste, lead paint in older buildings, toxic herbicides and pesticides in agriculture, or activities of militaries around the globe, environmental justice cannot be achieved without SDE that fosters a 'new set of values based on social responsibility and global citizenship; equity, justice and inclusiveness; the needs and rights of future generations; the value of diversity; and the environmental limits to human activity' (Blewitt, 2000). Eco-feminist philosophy shows how and why patriarchal values, beliefs, assumptions and behaviours systematically promote social injustice, exclusivity and the denial of the needs and rights of present generations of women and other human Others; threaten ecological and cultural diversity; and exceed environmental limits to human activity.

SIGNIFICANCE OF AN ECO-FEMINIST PHILOSOPHICAL PERSPECTIVE FOR SDE

The explosion of gender scholarship during the last three decades has shown the ways in which the mainstream curriculum has been male-gender biased (Cohee et al, 1998). The transformation of the 'malestream curriculum' to make it inclusive of women has impacted upon every academic discipline, interdisciplinary programme and continuing education ('life-long learning'; Warren, 1998). Initially, feminist transformation projects were conceived in terms of content areas rather than goals. But that approach proved to yield surface results in gender-resistant fields, such as mathematics, physics and chemistry. An inclusive, multidimensional, cross-disciplinary and interdisciplinary goal-oriented model of feminist curricular transformation efforts proved to be more successful (Warren, 1998). As this section argues, a similar goal-oriented eco-feminist philosophical approach has the potential to achieve widespread, multidimensional, cross-disciplinary and interdisciplinary goals and results in curricular transformation around SD issues that Chapter 36 of Agenda 21 envisioned for SDE. It can, for example, foster a change in people's environmental and ethical awareness, ways of thinking (or conceptual frameworks), values, skills and behaviours in ways that are necessary for SD and for effective and inclusive public participation in decision-making.

There are at least eight curricular domains involving WESDE interconnections in which eco-feminist philosophical transformation projects are both necessary and desirable if the goals of SDE are to be achieved:

1 primary content subject areas;
2 secondary content areas (for example, illustrations and examples);
3 conceptual frameworks (or worldviews) and tools;

4   methodology;
5   research design;
6   ethical awareness, values and behaviours;
7   science and epistemology; and
8   environmental awareness.

Primary content areas

There are 'information gaps' in the subject (or content) matter of mainstream disciplines concerning gender issues with SD and SDE. Typically, these gaps are the result of one of two kinds of biases. *Empirical* bias arises when generalizations fail to pass what this chapter calls the '4-R test': a good generalization is based on *r*andom samples, *r*ight size samples, *r*epresentative samples, and *r*eplicable experiments or observations. Empirical bias can be minimized or eliminated by ensuring that the generalizations on which they are based pass the 4-R test. Insofar as eco-feminist philosophy rejects generalizations or claims about environmental degradation as faulty if they fail to take into account the sort of data about women offered in the previous section (for example, women as forest managers, water collectors and food producers), an eco-feminist philosophical perspective provides more accurate, because more inclusive, information to fill the 'information gap'.

The second sort of bias that contributes to 'information gaps' in the subject matter of mainstream disciplines is *conceptual* bias. When the claims, beliefs, values, attitudes, assumptions, concepts and distinctions that characterize oppressive (including patriarchal) conceptual frameworks are false or seriously problematic on conceptual (rather than empirical) grounds, an eco-feminist philosophical perspective can show how, where, when and why the conceptual bias occurred. We have seen, for example, how the three concepts of 'expert', 'development' and 'poverty' are conceptually biased insofar as they are based on false, faulty or misleading definitions. To achieve the goals of SDE, these 'conceptual blinders' must be recognized and removed.

Secondary content areas

The empirical data offered in the second section of this chapter provides ample evidence of the gender errors that occur within and across disciplinary areas when women are absent, invisible, side-stepped, ignored, misunderstood, devalued, neglected, marginalized, exploited or misanalysed in the examples used, data presented, generalizations made or arguments advanced. In a multidimensional, transformative eco-feminist philosophical approach, awareness of WESDE interconnections is necessary to correct these gender errors.

Conceptual frameworks and tools

Three key assumptions of orthodox forestry were presented in the second section of this chapter that are male biased; the effect that this bias has on who is considered an 'expert' in forest management, water collection and distribution work, or food production was discussed. As a philosophical position, eco-feminist philosophy is particularly well suited to unpacking the sorts of oppressive (including patriarchal) conceptual frameworks that doom SD and SDE projects to failure. An eco-feminist philosophical perspective provides a way of understanding the conceptual basis of interconnected 'isms of domination' and the sorts of conceptual tools – definitions, distinctions, critical thinking about basic assumptions, beliefs, values, attitudes, and behaviours – that are necessary to understanding the ways in which gender, race, socio-economic status and geographic location shape SD and SDE failures or successes. Shiva's distinction between 'subsistence poverty' and 'material poverty' offers an eco-feminist analysis that helps to explain 'the paradox and crisis of development' that mistakenly identifies culturally perceived poverty with real material poverty and the growth of commodity production as better satisfying needs. In fact, the empirical data suggests that 'there is less water, less fertile soil, less genetic wealth as a result of the development process' (Shiva, 1988, p13).

Methodology

An eco-feminist philosophical perspective gives rise to a host of questions that affect the methodologies used in SD and SDE. These questions, generally, are not asked for two sorts of reasons. First, the questions themselves may logically contradict the conceptual frameworks that give rise to them. As Minnich (1986, p11) says, 'One cannot simply add the idea that the world is round to the idea that the world is flat'. Second, the questions themselves presuppose a gendered perspective that may not be available to the questioner. For example:

- *What* are WESDE interconnections?
- *How* does knowledge of WESDE interconnections affect one's approach to SDE?
- *Who* decides what the SDE projects will or should be?
- *Who* is or should be included in the decision-making process?
- *Who* will get more or less work, more or less money, and more or less power or status as a result of the implementation of an SDE project?
- *Who* will gain or lose jobs by a particular development project?
- *Who* really are 'the knowers' in a particular context and *what* and *how* do they know what they know?
- *Which* tasks do or could women have to neglect or take up if a development project is implemented?

Third, as any eco-feminist philosopher will insist, the questions one asks affects the answers one gets and affects what counts as appropriate or adequate evidence. As such, the absence or inattention to gender-sensitive questions (such as those given above) contributes to male-biased methodologies.

Research design

An eco-feminist philosophical perspective encourages non-traditional research methods and ways of collecting data that can expose problems that may not emerge from either quantitative (for example, surveys) or qualitative (for example, focus group) research. Such methods include participatory exercises, use of traditional media (dramas, songs created by women) and modern technologies (such as Polaroid cameras or videos). The latter have been shown to be effective as a technology that can be used to provide a direct link 'between women and national policy-makers – who listened to their concerns' (Grieser and Rawlins, 2000, pp24–25).

Ethical awareness, values and behaviours

One of the main debates in contemporary ethics is the so-called 'justice versus care debate'. Distilled to the basics, the debate is about the centrality of one or the other of two distinct ethical perspectives, the 'justice' and 'care' perspectives. The justice perspective assesses moral conduct in terms of the basic rights and duties of relevant parties. From a justice perspective, ethics is about rights (for example, the rights of future generations to inherit a sustainable environment), duties (for example, the duties of the present generation to meet its needs without compromising the ability of future generations to meet their own needs), and rules or principles that provide a universal ethical decision-making procedure for resolving ethical conflicts. In contrast, the care perspective assesses moral conduct in terms of such values as care, friendship and appropriate trust, which are themselves not reducible to talk of rights, duties, rules and universal principles. The ethical self is conceived as a relational, ecological, material, historically situated being in relationships, including relationships to the non-human environment.

The sort of 'ethical awareness, values and behaviours' that an eco-feminist philosophical perspective can help SDE cultivate is a combination of both the justice and care perspectives. It would involve both the recognition of the fundamental rights and duties of humans as ecological citizens of the globe, and the development of what wildlife biologist Aldo Leopold called an 'ecological conscience', 'an internal change in our intellectual emphasis, loyalties, affections, and convictions' (Leopold, 1997, pp209–210). In his defence of 'the land ethic', Leopold claimed: 'It is inconceivable to me that an ethical relation to land can exist without love, respect, and admiration for land. . . We can be ethical only in relation to something we can see, feel, understand, love or otherwise have faith in' (Leopold, 1997, pp200–223). Eco-feminist philosophical ethics, like both Leopold's land ethic and SDE, calls for just these sorts of internal changes in our ethical and environmental awareness, and in the values we practice in our interactions with the non-human natural world.

Science and epistemology

Acknowledgement of women's 'epistemic privilege' in particular contexts and the ITK of native peoples challenges traditional assumptions about both the gender neutrality of science and the time-honoured philosophical conceptions of knowledge and 'knowers' as objective, detached, impersonal, impartial, disinterested observers. Instead, like many feminist philosophies of science and feminist epistemology, eco-feminist philosophy supports a view of 'situated sciences' and partial, perspectival or 'situated knowledges' (Haraway, 1988, pp592–593). As Harding (1993, p54) argues:

> The social location of the knower is crucial to understanding and assessing epistemological claims. . .[T]he activities of those at the bottom of. . .social hierarchies can provide starting points for thought– for everyone's research and scholarship – from which humans' relations with each other and the natural world can become visible.

Environmental awareness

Environmental awareness includes a recognition of the interrelationship between ecological (or biological) and cultural diversity. 'Biological diversity' refers to the total of all biotic and abiotic genes, populations, species and ecosystems on the Earth at any one time. A primary value of biodiversity is that it provides long-term ecological stability, which, in turn, provides conditions for environmental sustainability. Where there is biodiversity, there is cultural diversity; distinctive aspects of diverse human cultures – the language, rituals, symbol systems, myths, stories, food production processes, relationships to the lands – emerge from the distinctiveness of the bio-regions and ecosystems in which people live and engage in productive activity. The sort of 'environmental awareness' that is needed to support SD and SDE must involve the promotion of ecological and cultural diversity.

CONCLUSIONS

This chapter has provided empirical data, conceptual analysis and philosophical argumentation to show how and why an eco-feminist philosophical perspective provides important insights concerning WESDE interconnections that are necessary for any successful understanding and implementation of the goals of sustainability in both development and education. It has also identified eight different areas in which an eco-feminist philosophical transformation of the mainstream (college and university) curriculum is important. If what has been argued is plausible, then these eco-feminist insights are important to any gender analysis of, and solution to, the invisibility, marginalization or exclusivity of women in SD and SDE programmes. Any successful 'learning-to-last' programme cannot afford the luxury of ignoring or overlooking them.

NOTE

1   Some of the material in this section and the second section of this chapter is drawn from Warren (2000).

REFERENCES

Blewitt, J (2002) 'Introduction: Learning and Sustainability', in Cohen, J and James, S (eds) *Learning to Last: Skills, Sustainability, and Strategy*, London, The Learning and Skills Development Agency, pp2–21

Brown, L (ed) (1992) *State of the World*, New York, W W Norton and Co

Buckingham-Hatfield, S (2000) *Gender and Environment*, London, Routledge

Buvinik, M and Yudelman, S (1989) *Women, Poverty and Progress in the Third World*, New York, Foreign Policy Association

Cohee, G E, Daumer, E, Kemp T D, Krebs, P M, Kafky, S and Runzo, S, (eds) (1998) *The Feminist Teacher Anthology: Pedagogies and Classroom Strategies*, New York, Columbia University

Cohen, J and James, S (eds) (2000) *Learning to Last: Skills, Sustainability, and Strategy*, London, The Learning and Skills Development Agency

Commission for Racial Justice (1987) *Toxic Waste and Race in the United States: A National Report on the Racial and Socioeconomic Characteristics of Communities with Hazardous Waste Sites*, New York, Commission for Racial Justice, United Church of Christ

Fortmann, L and Fairfax, S (1988) 'American Forestry Professionalism in the Third World: Some Preliminary Observations on Effects,' in *Women Creating Wealth: Transforming Economic Development*, Selected Papers and Speeches from the Association of Women in Development Conference, Washington, DC, pp105–108 Food and Agriculture Organization of the UN (FAO) (1991), available at www.fao.org/sd/EPdirect/EPre0023.htm

Gaard, G and Gruen, L (2004) 'Toward Global Health and Planetary Justice', in Zimmerman, M et al (eds) *Environmental Philosophy: From Animal Rights to Radical Ecology*, Fourth EditionUpper Saddle River, NJ, Prentice-Hall

Goodland, R (1995) 'South Africa: Environmental Sustainability Means the Empowerment of Women', in Westra, L and Wenz, P (eds) *Faces of Environmental Racism: Confronting Issues of Social Justice*, Lanham, MD, Rowman and Littlefield, pp207–225

Gray, E (1981) *Green Paradise Lost*, Wellesley, MA, Roundtable Press

Grieser, M and Rawlins, B (2000) 'Gender Matters', in Day, B and Monroe, M (eds) *Environmental Education and Communication for a Sustainable World: Handbook for International Practitioners*, Washington, DC, GreenCom (Environmental Education

Communication Project of the US Agency for International Development, Academy for Educational Development),pp23–31, www.usaid.gov/environment

Gruen, L (1996) 'On the Oppression of Women and Animals', *Environmental Ethics*, vol 18, no 4, pp441–444

Hamilton, C (1991) 'Women, Home and Community,' *Woman of Power: A Magazine of Feminism, Spirituality and Politics*, vol 20 (spring), pp42–53

Haraway, D (1988) 'Situated Knowledges: The Science Question in Feminism and the Privilege of Partial Perspective', *Feminist Studies*, vol 14, no 3, pp575–599

Harding, S (1993) 'Rethinking Standpoint Epistemology: What is "Strong Objectivity"?', in Alcoff, L and Potter, E (eds) *Feminist Epistemologies*, New York, Routledge, pp49–82

LaDuke, W (1993) 'A Society Based on Conquest Cannot Be Sustained: Native Peoples and the Environmental Crisis, in Hofrichter, R (ed) *Toxic Struggles: The Theory and Practice of Environmental Justice*, Philadelphia, PA, New Society Publishers, pp98–106

LaDuke, W (1999) *All Our Relations: Native Struggles for Land and Life,* Cambridge, MA, South End Press

LaDuke, W (2002) *The Winona LaDuke Reader: A Collection of Essential Writings*, Stillwater, MN, Voyageur Press

Leopold, A (1997) *A Sand County Almanac and Sketches Here and There,* New York, Oxford University Press

Mies, M and Shiva, V (1993) *Ecofeminism,* New Jersey, Zed Books

Minnich, E (1986) 'Conceptual Errors Across the Curriculum: Towards a Transformation of the Curriculum', in *The Research Clearinghouse: A Curriculum Integration Project at the Center for Research on Women*, Memphis, TN, Memphis State University

Minnich, E (1987) *Restoring the Balance: Women and Forest Resources*, Rome, Food and Culture Organization and Swedish International Development Authority

Parkin, S and Howard, U (2000) 'Foreword', in Cohen, J and James, S (eds) *Learning to Last: Skills, Sustainability, and Strategy*, London, The Learning and Skills Development Agency

Parkin, S and Howard, U (2002) 'Foreword', in J Cohen, S James and J Blewitt, *Learning to Last: Skills, Sustainability and Strategy*, London, LSDA

Seager, J (1997) *The State of Women in the World Atlas*, London, Penguin

Shiva, V (1988) *Staying Alive: Women, Ecology and Development,* London, Zed Books

Shiva, V (1994) *Close to Home: Women Reconnect Ecology, Health and Development Worldwide*, Philadelphia, PA, New Society Publishers

Shiva, V (2001) 'The Impoverishment of the Environment: Women and Children Last', in Zimmerman, M et al (ed) *Environmental Philosophy: From Animal Rights to Radical Ecology, Fourth Edition,* Upper Saddle River, NJ, Prentice-Hall, pp287–304

Simons, M (ed) (1995) *Feminist Interpretations of Simone de Beauvoir*, Philadelphia, PA, Pennsylvania State University Press

United Nations (1995) *The World's Women, 1995: Trends and Statistics,* New York, United Nations

Warren, K (1998) 'Rewriting the Future: The Feminist Challenge to the Malestream Curriculum', in Cohee, G et al (eds) *The Feminist Teacher Anthology*, New York, Columbia University, pp45–60

Warren, K (2000) *Ecofeminist Philosophy: A Western Perspective on What It Is and Why It Matters*, Lanham, MD, Rowman and Littlefield

WCED (1987) *Our Common Future,* Oxford, World Commission on Environment and Development and Oxford University Press

Wijkman, A and Timberlake, L (1988) *Natural Disasters: Acts of God or Acts of Man?* Philadelphia, New Society Publishers

Zimmerman, M et al (eds) (2001) *Environmental Philosophy: From Animal Rights to Radical Ecology, Fourth Edition,* Upper Saddle River, NJ, Prentice-Hall

Part 2

Chapter 9

Sustainability and Education in the Built Environment

Brian Edwards

THE DEBT TO VITRUVIUS

Environmental design only became a coherent theme of education in the construction industry during the 1960s. Even then it was preoccupied with energy rather than the broader concerns of sustainable development. Conceptually, however, the environmental tradition exists in texts that are the very bedrock of architecture and building design. In Vitruvius, for instance, comfort and climate are central to the tripartite model of utility, beauty and commodity. Vitruvius declared that the site of cities, the direction of streets and the orientation of buildings should be determined by environmental factors (Hawkes, 1996, pp10–11). The very nature of building design was the primary agent in the mediation between internal comfort and the external environment. Vitruvius was the first theoretician to recognize that architecture had a part to play in affording shelter which exploited the resources of nature (sun and wind) rather than excluded them.

The Vitruvian model is still reflected in the curricular division between design, technology and social studies that occurs in many schools of architecture. It, too, is found in the dialogue between science and art which underpins much of the education in the built environment disciplines. The idea of sustainability, therefore, draws upon a foundation that is deeply embedded in societal and technological ideals. However, the concept of bio-climatic design is more recent and owes much to visionaries from the 1960s, such as Buckminster Fuller and Reyner Banham. Fuller took the Vitruvian paradigm of comfort by suggesting enclosing the whole of urban activities in a glass envelope. Beneath a huge glazed embrace, Fuller envisaged that food would be grown, waste recycled as compost, energy demands reduced and social interactions enhanced. His utopianism has left a mark on today's practitioners in the form of the Great Court at the British Museum by the architect Lord Foster, the Eden Project in Cornwall by Sir Nicholas Grimshaw and the glazed wrapping of the South Bank in London by Lord Rogers. These initiatives, though seen as feats of engineering, are equally exercises in bio-climatic design whose roots go back to Vitruvius.

THE SEARCH FOR A WELL-TEMPERED ENVIRONMENT

Reyner Banham, the other key influence on contemporary sustainable practice, was more a theorist than practitioner. His book *The Architecture of the Well Tempered Environment*, published in 1969, put the environmental function of buildings to the fore in the history of architecture. To Banham, the technology of environmental control held the key to an alternative understanding of modern architecture. He openly challenged the thesis promulgated by Nikolaus Pevsner that structure and construction were central to giving form to architecture, not environmental design. Until Banham voiced his concerns, the relationship between energy use and building design was a subject for specialists with their own ethics, values and professional bodies, rather than architects. As such, a typical student of architecture during the 1960s (like the author) was encouraged to believe that heat, light, comfort and sound were design problems to be handed 'over to the emerging profession of mechanical and electrical consultants' (Robert Maxwell cited in Hawkes, 1996, p6). Banham argued with well-chosen case studies that environmental technologies were as important as the emergence of reinforced concrete or steel-framed construction in giving shape to 20th-century architecture.

THE OXFORD CONFERENCE

Banham's ideas gave impetus to a movement whose origins lay in the Oxford Conference of Architectural Education sponsored by the Royal Institute of British Architects (RIBA) in 1958. RIBA sought to ensure that education for the profession was based upon university-level provision, and with it went a preoccupation with rational design methods underpinned by research. The former art college tradition and office-based system of pupilage were gradually replaced by one where acquiring knowledge and transferable skills was seen as being as important as drawing and professional know-how (Crinson and Lubbock, 1994, pp139–140). In this shift in emphasis there was a recognition that the environmental design of buildings was an important criteria in the assessment of architectural performance. Building science emerged as a discipline as important as architecture itself. The aesthetics of design were absorbed within a wider lexicon of environmental concerns, a movement which gained momentum with the energy crisis of the 1970s.

Schools of architecture responded in different ways. Some, such as Strathclyde, became schools of architecture and building science; others adopted the title of centres for building design engineering, where architecture existed alongside the portfolio of new disciplines. The ambiguity of nomenclature allowed research and teaching to embrace the concept of architects becoming scientists and scientists becoming architects. The outcome was a mushrooming of interest in the measurable world of climatic responsive design and, ultimately, of sustainability.

Modernist educators became the new heads of schools of architecture formed in the wake of the Oxford Conference. The change in culture of architecture as a scientific rather than artistic discipline benefited the teaching of environmental science and, ultimately, of sustainable design. The former Beaux-Arts tradition had a coherent and consistent approach to design that largely denied the presence of the environmental agenda. Low-energy design existed only in the orientation of buildings to afford either sun traps or to cast powerful shadow patterns onto classical façades. What the post-Oxford Conference schools of architecture offered was a system of university education with an emphasis upon scientific method and upon research underpinning professional teaching. It also led to architecture schools being placed in faculties containing other built environment disciplines, such as civil engineering, surveying and construction management.

The effect was to foster environmental understanding at the expense of the artistic tradition. During the 1970s, 1980s and 1990s, those schools of architecture which tended to score well in government research assessment exercises (RAEs) were not separate small institutions but parts of bigger construction-based faculty units. The research upon which they concentrated was often in environmental science or areas of low energy design. The momentum created by schools of architecture at Cambridge, the Bartlett, University College London, Sheffield, Strathclyde and Cardiff had the effect of raising environmental awareness throughout the larger community of schools of architecture in the UK.

CONCEPT OF 'LONG LIFE, LOOSE FIT, LOW ENERGY'

Another significant response was the election in 1970 of a president of the RIBA sympathetic to the environmental cause. Alex Gordon, whose presidential tenure ran from 1970–1972, had served on the RIBA council since 1960 and helped to steer the post-Oxford reforms. He had made his name in public service mainly as chief architect for Birmingham City Council and approached building design from the angle of social reform. Gordon combined his utopianism within a deep sense of environmental awareness. He is largely remembered today for coining the mantra 'long life, loose fit, low energy' as the basis for architectural design. It is a legacy that combined elements of thinking from the Archigram Group, Buckminster Fuller and E F Schumacher, whose *Small is Beautiful* was published in the UK during his tenure in Portland Place. Many of today's architects, such as Richard Rogers (Lord Rogers of Riverside) and Michael Hopkins, purport to adopt the phrase as a design principle.

Although the Oxford conference had little to say about the detailed content of the curriculum, this was addressed by the Layton report of 1962 (Layton, 1962, p2). This report introduced the notion that architectural education should be diversified by introducing technical specialisms, such as building services design. The latter was one of eight 'scientific' specialisms that were intended to ensure that graduating architects had a sound general knowledge, including a detailed grounding in one or more specific technical area. So, whereas the Oxford conference introduced the quasi-scientific approach, the report of 1962 reinforced this by requiring the teaching of technology-based specialisms. As each specialism was intended to be underpinned by research enquiry and tested through studio-based projects, the effect was to give further weight to the emergence of environmental design as a complementary arm to building design.

In spite of these changes architectural education was largely conducted in a self-contained world. It was not possible for students of engineering or surveying to acquire sufficient credits to gain entry into the architectural profession or to enter via a graduate route (as is the case in the US or Germany). Architectural training was and remains a closed system with open edges for those architectural graduates wishing to diversify, but few routes into the centre for those from other disciplines. The most significant 'edge' is sustainability, and this is a concern across the construction industry – although architecture was arguably the first profession to embrace the topic in its entirety.

Environmental Duty of Care

The RIBA and, more recently, the Architects Registration Board (ARB) have adopted standards of professional behaviour that place an environmental duty of care upon practitioners. Inevitably, this has also been adopted in curriculum revisions since the late 1990s. Unlike the impetus for environmental understanding following the Oxford conference and the Layton report, whose origins were quasi-scientific, the code of professional conduct changes have, at their core, an ethical basis. Environmental ethics have emerged now to stand alongside the wider professional responsibilities adopted by architects. Ethics and the concept of environmental duty of care have a long taproot in professional perceptions.

The ethical basis for architectural practice in the 20th century evolved from a duty of care to the client, to one of a responsibility to society as a whole, to one where the architect has to consider the environmental impact of the decisions taken. In 1962 Sir Robert Matthew, in his presidential address to RIBA, declared that 'architecture today. . .is a service to the client and the community' (Senior, 1964, p23). Until then, the interests of the client were uppermost; often this ran counter to wider social or environmental interests. Matthew was the first president who voiced the legitimate interests of society as a whole. To Matthew, the ethical function of architecture was to help articulate a shared ethos – a compact between the client who commissions and pays for building work and the community at large who uses the building. It was a foundation of sufficient breadth to allow the absorption of subsequent environmental concerns. After all, 'a strict professional ethic, even if self-regarding in origin and imprecisely formulated, inevitably tends to generate an ideal of social service' (Senior, 1964, p23, clause 11.3). This view, when applied to sustainability, allowed the UK government-sponsored Sustainable Development Education Panel to suggest in 2000 that 'acting in accordance with sustainability principles [is] a defining characteristic of being a professional' (HMSO, 2000).

THE EUROPEAN DIMENSION

As ethical codes evolved, a parallel impetus appeared during the mid 1980s, not from RIBA but the European Union (EU). The Architects' Directive 85/384/EEC required consistent standards of education, professional standards and codes of conduct to ensure the free movement of architects across Europe. The Single European Act of 1986 introduced a number of minimum standards in order to ensure harmonization of architectural services across the diverse professional landscape of Europe. The impact was felt particularly acutely in terms of architectural education. A harmonized system of education for architects across Europe, implemented in 1987, required students to master 11 areas of study. Two specifically refer to environmental awareness: students are required to have an 'understanding of the relationship between people, comfort and buildings, and between buildings and the environment' (Architects Directive 85/384/EEC, clause 11.2). This open agenda of understanding suggests a tripartite synthesis of people, buildings and environment with Vitruvian overtones. Later in the directive, studies have to ensure the acquisition of an 'adequate knowledge of physical problems and technologies. . .so as to provide. . .internal conditions of comfort and protection against climate' (Architects Directive 85/384/EEC, clause 11.3). These clauses substantially increased the level of environmental teaching in schools of architecture and required visiting boards of RIBA and ARB (the latter body given specific responsibility to ensure that the directive was implemented in the UK) to vet schools on a regular basis. The wording of the two environmental clauses had the effect of broadening the perception of the environment to embrace interests beyond low-energy design. Questions of climate-responsive design, comfort, global warming and the bigger agenda of sustainable development now crept into the curriculum.

WIDER ENVIRONMENTAL CONCERNS

1992 was an important year in other respects, too. The UN Earth Summit held in Rio de Janeiro alerted world governments to the looming environmental and ecological problems associated with urban development. In 1992, 182 governments across the world signed up to a series of declarations not only aimed at reducing adverse environmental impacts, but at adopting action – such as Agenda 21. The impetus from the declaration influenced the construction industry professions in the UK, some of which subsequently adopted new codes and standards. RIBA took the lead, instituting a new committee to steer action. Known originally as the Energy Committee (from 1992), then the Energy and Environment (from 1994), it became the Sustainable Futures Committee in 1998. The changing title reflected the altering perception of environmental problems. Traditionally, the construction industry has concerned itself with low-energy design, supported enthusiastically by quasi-governmental bodies such as the Building Research Establishment (BRE). However, after the Earth Summit the emphasis shifted towards wider ecological concerns, such as rain-forest destruction and biodiversity. Initially, the design professions were slow to reorientate their environmental focus; but with government moves towards adopting the broad agenda of sustainable development, the professions and construction industry after 1995 saw the benefit to their members and clients of addressing these wider concerns.

One resource that gained particular attention was water. Although many understood that heating, lighting and ventilation of buildings was responsible for about 50 per cent of UK fossil-fuel energy use, few realized that about 60 per cent of all water consumption was building-related. With growing stress on water reserves, a series of droughts in the late 1990s and increasing water utility bills following industry privatization, architects and engineers began to design for water conservation. In parallel, the need to address the source of hardwood timbers employed in building meant that the building industry awoke to its central position in helping to address sustainability. The idea that local design decisions had an impact upon global problems began to be absorbed within higher education and the professions.

The Earth Summit provided a framework for development that has been adopted in many curriculum revisions, especially for those degree courses in sustainable design or sustainable architecture. Four main areas were addressed at the summit: energy conservation; rain-forest conservation and associated ecological management; biodiversity; and action plans for environmental recovery. The latter, known as Agenda 21 (action for the 21st century), led to momentum from central and local government, the professions, grassroots organizations and universities.

The adoption of the Maastricht Treaty in 1992 added further weight to the environmental argument. Various articles of the treaty strengthened laws on the environment, such as Article 130v, which introduced policies for 'preserving, improving and protecting the quality of the physical environment, protecting human health and encouraging the prudent use of natural resources' (Edwards, 1999, p9). Architects and educators in the built environment became increasingly aware of their environmental responsibilities and the impact of buildings upon the quality of life, health and resource consumption. The Maastricht Treaty also introduced four important principles that span sectoral interests, but which had serious implications for the way in which buildings were designed and architects educated. The first was an obligation to use best environmental knowledge: to incorporate the benefits of environmental innovation into building design. The second was to follow the 'precautionary principle', with the implication that risks should be assessed and caution exercised in the use of new materials and construction processes. The third was an obligation to rectify environmental damage at source, rather than disperse pollutants into air or water. Since many buildings pollute, the principle questioned the gas-guzzling technologies of much modern air-conditioned development. The final principle was the need to incorporate best environmental practice into local laws and codes of practice. By implication, this suggested a further revision of the Architects' Code of Conduct, a change which occurred in 1997.

REVISIONS TO THE CURRICULAR AS UNIVERSITIES RECOGNISE GLOBAL CHALLENGES

Education has had to adapt to these and other changes. Within higher education itself, the Toyne report of 1992 was an important milestone (HMSO, 1992). This report, under the chairmanship of Peter Toyne, vice chancellor of Liverpool John Moores University, advocated a range of measures, including the greening of courses that traditionally had ignored environmental issues. Cross-curricular greening, whereby undergraduates experience sustainability best practice from other courses, proved an important avenue for the broadening of environmental understanding in schools of architecture. Toyne also advocated the use of the university campus itself as the test bed for environmental innovation. As a consequence, a generation of Green buildings was constructed, some for built environment faculties, which were used in teaching and research (a good example is the School of Engineering building at de Montfort University, built in 1995). By the 1990s, therefore, there was pressure to incorporate sustainability into architectural education from three important quarters: changes to the code of conduct governing architectural services; European legislative reforms; and pressure from the university sector itself via the Toyne report.

It is necessary, at this point, to review the current framework of legislation and codes under which architects operate. Although these are specific to the architectural profession, similar provisions exist for other professions, such as the Institute of Civil Engineers, the Royal Institute of Chartered Surveyors and the Construction Industry Council. The Union of International Architects (UIA), the umbrella group that coordinates architectural institutes across the world, has adopted principles intended to be the framework for action at national level. Principle 2 states that 'architects have obligations to the public . . .and should thoughtfully consider the social and environmental impact of their professional activities' (Edwards, 2002, p16). Principle 3 goes further: architects , it states, 'shall strive to improve the environment and the quality of the life and habitat within it in a sustainable manner' (Edwards, 2002, p16). Hence, sustainability figures largely in the codes that have been established for architectural activity globally, even if at a national or local level action suggests the contrary. In 1999 the UK ARB amended its code with regard to the environment. The new code of conduct stated that while 'architects' primary responsibility is to their clients, they should nevertheless have due regard to their wider responsibility to conserve and enhance the quality of the environment and its natural resources' (Edwards, 2002, p16).

These code revisions have wide implications for architectural education: whereas ARB regulates 36 schools of architecture in the UK, RIBA helps to validate these and a further 70 worldwide. As a consequence, these professional bodies influence a whole generation of architects; in the case of RIBA, it influences the ethos and curriculum of around 25 per cent of architectural training globally. One repercussion is that sustainability now begins to assume subject importance in its own right rather than being taught as an aspect of technology. Ecologically sensitive design rather than a subject specialism, as it was during the 1980s, had by the year 2000 become centre stage in design projects. The latter is important since about half of all assessments in a typical school of architecture are design-based, and unless sustainability engages with the studio culture, it fails to address the process and philosophy of design education.

CHANGES TO THE CURRICULUM

In terms of architectural education, two main changes occurred in response to the greening of courses during the 1990s. The first was the incorporation of greater environmental awareness into undergraduate programmes (RIBA part-one level). The second was the introduction of specialist courses in sustainable design, primarily at postgraduate level. These two parallel curriculum adjustments were seen, on the one hand, as preparing students for the new world of work where basic sustainable practice was to the fore, and, on the other, of providing subject expertise beyond that required by code changes. For some students a deep knowledge of the science, technology and design skills implicit in sustainable practice offered better employment prospects than that provided by more orthodox courses. Unfortunately, at the time of writing few of the postgraduate courses in sustainable architecture or building design provide exemption from professional body examinations. As such, these mainly MSc courses are undersubscribed and fail to influence the wider culture of an architecture or engineering school. However, what the specialist courses do confirm is the validity of the Layton proposals of 1962 and, in their research bias, the wider reforms of the Oxford conference.

The architecture schools that have given priority to Green issues tend also to have a strong research culture. This is because much funding in building research is directed towards sustainability, especially that emanating from the Engineering and Physical Sciences Research Council (EPSRC) and the EU. The former has promoted research into smart materials and construction, much of it based upon green principles. The latter has been instrumental through the fourth and fifth frameworks in testing new renewable energy systems in the context of building development. Thus, in the schools, Green research has fed into teaching at undergraduate and postgraduate level. An example is the University of Sheffield, where the joint development of new steel flooring systems between the architecture and engineering departments has reduced energy demand in the construction and use of buildings. Again at Sheffield, research into the performance of low-energy designed hospitals has had an impact upon teaching, on the one hand, and on health building procurement by the National Health Service, on the other (see *Architectural Review*, 2002).

Research is one channel in which Green awareness can influence architectural teaching. Another is the model of education that seeks to prepare graduates for employment in the developing world. It is fair to say that in spite of code changes and new curricular specifications, most architecture courses in the UK pay scant regard to sustainability as a holistic concept. Although low-energy design is widely understood, the notion of social sustainability, of life-cycle costing and of alternative technology is given little timetable space. Typical of courses that do present this alternative view is the MSc in Building Design for Developing Countries, taught at the Bartlett School of Architecture and Planning at University College London (UCL). Set up in 1985, it attracts graduates who aim to work for Voluntary Service Overseas (VSO), the World Bank and governments in countries where resources are few and necessarily need to be used sustainably (Mitchell, 1996, pp163–182). Such a course challenges Western technological imperialism and encourages thought processes closer to ecological design. A similar course, though at undergraduate level, exists at the University of Huddersfield, where the architecture programme has its main design project in the third year set within the Middle East or North Africa. Students study on location for four weeks, often working with local voluntary organizations, and learn to apply technologies witnessed in the field, such as earth wall construction, sun-baked brick manufacture and wind towers, in their design exercises. Both of these courses set sustainable practice within a wide cultural, social and political context. Here, Green thinking is not about smart technologies but about students learning from local crafts and vernacular traditions. Uniquely, in the UK, the Huddersfield course enjoys professional recognition from RIBA and ARB.

Box 9.1 *Examples of sustainable design projects from the School of Architecture, University of Huddersfield*

(see plates between pp178 and 179)

1   Keith Dillon: design for a concert hall in Finland exploiting solar heating for melting façade ice.
2   Austen Smith: design for a de-mountable shelter for emergency housing.
3   Leigh Brown: design for a timber railway station.
4   Martin Bates: design for an architecture school.
5   Edward Highton: design for loose-fit, low-energy television offices.

THE CONTRIBUTION OF RICHARD ROGERS

The contribution to the culture of sustainability from the architect Richard Rogers (Lord Rogers of Riverside) should not be underestimated. His chairmanship of the Urban Task Force in 1999 has been influential in redirecting government attention towards urban sites and the value of sustainable design. One valuable principle set out in the subsequent report is that 'social well-being and environmental responsibility' is fundamental to 'design excellence' (*Towards an Urban Renaissance*, 1999). Through his Reith lectures of 1998, his books such as *Cities for a Small Planet* (Rogers, 1997) and the example of his buildings, Rogers's work has ensured that, by the opening of the 21st century, sustainable development has begun to significantly impact upon professional perceptions and now underpins most of the recognized courses in architecture in the UK.

It is evident from this brief overview that sustainability has been gaining a foothold on architectural education for at least a generation but, perhaps, most significantly over the past decade. Like many cultural changes, there needs to be sufficient time for organizations to adapt and a willingness to accept incremental advance. Although champions in the form of Rogers exist and the bedrock of theoretical appreciation established by Mumford and Banham is widely acknowledged, schools of architecture still require time and encouragement to meet the full agenda of the challenge of sustainability. This is why the professional bodies have been cautious in the demands made upon the education and the training of architects. In an industry where other pressures such as gender representation and protection from terrorism exist, sustainability has to be integrated into what many consider to be a bigger picture.

'GREENING' THE CRITERIA FOR VALIDATION

At the time of writing, a joint initiative of the RIBA/ARB on sustainability is being implemented in UK schools of architecture. It is less ambitious than many would have preferred; yet it marks an important milestone in corporate and professional responsibility. The revised 'criteria for validation' of architecture schools by RIBA (thereby influencing the training of some 20,000 architects a year worldwide) require greater emphasis being placed on 'knowledge and understanding of technology and environment and the ability to integrate this within design projects' (RIBA, 2002, p2). The key concept here is the integration of technology and environmental principles, not their separation into discrete lecture programmes. Design projects are expected to demonstrate that such knowledge and understanding have been applied in the real world of architectural design. Under the new criteria there are five thematic headings, one of which focuses entirely on sustainability. Students in part one are expected to demonstrate and integrate knowledge of environmental design in the context of 'human well-being, the welfare of future generations, the natural world

[and] consideration of a sustainable environment' (RIBA, 2002, p7). The terminology is unambiguous and the perception of sustainable design is widely drawn. In part two (the postgraduate programme), students are expected to go further. Here specific mention is made of the 'principles and theories associated with visual, thermal and acoustic environments' and their integration within 'coherent architectural designs' (RIBA, 2002, p7). The part-two criteria for validation go further, however; students are expected in their postgraduate studies to apply the principles of climatic design. The relationship between 'climate, built form, construction, lifestyle, energy consumption and human well-being' is now explicitly stated as a knowledge requirement to be demonstrated in design projects.

To a large extent, the views of early pioneers of Green design have become mainstream. Within a generation, authors such as Ian McHarg, whose book *Design with Nature* (McHarg, 1971) was almost underground reading during the early 1970s, find their principles now underpinning architectural education.

The broadcaster and journalist Jonathan Dimbleby, giving the first RIBA annual lecture in May 2002, went even further. He suggested that architects should refuse to undertake unsustainable jobs, arguing that the ethical basis of the profession was undermined by commissions that did not place sustainable design to the fore (*RIBA Journal*, 2002, p96). Dimbleby called for a new awareness of the 'broad picture of sustainability' where 'ecological concerns, economic development and community identity' were brought together. With such pressure from outside the profession, architectural education provides the opportunity to develop new approaches to sustainable design that could influence practice. The history of architectural training in the 20th century is one of growing technological awareness – of a shift from art to science as the basis for design education. Although the early years of the 21st century sees the re-emergence of art architects (such as Frank Gehry and Zaha Hadid), the agenda of sustainability will, in time, embrace both camps. Then sustainable design will become a cultural movement that unites art, science and nature.

Finally, however, a word of warning. The architectural profession has been slow to give financial support to appointing professors in sustainable design. Compared to the Royal Academy of Engineering, which directly funded five visiting chairs in sustainable development for the year 1998/1999 and a further five in 1999/2000 (HMSO, 2002), RIBA and the big architectural offices that dominate practice have yet to sponsor a professorial appointment in the area of sustainable design. In spite of the shift in ethical responsibilities and changing educational paradigms, industry has been slow to share its best practice with the academic community. As a consequence, the analysis of case studies, especially the performance of Green buildings, remains a resource which is in the province of big architectural practices rather than in the studio culture of a school of architecture where it could be employed to influence the next generation of architects.

REFERENCES

Banham, R (1969) *The Architecture of the Well Tempered Environment*, London, Architectural Press

Building Design (2003) 25 April, p6 (formerly *Architectural Review*)

Crinson, M and Lubbock, J (1994) *Architecture: Art or Profession?* Manchester, Manchester University Press

Edwards, B (1999) *Sustainable Architecture: European Directives and Building Design*, Oxford, Architectural Press

Edwards, B with Hyett, P (2002) *Rough Guide to Sustainability*, London, RIBA Publications

Hawkes, D (1996) *The Environmental Tradition: Studies in the Architecture of Environment*, London, E & F Spon

HMSO (1992) *Environmental Responsibilities: An Agenda for Further and Higher Education* (the Toyne Report), London, HMSO

HMSO (2000) *What Sustainable Development Education Means for the Professions*, London, HMSO, April

HMSO (2002) *What Sustainable Development Education Means for the Professions*, London, HMSO, April

Layton, E (1962) *Report on the Practical Training of Architects*, London, RIBA

Maxwell, R (1996) 'Introduction', in Hawkes, D, *The Environmental Tradition: Studies in the Architecture of Environment*, London, E & F Spon

McHarg, I (1971) *Design with Nature*, New York, Doubleday/Natural History Press

Mitchell, M (1996) 'Educating through Building: Architects, Appropriate Technology and Building Production', in Hamdi, N (ed) *Educating for Real*, London, Intermediate Technology Publications

RIBA (2002) *Criteria for Validation*, London, RIBA Publications, May

RIBA Journal (2002), vol 109, no 6

Rogers, R with Gumuchdjian, P (1997) *Cities for a Small Plan*, London, Faber and Faber

Schumacher, E F (1974) *Small is Beautiful*, London, Abacus

Senior, D (1964) *Your Architect*, London, Hodder and Stoughton

Towards an Urban Renaissance (Urban Task Force Report) (1999), London, E & F Spon

Chapter 10

Sustainable Transport and Logistics: Vision or Reality?

Colin Bamford

INTRODUCTION: THE TRANSPORT PROBLEM

On 25 November 2002, readers of the *Daily Telegraph* were provided with clear evidence of the critical state of the UK's transport system. In a substantial poll of its readers on 'What's wrong with Britain', the newspaper reported that of the 1420 on-line respondents:

- 85 per cent believed that because of congestion and frequent rail delays 'Britain is grinding to a halt'.
- 82 per cent were dissatisfied with the state of road traffic; 93 per cent expected the problems to get worse or remain unchanged.
- 61 per cent were dissatisfied with local transport; 86 per cent expected the quality to get worse or remain unchanged.

The same newspaper also contained an article on the deteriorating quality of the road network, as if regular road users were not already aware of the deficiencies. More specifically:

- Motorway travel was, on average, 30 per cent slower than in 1998.
- The western section of the M25 between junctions 10 and 21A was the most congested in the UK.
- The typical journey time from London to Leeds via the M1 was 14 per cent longer than in 1998 and was expected to increase by a further 15 per cent to 3.5 hours by 2006.
- The morning and evening peak periods for road traffic were now much more extensive, starting earlier and finishing later.

The above examples are indicative of a much wider problem that was identified a year earlier by the UK government's Commission for Integrated Transport (CfIT) (CfIT, 2001). In a major European best-practice benchmarking study, the CfIT stated that:

> *The evidence we are now publishing is a clear but stark demonstration of*
> *two generations of neglect, of a transport network starved of investment*
> *for half a century – a situation that forced people into their cars whether*
> *they wanted to or not. Here in the UK we have fallen a generation behind*
> *the best in Europe in planning transport in a holistic way.* (CfIT, 2000)

The main report made some stark comparisons with the rest of the European Union (EU), including that the UK has:

- more congestion than any other country;
- the most intensively used road network except for Spain;
- the longest commuter times in the EU;
- the most car-dominated economy; and
- the lowest level of public transport subsidy and the highest level of fares in any EU country.

It also stated that France invests half as much again as the UK in transport infrastructure and that Germany invests two-thirds more. About the only positive comparison was the UK's record on road safety, where it had the lowest death toll rate in the EU.

Nevertheless, the CfIT welcomed the UK government's ten-year transport plan (see the following section), although one must seriously question whether the resources that are being committed to transport will do much to improve the UK's European standing.

To appreciate why a more sustainable transport policy is required, one needs to be aware of traffic forecasts that have been used as the basis for policy decisions. In 1989, in putting forward the Roads for Prosperity programme, the Thatcher government was working on an estimated increase in vehicle miles of between 83 and 142 per cent by 2025. The most recent forecasts are a downward revision of these estimates (see Table 10.2). As things remain, the increase will still be in line with or just above projected gross domestic product (GDP) growth.

It should also be recognised that the private car is an inefficient means of transport. Not only does it consume vast amounts of energy; but, typically, vehicle occupancy rates are just 1.2 persons. Due to congestion, the average motorist spends around 5.4 days a year equivalent in traffic queues – this is a huge waste of resources that could be put to far more productive use.

Another relevant factor to take into account is the many side effects of vehicle use – for example:

- the link between increased vehicle use and the increased incidence of respiratory complaints such as asthma;
- the impact on child behaviour and learning experiences of children not being able to play freely in their home neighbourhood;
- the problems of waste disposal of vehicles at the end of their life cycle – tyre and battery disposal, in particular, pose enormous problems for global warming;

- the contribution of increased carbon dioxide (CO_2) emissions from vehicles, arguably the most serious environmental problem we face; any reduction of emissions from vehicle use will help us to meet our Kyoto Protocol commitment of a 20 per cent reduction on 1990 levels by 2010.

It is therefore not difficult to see why there are substantial concerns about the ways in which our transport system is not only organized and planned, but how we use it and the impact that this use has upon others. Unless there is a big change in transport policy, the future for transport users can only be described as bleak.

TRANSPORT POLICY AND SUSTAINABILITY: THE PRINCIPLES

It is appropriate to state the World Commission on Environment and Development's definition of a sustainable society (WCED, 1987). Popularly known as the Brundtland Report, it defined a sustainable society as one 'that meets the needs of the present without compromising the ability of future generations to meet their own needs.' Subsequently, this has been elaborated to argue that a physically sustainable society must meet three fundamental conditions. These are:

1   Its rates of use of renewable resources should not exceed their rates of regeneration.
2   Its rates of use of non-renewable resources should not exceed the rate at which sustainable renewable substitutes are developed.
3   Its rates of pollution emission should not exceed the capacity of the environment to assimilate them.

Only a cursory knowledge of transport is needed to realize that none of these conditions are close to being met. The UK's transport situation, however, should be put in perspective – a proper and effective understanding of sustainability should not only be global, but should also cover all activities that are net users of resources. Transport is just one of many areas of activity where there is a need for more sustainable outcomes.

From a UK perspective, the car and lorry are symbolic of the central problem of unsustainability (Whitelegg, 1994). To be more sustainable, not only has road use to fall (or at least the rate of increase must fall), but land-use policies and user attitudes have to change in order to move the focus away from a land-use planning and economic system that necessitates more and more use of road traffic.

There must also be improved integration in transport, particularly for interchange between modes. Where smoothly effected, switching from one mode to another enhances the quality of public transport provision and can have an impact upon modal choice. This is particularly true for car users, but also has significance for rail/car journeys.

The most sustainable of all transport modes are walking and cycling. Although some modest resource need is required for provision in towns and cities, the overall benefits that can result from people switching from private car transport are substantial, particularly at peak periods.

Figure 10.1 shows, in a highly simplified way, the rank order of transport modes in terms of their net use of resources.

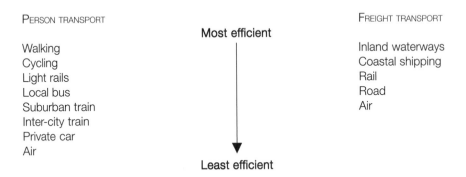

PERSON TRANSPORT		FREIGHT TRANSPORT
	Most efficient	
Walking		Inland waterways
Cycling		Coastal shipping
Light rails		Rail
Local bus		Road
Suburban train		Air
Inter-city train		
Private car		
Air		
	Least efficient	

Figure 10.1 *Transport modes and resource efficiency*

To put relative weightings on modal efficiency is a complex task. For person transport, local buses and light rail systems operating at high occupancy are around 30 times more efficient than the private car in terms of energy used. They are also substantially more efficient in terms of the space that is required for their operation. The position for freight is less complex – rail is more energy efficient than road and, where available, water transport for inland or coastal movements is, in turn, more efficient than rail. For person and goods transport, air is the least efficient by far. Although market forces mean that future demand will continue to grow, the outcome of this growth is far from sustainable. Under certain circumstances, however, air transport can produce important time savings and other benefits that should be offset against its energy use. Mass tourism growth most certainly does not constitute a sustainable outcome in transport, energy and resource terms.

In order to make a difference, a more sustainable transport policy should encompass measures that reduce the future demand for all forms of transport that are net users of energy. This will not be easy. It is not impossible, however, and could be achieved through the following:

- a deliberate policy to shift demand and supply to more sustainable modes of transport; the most obvious way to achieve this is to promote urban and inter-urban rail passenger and freight services at the expense of road transport;

- making fuel more expensive in real terms and taxing those vehicles that are heavy users of fuel in relation to their outputs more highly;
- improving fuel efficiency and promoting initiatives that spread best practice and innovation.

These should be the objectives, therefore, of a more sustainable transport policy.

A New Deal for Transport: Better for Everyone

New Labour's long-awaited transport policy strategy was published in July 1998 by the UK Department of the Environment, Transport and the Regions (DETR, 1998). This contained some interesting new developments, particularly from the economist's standpoint. The most important of these centred on a statement that there would be an increase in taxes to be paid by car drivers. Estimated at around UK£1 billion by 2005, the proposed tax increases took various forms, including:

- a commitment to increase the price of fuel in real terms of at least 6 per cent above the rate of inflation per annum (1 per cent higher than the previous government's policy);
- provision for introducing road user charges for access into city centres;
- access charges to popular countryside areas, such as parts of the national parks;
- new levies on city-centre workplace parking, both for new provision and for the use of spaces in seriously congested areas;
- the limited use of motorway charging.

To be effective, the demand for car transport must be price elastic – that is, the increased taxes should reduce the volume of travel. This is fine in theory. In reality, much personal travel is not price elastic. On the contrary, due to its necessity, it is more likely to be price inelastic, in which case demand will not fall by as much as the increase in the price of travel. This is particularly true of peak period travel into towns and cities. A further complication from a policy standpoint is that the burden of *specific* taxes tends to fall more heavily on the lowest paid, and those living in rural areas and who lack an adequate alternative. This is hardly consistent with the New Deal's statements on the need for improved transport inclusion.

Introducing the idea of hypothecation

This is the principle whereby resources raised through specific forms of taxation can be ring-fenced and then ear-marked for a very specific purpose. What this means is that the additional taxation raised from road users can be specifically allocated for new public transport projects. So, for example, the income raised from the UK£5 a day user charge for access into central London goes directly into subsidizing public transport fares or is allocated for new investment programmes for London's creaking transport system. This principle can be applied by any city that decides to introduce new road-pricing schemes, levies on workplace parking or similar taxes on car users. The principle is also being applied in the case of other taxes which apply on a national scale, such as increases in vehicle excise duty and fuel taxes.

Up to now, hypothecation has been a principle that economists have debated. Its application in transport is the first time that it has actually been applied in the UK, thereby avoiding the usual round of procedures where ministers make annual bids for a share of government expenditure.

The rationale behind it is that the government should recognize that more capital and, possibly, revenue resources are needed if it is to realize the stated objectives of the White Paper. At the same time there is a need for the prudent control of government spending, particularly in the light of the increased demands being made for increased expenditure on health, education, welfare payments and so on. In this way the country's transport infrastructure will benefit from the boost to public investment.

The costs and benefits of the main modes of freight transport were debated in the White Paper and have been further evaluated by the CfIT (CfIT, 2000). Economists have made a major contribution to this debate, especially through identifying and enumerating the respective costs and benefits of road and rail freight and through the extent to which heavier lorries can aid the competitiveness of UK businesses.

The New Deal for transport, therefore, has come in the form of a more sustainable transport system. As stated in paragraph 2.1, 'we need a transport system which doesn't damage our health but which provides a better quality of life for everyone, both now and in the future' (DETR, 1998, p271). For the first time, this White Paper has provided the vision that has been sadly lacking in the past.

TRANSPORT 2010: A TEN-YEAR PLAN

Almost exactly two years after the publication of the New Deal White Paper, and just two weeks before the election, the UK government published its ten-year transport plan (DETR, 2000a) Although plans for roads have been commonplace in the past, this is the first time that there has been an all-embracing plan covering all aspects of the future transport system. Logically, it can be seen as the means by which the New Deal strategy will be realized.

In resource terms, an estimated UK£180 billion of new investment and ongoing expenditure is being committed to modernizing the transport network. This is the largest sum ever allocated for transport projects. The objectives behind the plan are entirely consistent with those of the New Deal – namely to:

- reduce road congestion;
- lower CO_2 emissions and improve air quality;
- improve road and rail safety.

Like any plan, it also lays down targets for 2010. These include:

- a 50 per cent increase in passenger use of railways;
- a 10 per cent growth in bus passenger use;
- achieving the previously stated target for CO_2 reduction;

and to realize this:

- up to 25 new light rail projects;
- better bus services;
- major investment on London's Underground system; and, pointedly,
- 360 miles of trunk road and motorway widening;
- 100 new by-passes.

Table 10.1 *Planned transport investment and expenditure (2001/2002 to 2010/2011) (UK£ billion)*

	Public investment	Private investment	Total investment	Public resource expenditure[1]
Strategic roads	13.6	2.6	16.2	5.0
Railways	14.7	34.4	49.1	60.4
Local transport[2]	19.3	9.0	28.3	58.9
London	7.4	10.4	17.8	25.3
Other	0.7	–[4]	0.7	2.2
Unallocated	9.0	–[4]	9.0	–[4]
Charging income[3]	–[4]	–[4]	–[4]	2.7
Total	64.7	56.3	121.0	58.6

Notes: 1 includes revenue support for public transport, light rail feasibility studies and user charging feasibility projects
2 includes local roads and light rail
3 no allowance is made for funds generated during the life of the plan and hypothecated to public transport systems
4 not available
Source: DETR (2000a)

Table 10.1 shows the total allocation of resources. About one third will be derived from the private sector, particularly for new rail infrastructure and rolling stock. Contrary to earlier expectations, little private-sector investment in new toll roads is now expected. Significantly, one third of total expenditure is being provided for road construction and improvements. Although denied by the government, this is seen as a U-turn on its earlier New Deal strategy of 'no more major road-building projects'. It is also difficult to comprehend in the light of the commitment to a more sustainable transport policy.

A consequence of the plan's publication is that road traffic forecasts have been revised. These are shown in Table 10.2. The overall forecast suggests that there will be about 23 per cent less traffic than might have been expected without the plan. The largest fall is for the use of large goods vehicles, much of it a consequence of the 2001 implementation of 44-tonne operation. The increase in bus and coach use is a change from previous forecasts, which had been for a 'no change' situation.

The reduction in the rate of growth of road transport is clearly a more sustainable outcome than the 1995 traffic forecasts had indicated. So, too, is the increase in bus and coach use and the reduced rate of increase in the use of large goods vehicles. Despite its earlier intentions, it is undoubtedly true that these outcomes can only be achieved through providing considerable new investment in an already severely crowded road network.

It is one thing to produce a plan; it is an entirely different matter to see it through. This plan relies heavily on the contribution of the private sector. Recent problems on the railways must put this investment at risk. The government's own input could also be at risk if the economy moves into recession following the terrible events of 11 September 2001. There must also be doubts as to whether there is sufficient expertise available to plan and manage the many new road and light-rail projects that are envisaged to be operational by 2010.

Table 10.2 *Forecasts of road traffic to 2010 (2000 = 100)*

Vehicle kilometres	Without ten-year plan	With ten-year plan
Cars and taxis	121	117
Large goods vehicles	118	109
Light goods vehicles	125	123
Buses and coaches	109	118
All road traffic	122	117

Source: London Transport (2001, Table 4.8)

CONGESTION CHARGING: A MEANS OF RESTRICTING URBAN ROAD TRANSPORT

The problem of traffic congestion is the most intractable transport issue that the UK economy is currently experiencing. As should have already been observed, it is far too early to be certain of the effects of a more sustainable transport policy, especially the ways in which the public transport alternative is being enhanced. The disturbing evidence is that the costs of road traffic congestion are rising (the latest estimate is UK £20 billion a year). The consequence is one of increased business costs, millions of hours of potentially productive effort going to waste and genuine fears about competitiveness relative to other EU economies.

Economists are not well known for agreeing on things! But as far as congestion is concerned, there has been a consensus for some time that charging for the use of urban roads is the only way to combat congestion (Chartered Institute of Transport, 1990, 1992). Charging is viewed by economists as a means of correcting market failure – it so happens that if demand for urban road travel is elastic, then the reductions in traffic volumes will be substantial, meeting the objective of reducing congestion (Institute of Economic Affairs, 1998).

Transport planners also agree on the merits of charging: the obvious outcome, if the charge is at a meaningful level, is that traffic volumes will fall. They also see charges as providing an important source of hypothecated revenue for public transport projects.

User charges and road pricing may seem to be one and the same thing. To some extent they are; but, equally, in terms of objectives they differ. A user charge is any charge that is directly paid for the use of a particular road or section of road, or for entry into a designated zone. It does not vary with the level of demand. These charges can be levied for traffic entering or being used in a previously defined cordon, as recently introduced in Durham and in some Norwegian cities. They are usually flat rate charges and do not vary with traffic use or demand. Revenue from such charges must now be hypothecated into public transport projects.

A UK£5-a-day congestion charge was imposed for entry into central London in early 2003. It was the central pillar behind Mayor Livingstone's transport strategy for the capital and was expected to raise over UK£200 million a year. Most of this revenue is to be redirected to support the bus network and Underground, where fare reductions seem likely (Greater London Authority, 2001).

The toll zone covers an extensive cordon around the city centre. The charge applies to all vehicles, except for buses, taxis, motorcycles, emergency vehicles and orange badge holders. Drivers are required to pay the charge in advance or on the day and have their registration details installed on a database. Vehicles used within the cordon are monitored by cameras. Vehicles found not to have paid the charge are subject to a UK£80 fixed penalty, which will be reduced to UK£40 for prompt payment. Residents in the toll area are required to pay an annual fee of UK£130 for the unlimited use of their vehicles within the charging area.

The pioneering scheme for London is consistent with legislation that is now in place for other cities (DETR, 1998). Leicester and Bristol seem keen to follow London's lead, but not until 2006 or 2007. Other cities, such as Cambridge, Leeds, Birmingham and Manchester, have carried out feasibility studies.

The government recognizes the attraction of charging road users. In addition to directly reducing congestion, the revenue stream from the charges can improve city-centre access for public transport users. Charging, therefore, must not be seen in isolation from a much wider range of measures to enhance the overall quality of transport and accessibility in the cities involved.

The imminent introduction of congestion charges is an exciting new development. At last, politicians and planners have applied what economists have been saying for years. In London, for example, the UK£5 per day charge is expected to reduce traffic terminating in the charging area by 20 per cent (estimate made by Greater London Authority, 2000). At the same time, there should be an estimated 4 per cent increase in the use of public transport during morning peak hours. Despite the predictable criticism by pro-car organizations, alongside major improvements to public transport, congestion charging is the only feasible means left for tackling the intractable problem of road congestion. It is an important method of implementing a more sustainable transport policy.

44-TONNE LORRIES: MOVING GOODS IN A MORE SUSTAINABLE WAY

The use of heavy large-goods vehicles (or juggernauts, as they are popularly but wrongly called) is an emotive subject. In 1983, the maximum weight limit was increased to 38 tonnes, amidst massive protests in the media and on the streets. From 1 February 2001, following advice from the CfIT, the maximum weight limit increased to 44 tonnes, from the 41-tonne level that had been operational since 1999. This latest increase barely received a mention in the media.

Large goods vehicles, unlike buses and trains, do not have a good image. They are seen as noisy, dirty, intimidating, imposing and destructive. Few people really appreciate their role in the food chain and in the supply chains of businesses. They clearly have an important function and that is why, in 1998, the government asked the CfIT to investigate whether 44-tonne operation for general use should be introduced (it had previously applied to road–rail traffic only).

The CfIT's report follows a cost-benefit format, although it falls well short of a full cost-benefit analysis. On the surface, heavier lorries might appear to impose even greater negative externalities on the areas in which they are used and on the community, as a whole. Overall, this is not the case. Their main environmental benefit is that fewer vehicles are required for a given volume of work, their technical specification is more environmentally acceptable than older vehicles and they cause less wear and tear on road surfaces as they operate on a greater number of axles. They are entirely consistent with the principles and practices of a sustainable distribution strategy.

So why did the government find it necessary to ask the CfIT to investigate? The main reason was because of concerns over the impact of 44-tonne operations on the rail freight business, itself an important part of the government's sustainable transport policy. English, Welsh and Scottish Railway (EWS)'s rail freight market was thought to be vulnerable in business areas where the cross-elasticity of demand between road and rail freight charges was positive and elastic. This is the case for products such as coal and coke, chemicals and petroleum, where road has gained traffic from rail in recent years. There were also concerns about the impact on the mail deliveries and parcels traffic that EWS provides for Royal Mail.

The CfIT disagreed with the evidence provided by EWS that they stood to lose up to 19 per cent of their freight market with 44-tonne operation. However, they acknowledged that some traffic would be lost to road. The key question was whether the environmental disbenefit of the probable loss of some traffic from rail to road outweighed the environmental and economic advantages stemming from the more efficient use of heavier lorries.

The main business benefit arising from 44-tonne lorries is that they can carry a higher payload (the load that is generating revenue) than 38- and 41-tonne vehicles. Although it depends upon the volume of the load, for 44-tonne vehicles, this averages around 29 tonnes compared with 24 tonnes for 38-tonne vehicles. The heavier weight produces an internal economy of scale for those firms using them. It is quite difficult to estimate the actual savings in average costs (probably 6 to 8 per cent, compared with 38-tonne vehicles). The CfIT concluded that 44-tonne operation would:

- reduce traffic levels by 100 million vehicle kilometres per year (this amounts to 3 per cent of the total);
- mean that 1000 fewer lorries would be on the roads than would otherwise be the case;
- significantly result in annual savings of 80,000 to 100,000 tonnes of CO_2 emissions.

This is consistent with the government's policy of seeking to make distribution more sustainable. These benefits, along with cost savings for firms and reduced road wear, were deemed to offset the costs of some freight transferring to road from rail. They also do not take into account any measures that might improve the competitiveness of rail freight, such as increased infrastructure subsidies and grants and reduced track charges.

RAIL TRANSPORT: CENTRAL TO A MORE SUSTAINABLE TRANSPORT POLICY

The dramatic collapse of Railtrack and its plunge into 'public administration' occurred in October 2001. Although it might have been foreseen by a few observers, Railtrack's financial demise has cast serious doubts on the privatization model that was adopted in the 1993 Railways Act (Foster, 1994). It also confirms the scepticism amongst railway managers at that time (Edmonds J, 2000).

It is unclear what the future holds for the vertically separated railway. Apart from limited experiments in Sweden and Germany, there is no precedent. Railtrack has suffered considerable damage through the public perception of it as a profit-driven, yet seemingly negligent, monopoly. Under its new structure as a non-profit-making body, user confidence will return when punctuality and reliability levels improve. Investor confidence, so vital to its future, is more problematic. The signs at present are not good, with the scaling down of the West Coast main line project and serious doubts as to whether Railtrack can effect its obligations in the ten-year plan.

Rail is central to the realization of a more sustainable transport policy. The relatively new 'not-for-profit' Network Rail has a tremendous task ahead if it is to maintain, revitalize and upgrade the rail network to meet future needs.

THE PRICE OF FUEL

It is appropriate to finish this chapter with a few comments on the price of fuel. For all modes, this represents an important cost item, even greater if actual rather than perceived costs are used. In order to reduce road congestion and encourage a greater use of public transport, it has been government policy, until quite recently, to increase the price of fuel in real terms. This has not been without its problems.

Table 10.3 shows the pump price for unleaded petrol and diesel since 1995. As this indicates, the price of unleaded petrol has increased by 48 per cent to its peak in April 2000, while diesel has increased by over 50 per cent. Consequently, the UK has the highest-priced and highest-taxed fuel within the EU. Both of these facts have been used by industry pressure groups in their claims about the competitiveness of UK industry and transport relative to the rest of the EU.

The fuel prices shown in Table 10.3 have been determined, to some degree, by the world market. These market prices until November 2000 were then subject to the so-called fuel escalator, a deliberate policy to increase the price of fuel annually by 5 per cent (later 7 per cent) above the rate of inflation. The New Deal White Paper firmly committed the government to this policy.

Table 10.3 *Fuel prices in the UK, 1995–2001 (pence per litre)* [1]

	1995	1996	1997	1998	1999	2000	2001
Unleaded							
Price	54.1	55.2	59.2	65.8	70.2	80.0	75.9
All tax as percentage of price	73	77	77	82	82	76	76
Diesel[2]							
Price	54.7	56.4	60.2	66.8	73.2	81.1	77.3
All tax as percentage of price	72	76	76	82	83	75	74

Notes: 1 average pump price in April 2000
2 ultra-low sulphur diesel from 2000

As Table 10.3 shows, between 1999 and 2000, the price of fuel increased significantly, a consequence of a soaring world market price. This prompted an unprecedented range of protests from hauliers and farmers who were protesting at the effects of expensive fuel on their businesses. An added complication for the government was the much-publicized 'flagging out' of vehicles by well-known UK transport businesses such as Eddie Stobart.

The fuel escalator was abandoned in November 2000, when a 2 pence per litre fuel tax cut was announced. A further 2-pence cut followed in the March 2001 budget, pending low-sulphur petrol becoming more readily available. Subsequent falls in the world market price have reduced the price at the pump.

The government's reaction to the protests was obviously political. It could hardly have been anything otherwise. From a wider perspective, though, the scrapping of the fuel escalator is seen as a serious backward step in the government's commitment to a more sustainable transport policy.

THE 'FAILURE' OF HIGHER EDUCATION?

It should be clear from this evaluation that if the UK (and, indeed, other countries) is to get to grips with its serious transport problems, it needs an appropriate professional formation of problem-solvers who are able to take on the challenge. This is the role of the transport planner.

Transport planners come from a wide variety of backgrounds. Traditionally, this has included town planning, geography, economics and certain types of engineering. More recently, as transport issues have become more complex and more multidimensional, graduates from environmental sciences, sociology, marketing and design have been employed by a wide range of organizations. Typically, transport planners are employed by:

- central and local government;
- professional consultancies;
- non-governmental organizations (NGOs) responsible for strategic transport developments;
- bus, rail and logistics operators;
- universities and transport research organizations.

Bearing in mind the current direction and priorities of national transport policies, transport planners are involved in a wide range of activities, including:

- preparation of regional and local strategic transport plans;
- planning of new light rail systems and other types of transport infrastructure;
- preparation of new road schemes and local traffic management systems;
- cost-benefit studies on the likely impact of new transport developments;
- preparation and implementation of Green travel plans;
- in-depth research into a wide range of operational, infrastructure and strategic issues.

A small number of universities (including Huddersfield) provide under-graduate and postgraduate courses. There is a serious problem, however – namely, the current demand for transport planners exceeds supply. After a generation of neglect, both politically and educationally, the profession is desperate to attract new blood to meet the increased requirements that have now been placed upon it.

This so-called 'skills gap' has recently been acknowledged by the Transport Planning Society, the leading professional body, with members drawn from the private and public sectors and from academic institutions. It is the view of its members that, in the short term, the only realistic solution to the problem is to upgrade the skills from within organizations by means of an appropriate professional development programme. In the longer term, transport planning has to be seen as an appropriate and challenging career by an increased number of graduates. Universities should also play a part through developing more postgraduate courses and providing additional funding for more students on existing postgraduate courses.

This sounds fine in principle. In practice, it is far easier said than done from the universities' standpoint. Obstacles include:

- lack of funding and high fees that have to be charged for postgraduate courses at a time when undergraduate student debt is escalating;
- declining resource base in many universities;
- lack of specialist university departments capable of providing meaningful education and training programmes.

One might easily lay the blame for this state of affairs on the universities for not anticipating the skills gap before now. This is rather unfair. A large part of the blame must lie with government. After many years of neglect, transport problems have been elevated in importance. The reality of the situation is that there has been underinvestment, not only in transport itself, but also in the provision of relevant higher education courses. If we are serious about meeting the many transport challenges we face, the present shortfall has to be addressed as a matter of urgency. A model similar to that which encourages more young people into secondary school teaching, for example, would go a long way to meeting future need. In order to share the cost, employers could be asked to contribute. Education is an investment in human capital, whether it is made directly in a classroom situation or more indirectly in those vital areas of the economy and society where a need has been clearly identified. In the case of transport planners, the cost of no further action is one that has serious implications for the next generation of transport users.

VISION OR REALITY?

As this chapter has indicated, there is very clear evidence of the UK government's commitment to a more sustainable policy regarding the ways in which people and goods should move around the country in the future. This evidence comes from :

- policy statements, consultation documents and a ten-year transport plan;
- new structures that provide every opportunity to plan transport and logistics in a strategic way;
- investment in transport infrastructure from the private and public sector at an all-time high;
- a growing awareness amongst many road users that the present state of affairs cannot persist and that user charging is essential in many of our cities if demand is to be reduced;
- a slowing down in the growth rate of road transport use, an increased use of trains and buses and more freight being carried by rail.

If realized, this is the vision that will produce a more sustainable transport and logistics systems than is the case at present.

There are, however, increasingly worrying signs that sustainability may be fine in principle, but not so fine in reality. More specifically:

- A U-turn in government policy on fuel prices, for political and transport-related reasons, has seriously undermined one of the main ways in which fuel use might be reduced.
- The ten-year transport plan allocation of funds to strategic roads, as well as local improvements, has backtracked on an earlier statement that no more major new road schemes would be approved.
- There is increasing doubt over whether Railtrack, its contractors and the train-operating companies can meet their projected obligations as set out in the ten-year plan.
- Road transport demand continues to increase, albeit at a slightly reduced rate of growth.
- Depending upon the speed with which urban public-transport systems can be developed and whether, on completion, car drivers may yet have the motivation and confidence to switch modes.

This is the reality of the situation today.

REFERENCES

Chartered Institute of Transport (1990) *Paying for Progress*, London, CIT
Chartered Institute of Transport (1992) *Paying for Progress*, London, CIT
CfIT (2000) *Permitting 44 Tonne Lorries for General Use in the UK*, London, HMSO
CfIT (2001) *European Benchmarking Study*, London, HMSO
DETR (1998) *A New Deal for Transport – Better for Everyone*, London, HMSO
DETR (2000a) *Transport 2010 – A 10 Year Plan for Transport*, London, HMSO
DETR (2000b) *Breaking the Logjam*, London, HMSO

Edmonds, J (2000) in Freeman, G and Shaw, J (eds) *British Rail Privatisation*, Maidenhead, McGraw-Hill

Foster, C (1994) *The Economics of Rail Privatisation*, London, Centre of the Study of Regulated Industries

Greater London Authority (2001) 'Congestion Pricing', *London Lines*, vol 18, no 4

Institute of Economic Affairs (1998) *Economic Affairs*, vol 18, no 4

WCED (1987) *Our Common Future*, Oxford, World Commission on Environment and Development and Oxford University Press

Whitelegg, J (1994) *Transport for Sustainable Future*, Chichester, Wiley

Chapter 11

Accounting Education for Sustainability

Christopher Cowton

INTRODUCTION

At first sight, accounting and sustainability might be thought to have little connection. However, sustainability is one of the major challenges facing society; and accounting is a major component of modern organizational and social management (Burchell et al, 1980). What is accounted for influences views of what is important and helps to determine the terms in which issues are debated; and what accountants fail to identify and measure can easily be omitted from policy discussions and decisions at many different levels. Unfortunately, environmental sustainability is something that does not fit easily into conventional approaches to accounting, not least because accountants tend to base their figures on economic transactions entered into by the entity being accounted for, and thus are prone to ignore what economists refer to as 'externalities' – including harmful environmental consequences. Stated in this way, there would appear to be scope for exploring the relationship between accounting and sustainability; but it begins to look like a somewhat negative exercise, with accounting being part of 'the problem' of *un*sustainable development.

However, beginning with an early flowering of writing during the 1970s and, more recently, a renaissance during the 1990s and the early years of the 21st century, there has not only been a wider realization of the shortcomings of conventional accounting, but also a steadily growing appreciation of the possibility of a more positive link between accounting and the environment, if not with sustainable development as such. Academic research and scholarship, more recently accompanied by some interesting practical initiatives, have brought into being a set of ideas and developments that might, for convenience, be broadly grouped under the heading of 'social accounting'.

With the above background in mind, this chapter reflects on the question of how sustainability might figure in degree programmes in accounting.

Before outlining the structure of the remainder of the chapter, some explanatory remarks are probably in order. First, the chapter will concentrate on undergraduate education because that accounts for the bulk of accounting education provided in UK universities. There are postgraduate programmes, too; but they are on a relatively small scale, though it should also be noted that many graduates who enter the accountancy profession will not have studied accounting at university, and the profession is not exclusively graduate entry. Second, the chapter does not aim to specify the detailed content of a degree programme that takes sustainability seriously, providing guidelines, for example, for detailed syllabi. Rather, the chapter focuses upon how sustainability might come to figure in such programmes. Finally, the chapter will not define sustainability (or sustainable development) because nothing significant for the argument hangs on the question of a precise definition within the parameters of conventional usage of the term(s). Some of the activities or topics to which this chapter alludes might seem to fall short of a proper treatment of sustainability; but the points it makes apply *a fortiori* to sustainability.

The chapter begins by exploring in a little more detail the relationship between accounting and sustainability. The state of sustainability in undergraduate accounting education in the UK is then examined. The third main section discusses the prospects for reflecting sustainability in accounting education, paying particular attention to the role that the accounting profession might play.

ACCOUNTING AND SUSTAINABILITY

The field where the relationship between accounting and sustainability is most obviously addressed is 'social accounting', which is concerned with reflecting those features of corporate activity of ethical and social significance that are generally omitted from conventional transactions-based, profit-focused accounting. Accounting statements, such as the profit-and-loss account and the balance sheet, are incomplete depictions of performance and position, particularly to the extent that they fail to capture externalities:

> *As soon as we recognize that. . .trade-offs between (organizational) success and (societal/environmental) degradation or contribution are not trivial, we must accept that the business is not* just *an economic entity and its* overall *success or failure is* not *captured by the accounting numbers and the bottom line. There is a very real danger at this point that accounting and reporting are sending some seriously misleading signals.* (Gray et al, 1997, p179)

Social accounting is a broad umbrella term for a variety of approaches that are intended to remedy some or all of the deficiencies of conventional accounting. For example, Rubenstein (1992), in the context of 'Green accounting', suggests creating an accounting asset for essential natural resources upon which the enterprise is economically dependent. As these resources are degraded, a natural resource expense could be recorded in the enterprise's financial system. Different approaches and terminology abound, and during the latter part of the 1990s the more comprehensively descriptive acronym SEAAR (social and ethical accounting, auditing and reporting) became increasingly popular (Owen et al, 2000; Zadek et al, 1997). However, although social accounting is an amorphous and shifting field, its mission is, above all, to extend the accountability of organizations beyond their traditional role of simply providing a financial account to providers of capital, particularly shareholders (Owen et al, 1997). Occasionally it might be taken to include environmental accounting; in other instances the two might be distinguished from each other, particularly where a point or line of argument about the environment or 'Green' issues is being pursued. This chapter tends to use the term 'social accounting' in the more inclusive sense.

Social accounting has come a long way since Gray et al (1987, p204) lamented that 'the omens for increased recognition of corporate social responsibilities and accountability. . .could hardly look more unpromising'. The current situation is much more positive for, as Owen and Swift (2001, p4) more recently note, 'We are currently witnessing a dramatic resurgence of academic, professional and corporate interest in social accounting and auditing that has been largely dormant since the 1970s.' Zadek et al (1997) suggest that the emergence of ethical investment funds (Cowton, 1997, 1999; Sparkes, 2002) was an important influence on the 'renaissance' of social accounting at the end of the 1980s. But probably the most influential factor was the dramatic increase in concern about the natural environment around 1990: during much of the 1990s attention in social accounting was 'overwhelmingly focused on one element – the environment' (Owen et al, 1998, p143; Deegan and Rankin, 1997, 1999; Gray, 1990; Owen, 1992). Thus, the environment moved from being an 'also' to being a matter of 'central importance' (Gray, 1992, p400), almost to the extent of displacing other elements of social accounting for a time (Mathews, 1997).

However, there is more to sustainability than the natural environment alone, and the recognition of the social dimensions of sustainability, or – at least – increasing ethical concern about several other dimensions of business behaviour, has led to revitalizing the broader social accounting agenda. This has been accompanied by a new wave of social reporting, including the emergence of the notion of 'triple bottom line' reporting, which is intended to provide a more comprehensive picture of corporate reporting in terms of economic prosperity, environmental quality and social justice (Elkington, 1997). Such initiatives, first by value-driven organizations (Zadek et al, 1997) and then by some prominent companies – examples include Royal Dutch Shell, British Telecom (BT), Camelot, Six Continents and British American Tobacco (BAT), to name just five – provide a valuable complement to the academic debates.

However, encouraging though these developments might appear to be, some leading social accounting academics sound a note of caution (Gray, 2001; Owen et al, 2000; Owen and Swift, 2001). Some are sceptical of the motives for, and question the usefulness of, company initiatives; and in the opinion of Gray (2001, p11), 'it is not obvious that we have learned a great deal' during the past

30 years. Perhaps such comments are unduly negative; but to the extent that recent developments do have value, there remains the question of whether they represent just a faddish phase that will pass. This is something that concerned Lewis and her colleagues, who commented on the importance of education in supporting attempts to incorporate environmental concerns within accounting practice: 'In our view, for "green" accounting in the 1990s to avoid the fate of "social" accounting in the 1970s there is a clear need for the subject and all its relevant issues to be explored in the context of the teaching function' (Lewis et al, 1992, p219). Their suggestion is that, if social accounting (including its environmental manifestations) is to become embedded in practice, the next generation of accountants needs to be properly exposed to it. The current situation regarding coverage of sustainability, or at least environmental issues, in UK undergraduate degree programmes in accounting is the subject of the next section.

SUSTAINABILITY IN ACCOUNTING EDUCATION

As interest in, and concern about, the natural environment grew during the 1990s, research was conducted to determine whether this was reflected in the education of accountants. Owen et al (1994) undertook a study sponsored by the Chartered Association of Certified Accountants, the principle aims of which were to identify the extent to which undergraduate students were exposed to social and environmental accounting material in their studies, and to explore issues including the aims of such teaching and the nature of the material covered, or, alternatively, reasons for neglecting the subject area. The key findings from their questionnaire survey and the interviews that they conducted included the following:

- The coverage of social and environmental accounting material in many programmes was, at best, peripheral and, in many cases, was totally absent.
- When covered, such material tended to be taught as a final year option, with a generally low student take-up rate, or as a minor element of another accounting course – usually one concerned with 'financial accounting' – that is, the reporting of information to external parties.
- The initiative of individual members of staff played a crucial role in the establishment of new courses in social and environmental accounting and, indeed, in the maintenance of existing ones. This was often associated with the member of staff's personal research interest in the subject.
- There was, at the time, a developing dominance of 'environmental' over 'social' issues. However, that balance may have reflected the trajectory of social accounting when the survey was conducted, as was explained in the previous section; therefore, it is possible that it is no longer the case.
- Student expectations and perceived professional accreditation require-ments play a key role in shaping views of what is considered to be 'core'

accounting degree material and, hence, the acceptability, or otherwise, of social and environmental accounting teaching.

- Increasingly, severe resource constraints in higher education and the 'short-termism' engendered by research selectivity exercises place serious obstacles in the way of developing innovative courses in social and environmental accounting.

As this summary of key findings indicates, the research identified several significant issues and provided a useful snapshot; but it is some years since it was conducted. Is there any reason to suppose that the situation in now markedly different? Many academics would testify that the last point still applies, only with more force! Of more direct relevance is a report for the Institute of Chartered Accountants of Scotland (Gray et al, 2001), which consulted a wider range of constituencies than Owen et al (1994) (for example, practitioners, and undergraduates). It concluded that those accounting undergraduates who study environmental (and social) accounting find the experience enjoyable and stimulating. However, students who choose to study it are only a minority. Most students do not opt to study this field, a major factor apparently being a perceived lack of career relevance. Gray et al (2001) found that those students also enjoyed their own option choices; but this positive view was aligned with how they saw their career progressing rather than a more intrinsic regard for the nature of what they were studying.

The picture that emerges from these two studies of environmental accounting education resonates with findings from research conducted by Roberta Bampton at the University of Huddersfield (Bampton and Cowton, 2002a, 2002b). Her research data, and the analysis we have performed upon it, is concerned with more general ethical issues, but in the particular context of the teaching of management accounting – which may be defined as that part of accounting 'concerned with the provision of information to people within the organization to help them make better decisions and improve the efficiency and effectiveness of existing operations' (Drury, 2000, pp4–5). This contrasts with 'financial accounting', mentioned above. The findings indicate that the environment features as a significant ethical issue; but only a minority of management accounting lecturers integrate ethical issues in an explicit manner within their teaching of the subject. Two particular problems stood out for those lecturers who said that they would like to increase their coverage of ethical issues, including those who wish to address them explicitly for the first time. First, they complained of a shortage of material, particularly the general lack of coverage of ethical issues in management accounting textbooks. Second, they complained of the difficulty of finding space in an already overcrowded curriculum and timetable. This is a familiar reason or 'excuse' for not addressing ethical issues in business and management studies, generally; but in the case of accounting it might be given added force by the accreditation requirements of professional bodies when they validate degree programmes – or, at least, by academics' perceptions of those requirements. The overall picture that emerges, then, might best be described as follows:

ethical (including environmental) issues are 'squeezed into' the curriculum by a minority of lecturers who might be identified as enthusiasts or pioneers (Bampton and Cowton, 2002b); but beyond that there is virtually no coverage. There is no sign here, then, of sustainability taking root in individual courses within accounting degree programmes, just as there is no sign of the widespread adoption of courses devoted to sustainability or related concepts.

What of the future?

WHAT ARE THE PROSPECTS?

In many ways, the prospects for treating sustainability seriously in the undergraduate accounting curriculum look good. First, there has been more than a decade of sustained effort, particularly regarding the environment, by a group of accounting researchers who have built on the work of the 1970s to produce a significant body of scholarly work in academic journals for other interested academics to draw upon, should they wish to develop their own interest and teaching in the area. There are also books that might provide foundational material for students to read – for example, *Accounting and Accountability: Changes and Challenges in Corporate Social and Environmental Accounting* by Gray et al (1996) and the more tightly focused *Accounting and the Environment* by Gray and Bebbington (2001), which contains a chapter on sustainability. Other textbooks which have also covered relevant material include *Accounting and Society* by Perks (1993) and *Socially Responsible Accounting* by Mathews (1993). During the early 1990s the magazines of the professional accountancy bodies also included numerous articles on the environment, some of which were found useful by accounting lecturers (Gray et al, 2001).

Second, turning to the so-called 'real world' of practice, there are many examples today of social reporting in the public domain that often contain a considerable amount of material of relevance to sustainability concerns. Again, it is easy to be critical of, or even cynical about, such efforts; but much more has been accomplished than might have been expected just a few years ago, and each social report provides an example from which students can learn and from which they can hone their critical skills. The material produced is a valuable complement to the academic literature, some of which is likely to appear narrowly esoteric or unduly abstract to undergraduate students.

Third, professional accounting bodies have shown themselves willing to engage with the issues. For example, they have sponsored research on both social accounting practice and teaching, some of which has been referred to in this chapter. And they have engaged in other activities that have investigated the possible implications of the environment for the accounting profession (see, for example, Macve and Carey, 1992).

However, encouraging though these signs are, some leading social and environmental accounting academics have wondered whether they really presage significant change. With the experience of the earlier flowering of social accounting during the 1970s in mind, they began to experience a sense of déjà vu, with academic research and policy advocacy by professional bodies seemingly running well ahead of the everyday practice of the vast majority of accountants. As mentioned earlier, Lewis et al (1992) pointed to the need to reflect upon environmental issues in the context of teaching. Towards the end of the decade, Owen et al (1998, p143) felt able to comment that there is little evidence of any significant response from accounting practitioners towards the developing social and environmental agenda. Suggestions that deficiencies in accounting education are, in part, to blame for this current impasse are achieving increasing prominence.

This may be the case; but given the insignificance of ethical issues in accountancy courses, what is needed to bring about change in accounting education? Research interest and the personal enthusiasm of individuals can only accomplish so much, offering isolated optional courses and building a body of knowledge upon which other lecturers might draw. But what would encourage other lecturers to take advantage of the pioneers' efforts? If serious consideration of sustainability became the norm in most other parts of the university, this would, no doubt, have an impact. However, perhaps in the case of accounting we should look beyond the boundaries of the university itself.

It was noted earlier that many students take extremely seriously their perception of what is required to become a professional accountant. At present, they see social accounting and its ilk very much as 'optional extras' that have little relevance to the pursuit of their career aspirations. It was also noted that academics often claim that there is insufficient flexibility within the curriculum to treat social accounting and sustainability seriously, with professional accreditation requirements being at least partly to blame. If this analysis is broadly correct, then it would seem that the professional bodies hold the key in the form of their education and training requirements. If the profession were to say that sustainability must be treated seriously in accountancy training, and that it has particular relevance to universities in educating accountants, it seems highly likely that university curricula would fall into line, drawing upon the pioneering work that has already been done by enthusiastic scholars over recent years.

Is such a move by the profession likely? Probably not. However, without such action it appears that, in their high-level advocacy of environmental issues and sponsorship of research, welcome though these activities are, professional bodies are merely engaging in 'window-dressing', designed to provide a response to external trends while changing little or nothing about the way in which the profession actually operates. Given Enron and various other accounting scandals, this is probably a risky strategy. Furthermore, there are also important ethical initiatives in the business and financial world to which accountants need to be able to respond and in which they might participate. Whether addressing sustainability head-on, or as part of a broader approach that seeks to re-establish the ethical credibility of the accountancy profession, many commentators think that something real and lasting needs to happen in the accounting profession. The university undergraduate accounting curriculum might be one arena for such action, and probably one of the easier ones in which to make progress.

CONCLUSION

It might be true to say that if you are going to change the world, do not start with accounting. However, this might fail to appreciate the major role that the apparently mundane practices of accountancy play in modern organizational and social management. Although it has not always been well understood outside of accounting circles, significant choices are made in identifying what and how to measure, and those choices are far from neutral in their effects. Accountancy matters – and not just to accountants. It even matters to the environment!

Some of the issues touched upon in this chapter are common across most, if not all, of the university undergraduate curriculum. However, while the chapter has tried to highlight and pursue those issues that are pertinent for accounting, it is in the hope that as a 'case study' of an area with strong vocational roots these issues will also be of interest to readers from other fields. Essentially, the argument of the chapter can be summarized as follows. Although there is much work that remains to be done, the research and associated scholarly activity of the past decade and more have established the potential for sustainability to be incorporated much more widely into the teaching of accounting at undergraduate level than has hitherto been the case. Nevertheless, in order for that potential to be realized, professional accountancy bodies, which have been supportive of some of the research that has taken place, will have to insist on incorporating sustainability within the undergraduate curriculum. Only then will the majority of accounting staff and students in universities take sustainability seriously.

REFERENCES

Bampton, R and Cowton, C J (2002a) 'The teaching of ethics in management accounting: Progress and prospects', *Business Ethics: A European Review*, vol 11, no 1, pp52–61

Bampton, R and Cowton, C J (2002b) 'Pioneering in ethics teaching: The case of management accounting in universities in the British Isles', *Teaching Business Ethics*, vol 6, no 3, pp279–295

Burchell, S, Clubb, C, Hopwood, A, Hughes, J and Nahapiet, J (1980) 'The roles of accounting in organizations and society', *Accounting, Organizations and Society*, vol 5, no 1, pp5–27

Cowton, C J (1997) 'Socially responsible investment', in Chadwick, R (ed) *Encyclopedia of Applied Ethics*, volume 4, pp181–190, New York, Academic Press

Cowton, C J (1999) 'Accounting and financial ethics: From margin to mainstream?', *Business Ethics: A European Review*, vol 8, no 2, pp99–107

Deegan, C and Rankin, M (1997) 'The materiality of environmental information to users of annual reports', *Accounting, Auditing and Accountability Journal*, vol 10, no 4, pp562–583

Deegan, C and Rankin, M (1999) 'The environmental reporting expectations gap: Australian evidence', *British Accounting Review*, vol 31, no 3, pp313–346

Drury, C (2000) *Management and Cost Accounting*, fifth edition, London, Thomson Learning

Elkington, J (1997) *Cannibals with Forks: The Triple Bottom Line of 21st Century Business*, Oxford, Capstone

Gray, R, Owen, D and Maunders, K (1987) *Corporate Social Reporting: Accounting and Accountability*, Hemel Hempstead, Prentice-Hall

Gray, R H (1990) *The Greening of Accountancy: The Profession after Pearce*, London, Certified Accountants Publications

Gray, R H (1992), 'Accounting and environmentalism: An exploration of the challenge of gently accounting for accountability, transparency and sustainability', *Accounting, Organizations and Society*, vol 17, no 3, pp399–425

Gray, R (2001), 'Thirty years of social accounting, reporting and auditing: What (if anything) have we learnt?', *Business Ethics: A European Review*, vol 10, no 1, pp9–15

Gray, R, Owen, D and Adams, C (1996) *Accounting and Accountability: Changes and Challenges in Corporate Social and Environmental Accounting*, Hemel Hempstead, Prentice Hall

Gray, R, Collinson, D and Bebbington, J (1997) 'Environmental and social accounting and reporting', in Fisher, L (ed) *Financial Reporting Today: Current and Emerging Issues: The 1998 Edition*, Milton Keynes, Accountancy Books, pp179–214

Gray, R and Bebbington, J (2001) *Accounting for the Environment*, second edition, London, Sage

Gray, R, Collinson, D, French, J, McPhail, K and Stevenson, L (2001) *The Professional Accountancy Bodies and the Provision of Education and Training in Relation to Environmental Issues*, Edinburgh, Institute of Chartered Accountants of Scotland

Lewis, L, Humphrey, C and Owen, D (1992) 'Accounting and the social: A pedagogic perspective', *British Accounting Review*, vol 24, 3, pp219–233

Macve, R and Carey, A (eds) (1992) *Business, Accountancy and the Environment: A Policy and Research Agenda*, London, Institute of Chartered Accountants in England and Wales

Mathews, M R (1993) *Socially Responsible Accounting*, London, Chapman and Hall

Mathews, M R (1997) 'Twenty-five years of social and environmental accounting research: Is there a silver jubilee to celebrate?', *Accounting, Auditing and Accountability Journal*, vol 10, no 4, pp481–531

Owen, D L (ed) (1992) *Green Reporting: Accountancy and the Challenge of the Nineties*, London, Chapman and Hall

Owen, D, Humphrey, C and Lewis, L (1994) *Social and Environmental Accounting Education in British Universities*, Certified Research Report 39, London, Chartered Association of Certified Accountants

Owen, D, Gray, R and Bebbington, J (1997) 'Green accounting: Cosmetic irrelevance or radical agenda for change?', *Asia-Pacific Journal of Accounting*, vol 4, no 2, pp175–198

Owen, D, Humphrey, C and Lewis, L (1998) 'Social and environmental accounting education in British universities', in Wilson, R M S, Hassall, T and Murphy, B (eds) *Selected Papers in Accounting Education*, Sheffield, Sheffield Hallam University Press, pp143–145

Owen, D L, Swift, T A, Humphrey, C and Bowerman, M (2000) 'The new social audits: Accountability, managerial capture or the agenda of social champions?', *European Accounting Review*, vol 9, no 1, pp81–98

Owen, D and Swift, T (2001) 'Social accounting, reporting and auditing: Beyond the rhetoric?', *Business Ethics: A European Review*, vol 10, no 1, pp4–8

Perks, R W (1993) *Accounting and Society*, London: Chapman and Hall

Rubenstein, D B (1992) 'Bridging the gap between green accounting and black ink', *Accounting, Organizations and Society*, vol 17, no 5, pp501–508

Sparkes, R (2002) *Socially Responsible Investment: A Global Revolution*, Chichester, Wiley

Zadek, S, Pruzan, P and Evans, R (eds) (1997) *Building Corporate Accountability: Emerging Practices in Social and Ethical Accounting, Auditing and Reporting*, London, Earthscan

Chapter 12

Towards a New Economics?

Mark Baimbridge

INTRODUCTION

Economics sits uneasily in the social sciences. Although its central themes analyse relationships between people (albeit in the form of consumers, firms and government), concern regarding actual people often only plays a small element in the final analysis. When they do appear, a basic assumption is that they act in a rational, personal benefit-driven manner. Moreover, the route followed by mainstream economics over the last century has been one of increasing reliance on the abstracting of issues into mathematical and statistical models. Consequently, those who wish to study the environment via the medium of economics are divided on the degree to which analysis is facilitated by conventional economics. In some aspects, such as the inclusion of environmental loss estimates within cost-benefit calculations, there have been highly useful contributions. However, such valuations are inevitably imprecise and could easily underestimate the inestimable.

This chapter examines the attitude of economics in relation to the concept of sustainable development. First, it explores the various aspects of what might be called the 'greening' of economics, where the discourse, structure, methodology and paradigms of mainstream economics are reviewed in light of the need for the subject to address issues of sustainability. Second, it illustrates how economics has begun to address these concerns in terms of developing alternative approaches to determining well-being, and, in particular, how utility/welfare is thought of and measured in relation to national product and social indicators. In addition to such modifications to familiar aspects of economics, the discipline has also sought to embrace alternative perspectives, such as sociology, which offer alternative routes to analyse contemporary issues such as sustainability. Finally, the chapter outlines how economics is broadening its scope to encompass the sustainability debate, focusing upon two specific issues: economics and social cohesion, together with economic growth and environmental sustainability.

THE 'GREENING' OF ECONOMICS

Like many academic disciplines, the discourse of economics is conducted in terminology that is morally neutral; however, within this context it has been argued that the 'most impressive example of discourse manipulation is the concept of sustainable development' (Scott Cato and Kennett, 1999, p3). According to traditional economic thought, growth – rather than being the problem – offers the only solution. Hence, according to the concept of sustainable development, we can attain the 'holy grail' of sustainability and growth simultaneously without the need to restrain consumption per se by adjusting behaviour towards more environmentally sympathetic patterns.

It is this frequent inability to illustrate understanding of events that has resulted in the falling reputation of economics for many policy-makers. While the world has become increasingly complex, the subject has become increasing mathematical, assumption-based and founded upon simplification. However, from an environmental perspective the notion that human behaviour is predictable and can be modelled is erroneous. Given the above caveats, one can sympathize with the view that 'the world needs to create a new economics more than it needs a new anything else' (Anderson, 1999, p16).

The environment, therefore, should not be regarded as an external concern, but one that is central to the operation of economies where there is a clear interaction between the natural world and human actions. Based upon this idea that economic life is undertaken by real human beings as opposed to impersonal representations as households and firms, it then follows that we should reconsider the fundamental assumption behind such human (economic) behaviour. The simplistic assumption of rationality does not coincide with numerous aspects of human behaviour. Consequently, such a broader view of economic life cannot be value free, which is an irresponsible form of economics. The difficulty is that for most mainstream economists such a fundamental questioning of basic paradigms is simply a step too far.

However, economics as it is currently conceived remains largely unperceptive regarding ecological problems even though there is no such thing as an economic system that is isolated from social, cultural or ecological systems. Inevitably, the more realistic a study of something is, the more encompassing and interdisciplinary it necessarily has to be. In that sense, it has been suggested that economics as such needs to come to an end, and even the newest and greenest of new economics will be too narrow in scope.

MEASURING LIFE?

In spite of this negative view of the future of economics, a movement has arisen within the field that suggests that utility should be given expression in terms of happiness and that happiness and well-being can, and should, be measured. For example, it has become clear that much observed human behaviour, such as giving to charities, cannot be fully explained by reference to self-concerned preferences alone. Moreover, many of the pleasures of life cannot be bought in markets, are not priced and are not for sale (Scitovsky, 1976; Frank, 1985, 1999). In addition, developments within the field of psychology on the concept and measurement of happiness have been adopted by empirical economists in contrast to the fundamental idea that it is impossible to measure utility, which is regarded as ordinal rather than cardinal (Frey and Stutzer, 2002). Following on from this broadening of economists' horizons, this section briefly outlines the principle developments in two areas that are intrinsically related to economic growth and sustainable development when assessing people's well-being: gross national product (GNP) and social indictors.

As previously discussed, economists like nothing more than to measure whatever is available, and measuring human welfare by constructing an overall measure of economic activity has not been an exception, with GNP the familiar measurement of economic development. GNP's initial advantage is that it is based upon analysing the relationships between individuals and firms involved in creating goods and services. However, it is faced with serious deficiencies if used as an indicator of well-being. In particular, it is, in general, not possible to aggregate from the level of individual consumers to the level of the economy, as a whole. Therefore, even in a narrowly utilitarian sense, higher levels of GNP do not necessarily deliver more aggregate welfare (Sen, 1979). Furthermore, GNP, as usually constituted, excludes a large part of social activities, while the actual 'destruction' of utility, such as commuting and other disamenities, is partly measured as output and thus, paradoxically, raises GNP. Finally, income distribution and its change are neglected, though it is known that relative income matters greatly for well-being.

Many different efforts have been undertaken to overcome these weaknesses, including deriving welfare measures for non-market activities, such as household production and the voluntary sector, which account for approximately 150 per cent of the conventional measure (Nordhaus and Tobin, 1972; Salamon and Anheier, 1997; Offer, 2001). More recently, and of significance for this chapter, the concept of sustainability has received special attention, defined as an aggregate utility level that can be maintained over an infinite period of time (Kirkby et al, 1995; van Kooten and Bulte, 2000; Pearce and Barbier, 2000; Rao, 2000). It has been theoretically demonstrated that the national product net of asset depletion caused by the use of non-renewable natural resources also describes the discounted sustainable productive potential of an economy (Weitzman, 1976).

The fundamental idea behind social indicators is that the availability and access to particular commodities, such as nutrition, housing, health, education and the quality of the environment, constitute a precondition for welfare or happiness. In contrast to the extensions of national product, social indicators are not measured in terms of money, although one of their obvious problems is that this leads to difficulties when assessing their relative importance for well-being. The move towards this extension for estimating the standard of living is not a new concept, with a United Nations expert group in 1954 recommending that, in addition to real per capita income, use should be made of quantitative measures in the fields of health, education, employment and housing for assessing the standard of living (Dasgupta, 1993).

Subsequently, there have been numerous variations regarding defining and measuring social indicators, ranging from the use of 'classical' social indicators most frequently found in the literature, such as life expectancy, school enrolment and access to fresh water, to reliance upon a sole indicator, such as quality-adjusted life years, which considers the number of years remaining until death corrected for the quality of health (Zeckhauser and Shepard, 1976). A compromise between these two positions is the adoption of combined sub-indices. For example, the best-known indicator now also used by the World Bank is the Human Development Index (HDI), which encompasses income per capita, life expectancy and education. However, the HDI is also excessively partial in that it is oblivious of political and civil liberties. In an attempt to address this issue, the United Nations Development Programme (UNDP, 1991) pursues the recent literature on basic freedoms by tabling indices, but then declines to purposefully incorporate this information (Dasgupta, 1990).

ECONOMIC SOCIOLOGY

The imperialist nature of economics is a familiar concept to those within the social sciences. However, in several key areas the roles have been reversed, with sociologists and psychologists bringing new insights into the usually fortress-like world of economics. In particular, the field of economic sociology has witnessed the appearance of several anthologies on the 'new economic sociology' (Friedland and Robertson, 1990; Zukin and DiMaggio, 1990; Granovetter and Swedberg, 1992; Swedberg, 1993; Smelser and Swedberg, 1994). Smelser (1963, pp27–28) defines this as 'the application of the frames of reference, variables and explanatory models of sociology to that complex of activities concerned with the production, distribution, exchange and consumption of scarce goods and services', where the variables and models of the economic sociologist include sociological perspectives of personal interaction, groups, social structures, social controls, social networks, gender and the cultural context (Granovetter, 1985; Zelizer, 1989).

The precise impetus for this opening-up of economics is unclear, with explanations ranging from 1970s stagflation to the Marxist revival of the 1960s and 1970s. However, whatever the combination of reasons, a number of economists came to the conclusion that mainstream economics was too narrowly defined and sought to extend it. This process gained momentum through 'behavioural economics' (Simon, 1987), which is closely allied with psychology. But it was the work of Becker (1957) and Downs (1957) that gained momentum during the 1970s to incorporate a social perspective within economics (Hirschman, 1970; Arrow, 1974; Tullock and McKenzie, 1975; Williamson, 1975; Becker, 1976; Akerlof, 1984; Solow, 1990). Moreover, a new school of institutionalism – new institutional economics – has appeared and

Table 12.1 *A comparison of economics and economic sociology*

	Economics	Economic Sociology
Concept of actor	The actor is not influenced by other actors	The actor is influenced by other actors and is part of groups and society
Economic action	All economic actions are assumed to be rational (rationality as assumption)	Many different types of economic action are used, including rational ones (rationality as variable)
Constraints on action	Economic actions are constrained by the tastes and scarcity of resources, including technology	Economic actions are constrained by the scarcity of resources, by the social structure and by meaning structures
Economy in relation to society	The market and the economy are the basic references; society is a 'given'	The economy is seen as an integral part of society; society is always the basic reference
Goal of analysis	Prediction and explanation; rarely description	Description and explanation; rarely prediction
Methods used	Formal, especially mathematical model-building; no data or only official data are often used ('clean' models)	Many different methods are used, including historical and comparative ones; the data is often produced by the analyst
Intellectual tradition	Smith, Ricardo, Mill, Marshall, Keynes, Samuelson; the classics belong to the past; emphasis on current theory and achievements	Marx, Weber, Durkheim, Schumpeter, Polanyi-Parsons, Smelser; the classics are constantly reinterpreted and taught

Source: Smelser and Swedberg (1994)

there are some signs of the revival of previous incarnations of institutional economics (Hodgson, 1994). Table 12.1 summarizes the major theoretical differences between these two lines of enquiry.

Given the above outlined approach of economic sociology, it is possible to briefly compare this approach with that of mainstream economics in relation to environmental analysis. According to Siebert (1992), the central message of environmental economics is an allocation problem, where the theoretical foundations exist in relation to externalities, public goods, general equilibrium and applied cost-benefit analysis (Kneese, 1987). Economists regard pollution, for example, as the result of absent prices for scarce environmental resources, with the policy solution being to introduce surrogate prices in the form of taxes or other penalties (Cropper and Oates, 1992). The solution is, therefore, to match marginal control costs and marginal damage costs in order to illustrate the 'optimal' level of pollution. Consequently, policies directed at the environmental resource base can only be derived from considerations of population change, intergenerational well-being, technological possibilities and the existing resource base. In the words of Dasgupta (1993, p280) 'they can't be pulled out of the air by mere reference to sustainable development'.

In contrast, an economic sociology analysis of environmental issues does not necessarily adhere to this optimality-driven marginal framework. First, it investigates the social causes and reasons for environmental degradation. These can explain why there is still an ecological gap even if the amount of pollution is 'optimal'. In this connection, special emphasis must be placed upon the compatibility of environmental and economic interests. Second, it focuses upon the repercussions of environmental damage on social systems and actors. Here, the focus is upon the idea that pollution, for example, is unequally distributed over the social strata and social groups as social systems differ regarding their interests in environmental protection. Finally, it seeks to develop a theory of the social choice mechanisms or social arrangements in order to balance ecological supply and demand. Such mechanisms are markets, hierarchies, private bargaining and moral discourses (Dryzek, 1987). Given such an approach, economic sociology studies the benefits and failures of these mechanisms in relation to protecting the environment.

In essence, the difference between the two approaches can be traced back to the theory of action upon which they rely. Within mainstream economics, individual decision-making depends upon the set of available alternatives, the opportunity structure and individual preferences. If preferences and resources delimiting the set of attainable alternatives are given, then choice is determined solely by the opportunity structure. Moreover, it should be noted that this structure does not need to be interpreted in the usual monetary terms. Hence, in contrast to the standard approach in mainstream economics, which assumes that preferences are exogenously given, the task of a broader socio-economic approach is to develop theories of endogenous preference formation (Berger, 1994).

Economics and Social Cohesion

As previously discussed, mainstream economists have increasingly appreciated the need to bring social structures into their understanding of households, firms and markets. Within the theme of social networks and economics, these ideas are embodied in the notion of 'social capital': defined as the extent of an individual's social networks and their effect upon individual well-being (Loury, 1977; Bourdieu, 1980; Coleman, 1988). However, the approach has attracted criticism amongst mainstream economists regarding the nature of research on social capital. First, the term 'social capital' refers to a multitude of distinct, yet closely related, ideas that are generally unsuitable for economic modelling. Second, while economic analysis has been applied to various non-market interactions, endogenous social interactions are difficult to accommodate. Consequently, economics has been largely isolated from the social capital literature. Nevertheless, there is a growing body of economic research that deals with many of the ideas central to the notion of social capital, in general, and economic development, in particular.

First, the concept of trust is central to social capital literature (Coleman, 1988) since it plays an important role in the functioning of an economy, together with the combination of reputation and trust in trading and contracting networks. While the idea of measuring a societal level of trust is quite vague, there is a growing body of research (McMillan and Woodruff, 1999; Banjerjee and Duflo, 2000) that gives empirical content to these notions. In terms of fragmentation, heterogeneity and participation, another predominant issue in the social capital literature is the idea of participation in groups and voluntary associations as a manifestation of social capital (Alesina and La Ferrara, 2000). Finally, the social capital literature has speculated on the relationship between an individual's social capital and his or her well-being, where (through tighter community interaction) an individual has a wider set of opportunities – for instance, in the access to informal credit, employment or insurance (Granovetter, 1995; Narayan and Prichett, 1999; Grootaert, 1999; Maluccio et al, 2000).

In relation to social networks and development issues, understanding how such networks operate should aid the advancement of economic development policy within areas as diverse as credit provision for small- and medium-sized enterprises, infant nutrition, health and agriculture. Traditional economic analysis does not concern itself with these types of human activity (Goldstein, 2002). The two main functions of networks that development economists are studying are information and enforcement. First, one of the ways in which network analysis contributes to development economics is in understanding how information is disseminated. The leading example of this is the examination of how new technologies spread within communities (Conley and Udry, 2001). Second, in addition to information, we might expect to see strong network effects in enforcement. Members of a network may have informal enforcement mechanisms at their disposal; combined with information, these could provide for more efficient ways of conducting transactions. Recent work on this has, for example, focused on the importance of ethnic ties in trade credit relations (Fafchamps, 2000).

While the above illustrates that progress has been made in understanding how social networks shape economic activities, economists have done less work on how activities shape or form the networks themselves. In addition, there are other dimensions that economists can add to their models in order to make them more accurate and, thus, more powerful. Rauch and Hamilton (2001) identify three directions developed by sociologists that economists may be able to utilize. The first is the fact that alliances in networks are dynamic and power tends to concentrate in certain nodes of a given network. Second, not all ties are equal – for example, those of differing strength will be able to sustain different demands. Finally, there is the idea that networks can be 'constructive' in the sense that they shape agents' identities and, thus, their preferences, in addition to their capacities to take action or rule. Although social capital was never embraced by economists as the unifying concept of the social sciences, this discussion illustrates that many of its multiple facets are present in economics. This appears to offer interesting new ideas and has stimulated new research in economics.

ECONOMIC GROWTH AND THE ENVIRONMENT

For the last quarter century, the environment has been one of the most salient issues of the day. There is hardly any topic that has preoccupied the public to a similar degree. New global threats have been added to old unsolved problems. Though it is difficult to give an overall account of the state of the environment, the feeling prevails that, after further decades of continued economic expansion in a form unconstrained by ecological considerations, environmental destruction has taken on frightening dimensions (Berger, 1994).

In contrast to the explicit calls for a wholesale reinterpretation of fundamental economic paradigms, an alternative approach has sought to make more subtle amendments to the theoretical and practical interaction between mainstream economics and sustainability. Key contributions that typify and elucidate such thinking include Ekins (2000) and Pearce and Barbier (2000). The starting point for such analysis remains combined exponential population growth and increases in economic activity, together with the introduction of technologies that are frequently incompatible with ecological cycles, which is leading to environmental degradation and loss. Hence, the conundrum once more becomes the ability to balance demographic momentum and global economic aspirations with environmentally sustainable economic growth.

However, rather than seeking to explore refined versions of economic optimization to solve this trade-off, Ekins (2000), for example, turns the question on its head. The emphasis becomes whether the sustainable use of environmental functions, when adopted as a prime objective of public policy, would exert a substantial constraint on economic growth. The objective function is the maximization of human well-being relative to sustainability, which is taken as fundamental to maintaining welfare but is difficult to measure with monetary values, such that they are removed from cost–benefit analysis. Hence, this approach focuses upon whether the constraint of environmentally sustainable use is binding upon economic growth and, if so, to what extent.

First, it is important to recognize that there are many commodities which do not result in environmental damage. Thus, if consumer preferences were to shift, or if production processes and consumption could be altered to reduce the environmental impacts associated with destructive goods and services, there is no reason why increasing incomes and consumer expenditure should not be associated with greatly reduced impacts so that important environmental functions are sustained. However, history has demonstrated that even under severe environmental pressures, shifts in consumer preference and the response of firms cannot be guaranteed. Consumer preferences derive from powerful social and cultural perceptions, while the primary goals of businesses are to maintain profit levels and this may make them relatively unresponsive to calls to modify their impacts on the environment.

Second, the necessary reductions of consumption and production will not be achieved without a determined policy stance. However, such a policy may be expected to constrain economic growth unless two conditions, in particular, hold regarding environmental policy. These conditions are that environmental policy must:

1   reduce economic distortions so that allocative efficiency is increased; and
2   reduce technical change that contributes to sustainability and increases labour productivity, at least to the same extent as would have occurred without the policy.

With regard to the first of these propositions, there are technologies that can improve both economic and environmental performance which are yet to be introduced. In addition, the tax system is frequently a source of inefficiency which may be reduced by introducing appropriate taxes or removing environmentally harmful subsidies. However, such inefficiencies can only be removed once, and the opportunity for such unilateral gains thereby diminishes over time. Consequently, the second condition of induced technical change necessarily becomes the long-term focus as the potential source of environmental sustainability combined with continued economic growth. Although it is impossible to predict comparative economic productivity following environmentally conserving technical change, the new generation of resource-efficient and low-pollution technologies are more economically productive compared to environmentally intensive predecessors. Hence, the possibility exists for technology to provide simultaneous economic and ecological gains.

Ekins (2000) concludes his thesis by suggesting that sustainability may ultimately require three possible changes to current consumption and production patterns:

1   Technologies with improved environmental performance must be used.
2   The overall package of desired commodities must be less damaging than at present.
3   Constraining wants which relate to commodities that persistently degrade the environment.

The first type of change constitutes the ecological modernization of industry, where production is transformed, while human goals that drive it remain unchanged. Indeed, it is probable that the technologies required to simultaneously increase value-added growth and to reduce environmental impacts could become available and are economically viable. In the meantime, there are market and government failures, distorting tax systems and unexploited technologies that provide immediate opportunities for both economic and environmental gains. The second type of change requires a transformation in consumer preferences, although there is little practical evidence of consumers in the Northern hemisphere adjusting their life-style patterns. The final type of change is that envisaged by those who believe that meeting the challenge of sustainability will result in placing limits on economic growth. Whatever the theoretical possibilities that either a technical fix, removal of inefficiencies/distortions or redefined consumer preferences will permit incomes to continue to grow indefinitely, this view does not accept that such a situation can be realized in practice.

A pragmatic response to the continuing uncertainty of the contribution of each of the three types of changes to sustainability might be to advocate allocation based on needs and requirements of locality, while demanding reduced environmental impacts from environmentally intensive sectors, even at the cost of reducing their economic activity.

CONCLUSION

While the calls for substantial paradigm shifts in economics are, in reality, too radical, the question still remains as to why the discipline has made only token steps. A potential explanation for this reluctance has been advanced by Anderson (1999) who agues that economics does not possess the internal tensions evident in other social sciences; in particular, it is exceptional in not having 'hard' and 'soft' elements. It just has the 'hard' side. Hence, those individuals attracted to the softer human and ecological issues of economics either have their concerns 'hardened', or the discussion of such issues is left to the remit of other disciplines. This hardness can be explained by the use of monetary values, in both measurement and calculations. Hence, when mainstream economics collides with areas of life that are not primarily about money, such as the impact of economic activity on the biosphere, it can only turn to its money-focused methodology to analyse issues. Furthermore, when environmental economics seeks to explore ethical issues, it is reduced to turning such judgements into consumer preferences and, in turn, interpreting these as a willingness to either pay or accept money. Consequently, economists who explore issues such as sustainable development find themselves caged in by the orthodox methodology where the 'hardness' of a money-orientated quantitative approach appears the only route for investigators.

The question, therefore, becomes one of how economists can find themselves a route out this theoretical, empirical and policy cul-de-sac. As we have seen, there are, essentially, two alternative directions for the discipline: first, the seismic upheaval of established economic paradigms, or, second, the opening-up of economics to new ideas, either from a profound rethinking of established concepts or from allied social sciences, such as sociology, psychology and social cohesion. In terms of practicality, it is this second option that appears to hold the greatest potential. Given the ongoing and frequently accelerating global environmental concerns, the debate between economic growth and sustainable development can be described as occurring between the opposing camps of growth pessimists and growth optimists. The former camp contends that conflict between exponential growth and limited resources cannot be reconciled, while growth optimists place faith in the scope for substitution, technical progress and structural change (World Bank, 1992). However, whatever the potential approaches – such as those advocated by Ekins (2000) and Pearce and Barbier (2000) – may bestow, the words of the famous Economist Kenneth Boulding remain a salutary reminder of the tasks ahead: 'Anyone who believes exponential growth can go on forever in a finite world is either a madman or an economist.'

REFERENCES

Akerlof, G (1984) *An Economic Theorist's Book of Tales*, Cambridge, Cambridge University Press

Alesina, A and La Ferrara, E (2000) 'Participation in heterogeneous communities', *Quarterly Journal of Economics*, vol 115, no 3, pp847–904

Anderson, V (1999) 'Can there be a sensible economics?', in Scott Cato, M and Kennett, M (eds) *Green Economics: Beyond Supply and Demand to Meeting People's Needs*, Aberystwyth, Green Audit

Arrow, K (1974) *The Limits of Organization*, New York, Norton

Banerjee, A V and Duflo, E (2000) 'Reputation effects and the limits of contracting: a study of the Indian software industry', *Quarterly Journal of Economics*, vol 115, no 3, pp989–1017

Becker, G (1957) *The Economics of Discrimination*, Chicago, University of Chicago Press

Becker, G (1976) *The Economic Approach to Human Life*, Chicago, University of Chicago Press

Berger, J (1994) 'The economy and the environment', in Smelser, N J and Swedberg, R (eds) *Handbook of Economic Sociology*, Princeton, Princeton University Press

Bourdieu, P (1980) 'Le capital social: notes provisoires', *Actes de la Recherche en Sciences Sociales*, vol 31, pp3–6

Coleman, J S (1988) 'Social capital in the creation of human capital', *American Journal of Sociology*, vol 100, no 400, Conference papers, pp1–32

Conley, T and Udry, C (2001) 'Social learning through networks: the adoption of new agricultural technologies', *American Journal of Agricultural Economics*, vol 83, no 3, pp 668–673

Cropper, M L and Oates, W E (1992) 'Environmental economics: a survey', *Journal of Economic Literature*, vol 30, pp675–740

Cruces, G (2002) 'Beyond the buzzword "social capital" in economics', *STICERD Review 2001*, London, London School of Economics

Dasgupta, P (1990) 'Well-being and the extent of its realization in poor countries', *Economic Journal*, vol 100, no 400, Conference papers, pp1–32

Dasgupta, P (1993) *An Inquiry into Well-Being and Destitution*, Oxford, Clarendon Press

Downs, A (1957) *An Economic Theory of Democracy*, New York, Harper and Row

Dryzek (1987) *Rational Ecology*, Oxford, Blackwells

Ekins, P (2000) E*conomic Growth and Environmental Sustainability: The Prospects for Green Growth*, London, Routledge

Fafchamps, M (2000) 'Ethnicity and credit in African manufacturing', *Journal of Development Economics*, vol 61, no 1, pp205–235

Frank, R H (1985) *Choosing the Right Pond*, Oxford, Oxford University Press

Frank, R H (1999) *Luxury Fever: Why Money Fails To Satisfy in an Era of Excess*, New York, Free Press

Frey, B S and Stutzer, A (2002) *Happiness and Economics: How the Economy and Institutions Affect Well-Being*, Princeton, Princeton University Press

Friedland, R and Robertson, A F (eds) (1990) *Beyond the Marketplace: Rethinking Economy and Society*, New York, Aldine de Gruyter

Goldstein, M (2002) 'Understanding social networks for development', *STICERD Review 2001*, London, London School of Economics

Granovetter, M (1985) 'Economic action and social structure: the problem of embeddedness', *American Journal of Sociology*, vol 91, pp481–510

Granovetter, M and Swedberg, R (eds) (1992) *The Sociology of Economic Life*, Boulder, CO, Westview Press

Granovetter, M (1995) *Getting a Job: A Study of Contact and Careers*, Chicago, University of Chicago Press

Grootaert, C (1999) *Social Capital, Household Welfare and Poverty in Indonesia*, World Bank Policy Research Working Paper, no 2148

Hirschman, A O (1970) *Exit, Voice and Loyalty: Responses to Decline in Firms, Organizations and States*, Cambridge, MA, Harvard University Press

Hodgson, G (1994) 'The return of institutional economics', in Smelser, N J and Swedberg, R (eds) *Handbook of Economic Sociology*, Princeton, Princeton University Press

Kirkby, J, O'Keefe, P and Timberlake, L (1995) *The Earthscan Reader in Sustainable Development*, London, Earthscan Publications

Kneese, A (1987) 'Environmental economics', in Eatwell, J, Milgate, M and Newman, P (eds) *The New Palgrave Dictionary of Economics*, London, Macmillan

Loury, G (1977) 'A dynamic theory of racial income differences', in Wallace, P A and Mund, A L (eds) *Women, Minorities and Employment Discrimination*, Lexington, MA, Lexington Books

Maluccio, J, Hadded, L and May, J (2000) 'Social capital and household welfare in South Africa, 1993–98', *Journal of Development Studies*, vol 36, no 6, pp54–81

McMillan. J and Woodruff, C (1999) 'Inter-firm relationships and informal credit in Vietnam', *Quarterly Journal of Economics*, vol 114, no 4, pp1285–1320

Narayan, D and Pritchett, L (1999) 'Cents and sociability: household income and social capital in rural Tanzania', *Economic Development and Cultural Change*, vol 47, no 4, pp871–897

Nordhaus, W and Tobin, J (1972) *Is Growth Obsolete?*, NBER General Series no 96, New York, Columbia University Press

Offer, A (2001) 'On economic welfare measurement and human well-being over the long-run', in David, P A, Solar, P and Thomas, M (eds) *The Economic Future in Historical Perspective*, London, British Academy

Pearce, D and Barbier, E B (2000) *Blueprint for a Sustainable Economy*, London, Earthscan

Rao, P K (2001) *Sustainable Development: Economics and Policy*, Oxford, Blackwell

Rauch, J and Hamilton, G (2001) 'Networks and markets: concepts for bridging disciplines', in Rauch, J and Casella, A (eds) *Networks and Markets*, New York, The Russell Sage Foundation

Salamon, L M and Anheier, H K (1997) *Defining the Nonprofit Sector: A Cross-national Analysis*, Manchester, Manchester University Press

Scitovsky, T (1976) *The Joyless Economy: An Inquiry into Human Satisfaction and Dissatisfaction*, Oxford, Oxford University Press

Scott Cato, M and Kennett, M (1999) 'An introduction to green economics', in Scott Cato, M and Kennett, M (eds) *Green Economics: Beyond Supply and Demand To Meeting People's Needs*, Aberystwyth, Green Audit

Sen, A (1979) 'The welfare basis of real income comparisons: a survey', *Journal of Economic Literature*, vol 17, no 1, pp1–45

Sen, A (1993) 'Capability and well-being', in Sen, A and Nussbaum, M (eds) *The Quality of Life*, Oxford, Oxford University Press

Siebert, H (1992) *Economics of the Environment: Theory and Policy*, Berlin

Simon, H (1987) 'Behavioral economics', in Eatwell, J, Milgate, M and Newman, P (eds) *The New Palgrave Dictionary of Economics*, London, Macmillan

Smelser, N J (1963) *The Sociology of Economic Life*, Englewood Cliffs, NJ, Prentice-Hall

Smelser, N J and Swedberg, R (1994) 'The sociological perspective on the economy', in Smelser, N J and Swedberg, R (eds) *Handbook of Economic Sociology*, Princeton, Princeton University Press

Solow, R M (1990) *The Labor Market as a Social Institution*, Oxford, Basil Blackwell

Swedberg, R (ed) (1993) *Explorations in Economic Sociology*, New York, Russell Sage Foundation

Tullock, G and McKenzie, R (1975) *The New World of Economics: Explorations into the Human Experience*, Homewood, IL, Richard D Irwin

UNDP (1991) *Human Development Report*, New York, United Nations Development Programme

van Kooten, G C and Bulte, E H (2000) *The Economics of Nature: Managing Biological Assets*, Oxford, Blackwell

Webley, P, Burgoyne, C B, Lea, S E G and Young, B M (2001) *The Economic Psychology of Everyday Life*, London, Routledge

Weitzman, M (1976) 'On the welfare significance of national product in a dynamic economy', *Quarterly Journal of Economics*, vol 90, no 1, pp156–162

Williamson, O (1975) *Markets and Hierarchies: Analysis and Antitrust Implications*, New York, The Free Press

World Bank (1992) *World Development Report 1992: Development and the Environment*, Oxford, Oxford University Press

Zeckhauser, R J and Shepard, D S (1976) 'Where now for saving lives?', *Law and Contemporary Problems*, vol 40, no 4, pp5–45

Zelizer, V (1989) 'Beyond the polemics of the market: establishing a theoretical and empirical agenda', *Social Forces*, vol 3, pp614–634

Zukin, S and DiMaggio, P (eds) (1990) *Structures of Capital: The Social Organisation of the Economy*, Cambridge, Cambridge University Press

From **Chapter 9**
Design for a concert hall in Finland exploiting solar heating for melting façade ice
(Keith Dillon, University of Huddersfield)

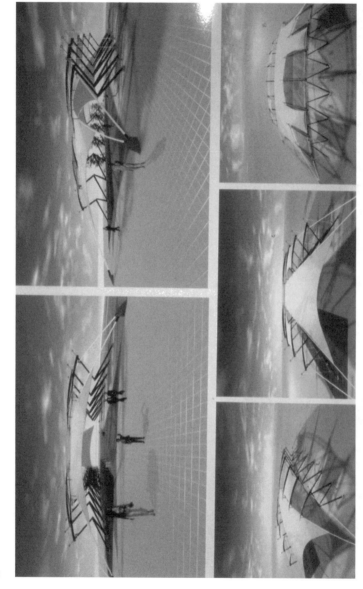

From **Chapter 9**
Design for a de-mountable shelter for emergency housing
(Austen Smith, University of Huddersfield)

From **Chapter 9**
Design for a timber railway station
(Leigh Brown, University of Huddersfield)

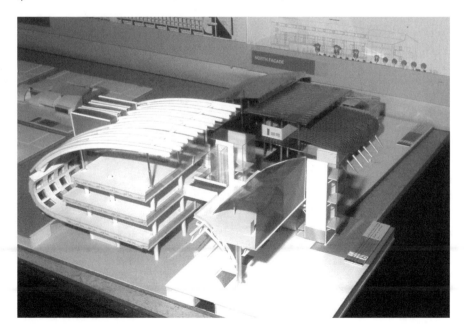

From **Chapter 9**
Design for an architecture school
(Martin Bates, University of Huddersfield)

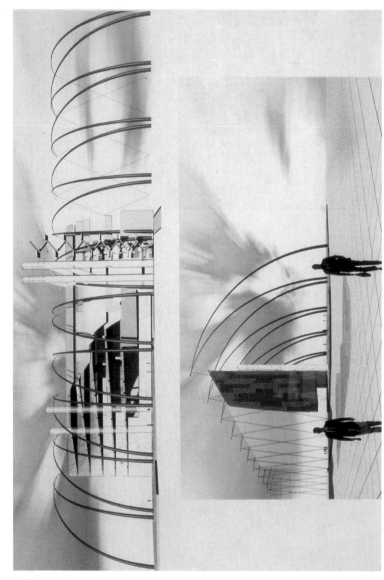

From **Chapter 9**
Design for a loose-fit, low-energy television offices
(Edward Highton, University of Huddersfield)

Chapter 13

Social Policy and Sustainable Development

Meg Huby

INTRODUCTION

This chapter begins by examining the nature of social policy as an academic subject. It argues that, even if social policy concerns are seen as restricted solely to the institutional arrangements for meeting needs through welfare services, there is a clear case for considering the environmental factors that can contribute to social disadvantage and for analysing the distributional effects of policies designed for environmental protection. Most interpretations of the concept of sustainable development recognize the importance of equity for achieving sustainability. An understanding of the linkages between social and environmental problems is essential if the goal of equitable access to resources and services for meeting needs is to be met.

Recent trends in social policy extend the remit of the subject to link studies of social disadvantage with wider issues. The idea of poverty, for example, is increasingly seen in the context of broader social exclusion, lack of connectedness and matters that deal with neighbourhoods and place. It is here that other principles of sustainable development come to the fore. Issues surrounding democracy and local participation in policy processes are remarkably similar on both the social exclusion and sustainable development agendas. Similarly, the need for more policy integration and planning is common to both approaches.

The implications for bringing ideas of sustainable development into the teaching of social policy in higher education can be identified on two levels. First, in order to appreciate the need for environmental protection policies, one must understand, albeit at a basic level, how the physical and biological environment works. Potential conflicts and tensions between policies for social and environment can then be analysed, particularly in relation to equity. Second, the principles of sustainable development can provide a unifying framework for studying wider aspects of social policy, informing many aspects of traditional courses and modules.

THE NATURE OF SOCIAL POLICY

At the beginning of the 21st century, there is no clear consensus on what social policy actually is. Debates about whether it constitutes a discipline in its own right, or simply a less well-defined multidisciplinary field of study, have been joined by arguments about what should properly constitute its main concerns. At one end of the spectrum of views on the nature of social policy is the idea that studies of social welfare should primarily take an applied administrative perspective, focusing on services and service delivery. At the other end is the argument that social policy should look beyond the provision of welfare services to examine the extent to which this provision improves wider aspects of well-being, living standards and the quality of life. It is from this position that the traditional academic boundaries between social policy, politics, sociology, economics and, increasingly, environmental studies appear as constraints to a deeper understanding of policy outcomes.

There is little doubt that 'social policy is still concerned with social disadvantage, with social problems, with needs, and with the collective response to these issues' (Spicker, 2002, p11). It seems naive to express concerns about social disadvantage and needs without considering the factors that lead to these, or to analyse collective responses to disadvantage without reference to the idea that their effectiveness must depend upon the environmental, political and economic context in which they are played out.

The notion that social concerns must be integrated with environmental protection if development is to be sustainable was popularized by the Brundtland Report (World Commission on Environment and Development [WCED], 1987) and endorsed by Agenda 21 at the Rio Earth Summit (United Nations Conference on Environment and Development [UNCED], 1992). Since then it has been embraced by representatives of all sections of society at international, national and local levels. Interpretations of the precise meaning of sustainable development differ widely, reflecting a range of theoretical and philosophical positions. At one end of the spectrum are 'light green' anthropocentric approaches, characterized by the idea that continuing economic growth, consumption and the reduction of poverty can go hand in hand with improvements in environmental quality. At the other end, 'deep green' eco-centric thinkers reject the necessity for further economic growth and industrialization, seeing the solutions to social and environmental problems in reductions in consumption, with radical changes in value systems and social and political structures. No proponents of sustainable development, however, dispute the salience of environmental conditions to social development.

MEETING NEEDS

Social policy has long-established concerns with institutional arrangements to improve welfare through meeting needs. Fulfilling human needs for water, food, domestic energy, housing, transport and leisure ultimately depends upon environmental resources. The use of these resources either for consumption or for the disposal of waste inevitably has an impact upon the environment (Huby, 1998; Cahill, 2002). As the state of the environment changes in response to human activity, problems arise that cause concern to people who value the environment in its own right. But even those who value the environment purely as a human resource must surely recognize the need to protect that resource, both for sustaining future patterns of use and because of the deleterious effects that a degraded environment can have on human health and well-being, on poverty and on livelihoods. Ultimately, environmental change influences the extent to which future human needs can be met.

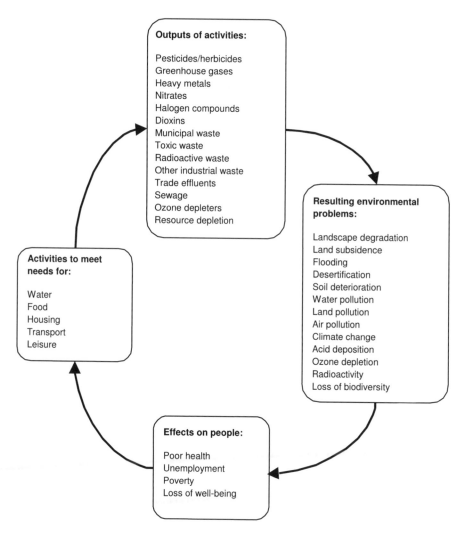

Figure 13.1 *Linkages between meeting needs and environmental problems*

An understanding of the vital importance of the environment in meeting human needs leads to a recognition of how environmental protection policies have potential social benefits. Tackling motor vehicle emissions, for example, through policies to reduce car use could lead to improved public transport systems and facilities for walkers and cyclists. Public health benefits could accrue from better air quality, fewer road traffic accidents and a population more inclined to take exercise. Access to workplaces, leisure facilities and services could be increased, especially for vulnerable groups of people. Environmental goals to reduce atmospheric carbon emissions could, for example, be achieved through policies to increase the efficiency of domestic energy use. The provision of insulation, double glazing and energy-efficient appliances could lead to a reduction in fuel bills that would particularly benefit lower-income households. Environmental policies to reduce waste by enabling and supporting high rates of recycling of municipal waste and the refurbishment and reuse of domestic appliances could create opportunities for new employment in economically deprived areas. A generally safer and healthier environment could produce long-term, lasting benefits not just locally, but on a wider geographical scale.

This rosy picture, however, ignores the complex problems that dog the development of integrated social and environmental policies. All too often solutions to environmental problems are applied in isolation with adverse and regressive distributional effects. Economic policy instruments, such as fuel taxes and road tolls, designed to reduce car use may do little to change the driving habits of the better off (Huby and Burkitt, 2000). They are, however, likely to cause hardship to people whose poor health or disability prevents them from walking, cycling or gaining access to public transport, to low-income families such as single parents for whom public transport costs are prohibitive, and to households in rural areas where services are poor or non-existent (Lucas et al, 2001). Similarly, domestic energy-efficiency measures that are currently available bring most benefit to people who can afford the initial costs of installing insulation or buying energy-efficient appliances such as washing machines and dryers. They are of little use to people whose low incomes require them to depend upon inefficient heating systems and second-hand appliances. Even the cost of low-energy light bulbs places them beyond the reach of some households.

Tensions like these, arising between policies to protect the environment and to improve social welfare, are most obviously apparent in debates surrounding water and energy pricing (Huby, 2002). Economic arguments point to the need to increase prices, reflecting the real costs of provision and incorporating the environmental externalities of energy generation and water abstraction, treatment and disposal (Royal Commission on Environmental Pollution, 2000; Office of Water Services, 2000). The links to traditional social policy concerns here are clear, particularly with regard to social security. Environmental taxes designed to emphasize the real value of natural resources and to act as incentives to conserve fuel and water will inevitably lead to disproportionate hardship for low-income households if they are introduced in isolation.

The Royal Commission on Environmental Pollution (2000), however, has suggested that the introduction of new carbon taxes could be accompanied by changes to the benefits system funded by ring-fencing a proportion of carbon tax revenue. Levels of mainstream benefits, cold weather payments and winter fuel payments could be increased; outreach systems could be improved to increase take-up; eligibility could be widened; and social housing stock could be improved to increase energy efficiency.

The effect of water price increases on social security benefit recipients has already been documented (Herbert and Kempson, 1995). The 1989 privatization of the water industry in England and Wales required the newly constituted water companies to take action for environmental protection. Because the regulatory framework allowed the extra costs resulting from environmental improvements to be passed on to consumers, water bills soared. Between 1989–1990 and 1994–1995, average household water and sewerage bills rose by 67 per cent (National Consumer Council, 1994). The impact of this on low-income households is reflected in the fact that over the same period there was a sixfold increase in the number of social security benefit claimants using the direct payment scheme for water (Huby and Anthony, 1997). In 1995, 4 per cent of all income support recipients paid for their water in this way (DSS Press Release, 30 November 1995).

The challenge, then, is to develop environmental policies in conjunction with social policy so that regressive distributional effects can be avoided. Social policy concerns with equity and the social disadvantages associated with income levels, class, gender, age, ethnicity, health and disability are of crucial relevance to the success of policies aiming to protect and enhance the environment. Social policy has a key role to play in explicitly accepting the need for environmental protection policies and in analysing how these can impact upon conditions of social disadvantage.

POVERTY, EQUITY AND SUSTAINABLE DEVELOPMENT

It is in the equitable meeting of human needs that the notion of sustainable development is most clearly pertinent to the goals of social policy: 'Sustainable development requires meeting the basic needs of all and extending to all the opportunity to satisfy their aspirations for a better life' (WCED, 1987, p44). The current shift in social policy, away from simply evaluating policy and administrative arrangements and towards broader themes of poverty and inequality, focuses attention on the underlying causes of social problems and the means to address these (*Social Policy Association News*, February/March 2002). The goal of sustainable development to ensure that people can meet their needs and achieve reasonable standards of welfare is indistinguishable from at least some of the goals of social policy.

The environmental aims of sustainable development are essentially incompatible with poverty and social injustice. Inequalities in resource distribution result in a polarization of very rich and very poor lifestyles, both of which are responsible for natural resource degradation. More prosperous consumers, for example, make greater use of water for 'luxury' uses such as car washing and watering gardens and contribute to demands for more intensive food production, particularly for meat and dairy products. They tend to live in bigger houses and consume more energy for heating and to operate electrical household appliances, such as dishwashers, computers and music systems. Over 60 per cent of households in Organisation for Economic Co-operation and Development (OECD) countries own at least one private car, and more affluent car owners make longer and more frequent journeys. Rising prosperity brings more opportunities for leisure, more trips to the countryside and more overseas holidays, as well as placing increasing demands on industry for the production of leisure goods. More affluent sectors of society are also responsible for the production of polluting waste. This includes the atmospheric pollution and greenhouse gases emitted from the use of energy for domestic purposes, transport and industry and the massive amounts of solid waste generated from packaging and used consumer goods.

At the other end of the scale, many people living in poverty have no choice but to make maximum use of the natural resources that are available to them. Their immediate livelihoods depend upon these resources; but, at the same time, growing poverty, population density and pressures on land mean that overuse results in environmental degradation. Developing countries, for example, are facing increasing problems of water scarcity, deforestation, desertification and pollution. The activities of poorer people in more affluent countries also have negative effects on the environment. The demand for cheap food puts pressure on agricultural intensification and on the provision of frozen and pre-packaged foods that are wasteful in terms of energy use and packaging. People living on low incomes are less likely to live in well-insulated homes and more likely to use resources inefficiently since they often cannot afford to buy energy- and water-efficient appliances. They are similarly less able to afford to buy Green products because these are usually more expensive than other brands.

Reducing social inequity can bring environmental benefits and these, in turn, can operate, at least in principle, to reduce social inequality. Even in a relatively rich country like the UK, there is a huge difference in the way that rich and poor groups of people experience environmental damage. The rich can usually afford to move away from problem areas, while poorer groups bear the brunt not only of the damage to which they have contributed themselves, but also of environmental degradation caused by the polluting activities of the rich. Sites for chemical plants, toxic waste incinerators, radioactive waste repositories, nuclear power stations, major roads, railways and airports are often located in socially and economically marginalized areas. These tend to have high unemployment and low-income levels, and the likelihood of local objections to proposed developments are minimized (Huby, 1998; Boardman, 1999). Environmental improvements in such areas can actually reduce social inequity by bringing disproportionate benefits to vulnerable groups of people.

Sustainable development demands that meeting current human needs must not undermine the ability of future generations to meet their needs. In other words, it requires both intra- and inter-generational equity. If future generations are to be considered, there is even more necessity to protect the environment upon which the meeting of future needs will depend.

DEMOCRACY AND PARTICIPATION

So far, we have seen how the goals of sustainable development and social policy coincide, and we have established the salience of environmental conditions to achieving social goals. Although the concept of sustainable development is complex and contested, social equity is a fundamental principle that seems to underpin all of its interpretations.

Another such principle is that of democracy: 'Sustainable development requires a political system that secures effective citizen participation in decision-making' (WCED, 1987, p65). Carter (2001) highlights the need for community participation through consultative processes, citizen initiatives and the strengthening of institutions of local democracy. He argues that this not only raises awareness of problems, but also increases the chances of successful, relevant policy implementation and raises public support for environmental policies.

It is well documented in the development literature that policies designed and imposed from above risk failure if they are not perceived as necessary or relevant by the people whose lives they affect directly (Chambers, 1983; Agrawal and Gibson, 1999; Adams, 2001). That this is increasingly being recognized by social policy analysts is evident from the growing body of literature on community participation studies (see, for example, Chanan, 1999; Taylor, 2000). Democracy and public participation are clearly principles that unify the interests of sustainable development and social policy.

POLICY INTEGRATION AND PLANNING

Carter (2001) identifies policy integration and planning as key principles underlying the pursuit of sustainable development policies. The diverse interests involved require extensive cooperation and coordination between a wide range of policy sectors. A similar phenomenon is already apparent in social policy, where the need to erode institutional borders between employment, social security, housing, education, social services and health is frequently identified.

However, if social policy is to take on the sustainable development mantle, it needs to widen its remit to consider the interactions of social welfare with other policy areas, including energy, transport, agriculture and industry. This is something of a tall order for academics, but even more so for policy-makers. Carter suggests that this level of integration constitutes a form of 'administrative revolution' involving 'the creation of new structures, the reform of existing institutions and the transformation of established policy-making processes' (Carter, 2001, p209).

Clearly, planning is of crucial importance. Most commentators would agree that sustainable development necessitates some government intervention; but questions are raised about its extent and nature. Social policy analysts are already familiar with debates surrounding relationships and divisions of responsibility between the state, market, the voluntary sector and individuals. Coming to terms with social policy as an integral component of wider sustainable development simply needs an extension of the debate to include a broader range of policy actors and consideration of more varied mixes of policy instruments. Whatever this entails, there remains a clear role for government in the strategy, design, coordination, planning and supervision of sustainable development policies.

IMPLICATIONS FOR SOCIAL POLICY IN HIGHER AND FURTHER EDUCATION

Cahill and Fitzpatrick (2001) argue for the realignment of social policy to recognize the environmental dimensions of all the topics traditionally covered by the subject. Here, we suggest that the incorporation of these dimensions might take place at two levels. First, there is a need to ensure that students in higher and further education are aware of the importance of environmental protection for social welfare. Attention must be paid to understanding environmental problems and their relevance to social science. Second, there is a huge potential for the principles of sustainable development – particularly equity, democracy, participation, policy integration and planning – to be used to construct a unifying framework for social policy, emphasizing the importance of achieving stable and long-term solutions to social problems.

Understanding environmental issues

The general need to raise environmental responsibility and awareness across the educational agenda in the UK was recognized by the Toyne Report (Toyne, 1993). This examined the present state of environmental education in England and Wales and recommended that all further and higher educational institutions should formulate strategies for developing environmental education and improving all aspects of their own environmental performance. Implicit in the report is the notion of sustainable development, albeit in its anthropocentric sense. It highlights the need to:

> . . .raise the level of environmental awareness across the population at large and promote far wider understanding of:

- *the way in which the planet's life-sustaining systems function (at least in outline);*
- *the importance of maintaining the delicate balance of these systems by living in harmony with them, and the skills this will require;*
- *the reasons why 'non-sustainable' activities come about, and the contribution which the individual makes to them.*
  (Toyne, 1993, p22)

Bringing environmental issues into higher education teaching is not entirely new in the social sciences. The relevance of the environment to sociology, philosophy, politics and economics, for example, has long been recognized. The study of environmental sociology and environmental philosophy has been established for at least the last decade (Yearley, 1991; Nash, 1989). Similarly, key works by Pearce et al (1989) and Dobson (1990) placed the environment squarely on the academic economic and political agendas, respectively.

It has taken rather longer for the environment to become an established part of the social policy agenda (Cahill, 1992; George and Wilding, 1994; Hill, 1996; Huby, 1998; Cahill, 2002). Yet, if we regard the goal of improving welfare as being social progress or change for the better, the implication is that such change should continue to bring lasting benefits. George and Wilding (1999) map the changes that have taken place in British society over the last half century, making particular reference to stability and sustainability and high-lighting the crucial importance of environmental change for social welfare. Social development has the potential to undermine its own resource base, the environment upon which all life ultimately depends. For social progress to be sustainable, it must take place without damaging the environment. There is clearly an argument for introducing basic environmental modules into social policy teaching and to use an understanding of the interdependence between social and environmental policies to inform many traditional modules.

Sustainable development as a unifying framework for social policy

Although social policy has developed and reshaped itself considerably over recent years, at its heart remains the notion of improving welfare for those people most in need. Ideas about need and poverty have, however, moved on. Early concerns that centered on financial and material aspects of poverty have been extended due to a growing recognition that social disadvantage encompasses much more than simply low income.

Certainly, a low income, either in or out of work, and a lack of wealth or assets remain key indicators of poverty. Social security is still a crucial part of the social policy agenda. But of equal importance is the impact of low income and wealth on people's living conditions. People with low incomes are more likely to live in poor housing, suffer poorer health, have more need of personal social services and have less access to education and training than those who are better off. Again, housing, health, social services and education remain key elements in the study of social policy.

Other aspects of poverty, however, are now coming to the fore. These include hardships associated with neighbourhood degradation – such as litter; crime and fear of crime; poor transport; and lack of access to health and leisure services, schools, shops and workplaces – as well as less tangible problems, such as marginalization, disempowerment and alienation. Not only are these elements of social disadvantage caused by financial poverty, but they tend, in turn, to exclude people from the means of improving their situations by increasing their incomes through paid work.

Taken together, these ideas have given rise to the concepts of 'unconnectedness' and social exclusion currently dominating social policy thinking. The establishment of the UK government's Social Exclusion Unit in 1997 is an explicit acknowledgement that many causes of social exclusion are structural. As a policy issue, social exclusion 'relates specifically to the values, processes and actions of agencies, organizations and institutions within a society which have the effect of systematically excluding certain individuals, groups or communities from the benefits of their policy decisions and practices' (Lucas, 2000, p15).

There is clear scope for integrated and well-planned policy interventions to ensure greater participation by, and inclusion of, socially disadvantaged groups. At the same time, the differing needs of people of different ages, gender, physical and mental ability and race or ethnicity are key to the success of policies to encourage social inclusion.

These themes of equity, participation, policy integration and planning are, of course, the very themes discussed above as constituting the underlying principles of sustainable development. Indeed, the similarities lead Lucas (2000) to provide a convincing argument for the integration of national policy strategies in order to tackle problems of social exclusion and to achieve sustainable development. Lucas presents a detailed analysis of the many potential synergies between social exclusion and sustainable development programmes. Housing improvements, for example, can meet the social objectives of improving health and reducing fuel poverty, while meeting sustainable development objectives of improving local neighbourhood environments and reducing carbon emissions. Sustainable development initiatives can lead to capacity-building in local communities as people gain knowledge, skills and confidence, developing a sense of ownership and pride in their physical environment. Both sustainable development and social exclusion programmes seek to increase participation and partnerships in policy formulation and planning through democratic processes that target vulnerable and excluded social groups.

However, Lucas also recognizes the conflicts and tensions that can arise between social and environmental policy objectives. The discussion above has illustrated how these operate with respect to energy and water pricing. Another example is the use of economic subsidies to open up transport options for people in excluded groups. Extending the benefits of private car use to more people is in direct conflict with environmental policies to reduce vehicle emissions by discouraging travel by car. Similarly, the use of green-field sites to build affordable housing to meet social exclusion goals has serious repercussions for policies to protect biodiversity by conserving natural habitats. While social exclusion issues have a key place in the sustainable development agenda, the same is not true for environmental issues in the agenda for combating social exclusion. Potential conflicts between social and environmental interests then point to the logic of subsuming social exclusion within the remit of sustainable development, rather than simply recognizing that the two strategies are, to some extent, complementary.

The commitment to reduce social exclusion (Social Exclusion Unit, 2001) sits easily within the wider government strategy for sustainable development (Department for the Environment, Transport and the Regions [DETR], 1999). The latter includes clear objectives for social progress to recognize the needs of everyone. But it also incorporates goals for protecting the environment by using natural resources prudently. Meeting all of these goals together is not likely to be easy. It will require far greater policy cohesion across a wide range of government departments. The value of this approach is, nevertheless, already recognized by many academics and policy-makers. The Local Government Bill 2000 places a duty on all local authorities to promote social, environmental and economic well-being together. From a social policy perspective, the use of sustainable development as a framework allows for the study of the key traditional issues in social welfare in the context of the environmental conditions upon which so much of social well-being depends.

REFERENCES

Adams, W M (2001) *Green Development: Environment and Sustainability in the Third World, 2nd Edition*, London, Routledge

Agrawal, A and Gibson, C C (1999) 'Enchantment and disenchantment: the role of community in natural resource conservation', *World Development*, vol 27, pp629–649

Boardman, B (1999) *Equity and the Environment: Guidelines for a Green and Socially Just Government*, London, Catalyst and Friends of the Earth

Cahill, M (1992) 'The greening of social policy', in Manning, N (ed) *Social Policy Review 1990– 1991*, London, Longman

Cahill, M (2002) *The Environment and Social Policy*, London, Routledge

Cahill, M and Fitzpatrick, T (2001) 'Special Issue: Environmental Issues and Social Welfare, Editorial Introduction', *Social Policy and Administration*, vol 35, no 5, pp469–471

Carter, N (2001) *The Politics of the Environment*, Cambridge, Cambridge University Press

Chambers, R (1983) *Rural Development: Putting the Last First*, London, Longman

Chanan, G (1999) *Regeneration and Sustainable Communities*, London, Community Development Foundation

DETR (1999) *A Better Quality of Life: A National Strategy for Sustainable Development*, London, The Stationery Office

Dobson, A (1990) *Green Political Thought*, London, Unwin Hyman

George, V and Wilding, P (1994) *Welfare and Ideology*, Hemel Hempstead, Harvester Wheatsheaf

George, V and Wilding, P (1999) *British Society and Social Welfare: Towards a Sustainable Society*, London, Macmillan Press

Herbert, A and Kempson, E (1995) *Water Debt and Disconnection*, London, Policy Studies Institute

Hill, M (1996) *Social Policy: A Comparative Analysis*, Hemel Hempstead, Prentice Hall

Huby, M (1998) *Social Policy and the Environment*, Buckingham, Open University Press

Huby, M (2002) 'The sustainable use of resources on a global scale', in Fitzpatrick, T and Cahill, M (eds) *Environmental Issues and Social Welfare*, Basingstoke, Macmillan

Huby, M and Anthony, K (1997) 'Regional inequalities in paying for water', *Policy Studies* vol 18, no 3/4, pp207–217

Huby, M and Burkitt, N (2000) 'Is the "New Deal for Transport" really "Better for Everyone"? The Social Policy Implications of the UK's 1998 Transport White Paper', *Environment and Planning C: Government and Policy*, vol 18, pp379–392

Lucas, K (2000) 'Two for One and One for All? Exploring the Potential for Integrating the Sustainable Development and Social Exclusion Policy Agendas in the UK', Centre for Sustainable Development, London, University of Westminster

Lucas, K, Grosvenor, T and Simpson, R (2001) *Transport, the Environment and Social Exclusion*, York, Joseph Rowntree Foundation

Nash, R (1989) *The Rights of Nature: A History of Environmental Ethics*, Madison, Wisconsin, University of Wisconsin Press

National Consumer Council (1994) *Water Price Controls: Key Consumer Concerns*, London, National Consumer Council

Office of Water Services (2000) *Representing Water Customers 1999–2000: Annual Report of the Ofwat National Customer Council and the Ten Regional Customer Service Committees*, Birmingham, Office of Water Services

Pearce, D, Markandya, A and Barbier, E (1989) *Blueprint for a Green Economy*, London, Earthscan

Royal Commission on Environmental Pollution (2000) *Twenty-second Report: Energy – The Changing Climate*, Cm 4749, London, The Stationery Office

Social Exclusion Unit (2001) *Preventing Social Exclusion*, London, The Stationery Office

Social Policy Association News (2002) February/March, Newsletter of the UK Social Policy Association

Spicker, P (2002) 'Social policy under threat', *SPA News May/June 2002*, Social Policy Association

Taylor, M (2000) *Top Down Meets Bottom Up: Neighbourhood Management*, York, Joseph Rowntree Foundation

Toyne, P (1993) *Environmental Responsibility: An Agenda for Further and Higher Education* (the Toyne Report), Report of a Committee on Environmental Education in Further and Higher Education, appointed by the Department for Education and the Welsh Office, London, HMSO

UNCED (1992) *Agenda 21: A Programme of Action for Sustainable Development*, New York, United Nations

WCED (1987) *Our Common Future*, Oxford, Oxford University Press

Yearley, S (1991) *The Green Case: A Sociology of Environmental Issues, Arguments and Politics*, London, HarperCollins

Chapter 14

Sustainable Development, Sociology and UK Higher Education

Matthew Smith, John Donnelly and Andrew Parker

Strategies to achieve sustainable development are situated in structural contexts, economies and societies in which individual and group interests often diverge. Their success depends on the efficacy of the intentional acts of human agents. In seeking answers to these issues of human agency and social structure we are necessarily drawn to the discipline of sociology (Redclift and Woodgate, 1994, p51).

Instead of sociological discourses being driven exclusively by disciplinary conventions and disputes, theorists should seriously engage the problems and language of argumentation of a public world of social and political conflict. (Seidman, 1998, p3)

INTRODUCTION

Karl Marx, unlike Max Weber, believed that the main purpose of studying society was to change it. If we follow Marx's reasoning, then surely, at a time of repellent levels of inequality connected with environmental exploitation and destruction, sociology should be fundamentally concerned with sustainable development (SD). However, what this concern might look like may be less clear. One of the authors of this chapter, when introducing the theme of sustainable development as part of a second-year undergraduate sociology course, uses the alternative interpretations of the term 'sustainability' by himself and Margaret Thatcher as indicative of the problems presented in trying to understand, let alone engender, SD. If we add to this the similarly contested terrain of sociology, we face a daunting prospect; there seems to be every chance for the authors to slip past each other as we try to find some purchase within the vast hangars of both sociology and SD. In seeking to avoid this, it is inevitable that this chapter does not provide a comprehensive picture. Instead, it aims to reflect upon the ways in which the discipline of sociology can intersect with the broader challenge that higher education (HE) faces in seeking to practice and engender SD.

The chapter is divided into three sections. The first considers the range of ways in which sociology's theoretical and substantive preoccupations resonate with the SD agenda. The second section explores the ways in which SD is treated in introductory sociology textbooks in order to illustrate issues raised in the preceding analysis, as well as to reveal some of the ways in which SD is currently dealt with in mainstream undergraduate sociology. Finally, the chapter considers the degree to which sociology can adequately engage with SD within a policy environment that privileges forms of knowledge which appear to centre primarily on the drive to satisfy broader economic needs.

CONNECTIONS: SOCIOLOGY AND SUSTAINABLE DEVELOPMENT

Following Benton and Redclift's comments on social theory and the environment (1994, p2), it is important to acknowledge the different possible dimensions to sociology's connection with SD. Debates around the latter may pose critical questions for mainstream social scientific thinking, as well as resonate with key social scientific theoretical concerns. At the same time, sociology may be able to make an important contribution to SD. One could also argue that through the pursuit of 'good' sociology, these dimensions should interconnect. A key starting point to mapping these possible connections is to acknowledge the contested nature of both sociology and SD. In terms of SD, we could choose to deploy the dominant reading of the Earth Summit at Rio, viewing SD as a tangible but distant notion centred around environmental concerns. On the other hand, the emphasis in the Johannesburg summit on SD on poverty alleviation (no matter how distorted the substance of the arguments) presents a whole new agenda – and, as this chapter will show, one with greater resonance in terms of sociology's particular concern with social relations and equity. Alternatively, perhaps grand policy statements are less important than the micro-practice of non-governmental organizations (NGOs) and voluntary associations, or the conceptual linking of SD with post-modernism or late modernity. Rather than discuss a particular formation of SD, our aim is to highlight sociology's particular strengths in engaging more fully with debates over the theory, policy and practice of SD.

To do this, the emphasis here is on sociology's subject matter – its theories, perspectives and methodologies – and how these may intersect with issues regarding SD education. Inevitably, this connects with concerns over the boundaries of sociology. While we do not aim to favour either teaching or research, the constraint of space, alongside the focus on sociology within a HE context, leads us to emphasize curriculum content. Implicit within this agenda is a notion of how a discipline might contribute to SD. In this instance, we focus on where SD resonates with elements of the sociological canon. This is, of course, highly partial, seeming to emphasize education about rather than for

SD. However, we make no apology for this; the failure to reflect before acting has underpinned a range of ill-advised development strategies and trajectories. Second, sociological knowledge, for us, exists to engender change in itself through its description and analysis of society, particularly in terms of inequality and injustice. How that informs change may take a variety of forms, from empowering students of sociology in their personal and political lives to shaping policy.

Sociology's increasing dispersal and diffusion through a wide range of sub-disciplines and areas makes exploring its engagement with SD similarly problematic. One could go further than this and suggest that this diversity may, in fact, undermine those engagements. For example, in discussing the ways in which social science may afford important environmental insights, Benton and Redclift clearly identify 'the sociology of social movements, policy-analysis, "global systems" sociology, sociology of science, "structuration theory" and phenomenology' (Benton and Redclift, 1994, p2). Mapping this onto SD, we might find social movement theory that seeks to explain the political processes, movements and campaigns which led to the rise of SD, as well as the groups opposing the 2002 Johannesburg Summit; environmental sociology that affords insights into competing conceptions of the environment; 'global sociology' that conceptualizes the transnational character of environmental concerns and the networks of governance that relate to this; and policy sociology that explores the social relations inherent in providing incentives for more SD. This simply demonstrates the ways in which sociology's diversity affords a range of potential engagements with SD. But it is also raises some important problems.

First, there are the risks that a fragmented engagement with SD presents. Engagement with SD as subsidiary aspects of sociology's sub-disciplines risks it being appended to particular specialized concerns, separating out the dimensions of SD (such as the environment, equity and 'politics'), as well as the competing debates around SD (such as those rooted in theory, policy or practice). This is not to suggest that SD should not be engaged with in policy sociology explorations of how to implement Agenda 21 (United Nations Conference on Environment and Development [UNCED], 1992, p47), for example; but it does raise concerns that the fundamental and paradigmatic shifts associated with a meaningful, complex and nuanced conception of SD may be missed. This relates to the second concern, that only treating SD in this way may distance it from the mainstream, positioning it as something separate from the core concerns of sociology, potentially ghettoizing it, and running the risk of perpetuating the misnomer that SD is exclusively about the environment. These problems, alongside the argument that debates around SD have much in common with the debates at the core of sociology, lead us to argue for a greater embedding of SD within mainstream sociology and, in particular, social theory. The case for this is perhaps made even stronger post the Johannesburg Summit and the more public association of SD with issues such as poverty, equity and justice, although the association may also extend to corporate strategy and trade liberalization. Ironically, the marketing reflected in the latter may also come into play in forcing sociology to engage with SD more directly, as demanded by its 'clients' in the HE market.

SUSTAINABLE DEVELOPMENT AND THE ROOTS OF SOCIOLOGY

Wherever one looks during the 19th century, social change inspired questions about the nature of individuals and collectivities and the connections between them: questions about the relationship of citizens or subjects to the state, and about individualism and the decline of moral community. Even today, in a world which has since been transformed – although not out of all recognition, globalization notwithstanding – understanding of social change and the problematic relationship between the individual and the collective remain fundamental to sociology. (Jenkins, 2002, p20)

Sustainable development is nothing if not concerned with change, individualism, community and morality: attempts to adequately define sustainable development grapple with the shifts and trade-offs required to transform trajectories of change. Identifying levels of action for sustainable development requires engaging with varied individual, and hence community, relationships with environmental resources and the ways in which this affects relationships with local and distant others. The recent NGO walkout at the end of the World Summit on Sustainable Development (WSSD) in Johannesburg in 2002 could be characterized as an attempt to highlight the failure of the new global moral community which the summit rhetoric promised.

Intrinsic to the argument is that analysing SD should be of central concern to sociology as a discipline, both in terms of theory and substantive examination. Second, such a concern should not be seen as requiring a new sub-discipline, given that sociology has been centrally concerned with understanding and explaining social change since its inception from both an analytical and, importantly, a critical stance. The concerns of Marx, Weber and Durkheim to *explain* (in their differing ways) the social impact of industrializing capitalism also contained *critical* views of the outcome of such change, whether in terms of the social condition of the proletariat, the constraining impact of rationalization and bureaucratization, or the anomic or coercive consequences of abnormal forms of the division of labour. Given the continuing impact of processes of globalizing capitalism upon economic, political and cultural life, in the context of the collapse of the party-state system and ongoing environmental concerns, it might reasonably be argued that SD should now be seen as the only viable alternative to the continuing ravages of capitalism. Thus, the critical intervention of SD as a normative conception of change concerned with relations between individuals, collectives and 'non-human' factors, and between nation states and the supra-territorial (Scholte, 2000, p46) should surely be positioned centrally within sociology. Linked to this, the associated balance between structure and agency – that is, between individual agency and volition, and the shaping of these by particular social, cultural, political or environmental formations – speaks directly to SD issues, the levels at which SD can be pursued and the ways in which we, as sociologists, understand the factors constraining it.

SUSTAINABLE DEVELOPMENT IN MODERN SOCIOLOGY TEXTBOOKS

Given sociology's concern with engaging with and understanding contemporary processes of social change, one might therefore expect SD to be a central issue for the sociological imagination and to lie at the core of the discipline's teaching. In considering whether this is, in fact, the case, this section reviews the way in which the issue of SD is approached in a number of recent key sociology textbooks and surveys. While not exhaustive, the works selected are generally highly regarded as key texts within the teaching of sociology at undergraduate level and the surveys as comprehensive reviews. Giddens (2001), Bilton et al (2002) and Fulcher and Scott (1999) might be seen as 'mainstream' texts, while Macionis and Plummer (2002) and Cohen and Kennedy (2000) both explicitly attempt to incorporate a more global perspective. Taylor (1999) and Burgess and Murcott (2001) seek to present accounts of the major trends in contemporary UK sociology. In subjecting these texts to critical review, our purpose is not to suggest that questions relating to SD are totally ignored by sociology – although it cannot be denied that until the last two decades, sociology was 'environmentally blind' and that the key theorists of the discipline did not really examine the relations between society and the environment except to see nature as a resource to be exploited/utilized in pursuit of 'development'. Nor do we deny the existence of a specialist literature in the sociology of development and theory that discusses these issues (see, for example, Beck, 1992, and Mellor, 1997). Rather, we argue that SD is sufficiently central to the prime concerns of sociology that it should feature prominently in the core textbooks of the discipline. If this proves not to be the case, this would be indicative that the topic is, to a large extent, being marginalized or, at best, simply being 'incorporated' as yet another sub-discipline, rather than being 'engaged' (Shove, 1994, pp257–265) with in a way that would do justice to the significance of the issue and that might also possibly generate new insights, allowing sociology to contribute to our understanding of environmental issues and social change.

Of the three 'mainstream' textbooks, only Giddens (2001) sees environmental issues as warranting detailed examination in their own right, and even he only devotes half a chapter to the 'ecological crisis'. Neither Bilton et al (2002) nor Fulcher and Scott (1999) provide any extensive discussions. There are no references to 'sustainability' or 'sustainable development' in Bilton et al (2002) and only isolated references to 'environment' or 'ecology'. While various chapters contain brief reference to, for example, 'threats to the global environment', 'ecological crisis', the environmental impact of transnational corporations (TNCs), the 1992 Earth Summit and the implications of US President Bush's refusal to sign the Kyoto Protocol, or the Green movement and the need for a new global politics, this general awareness of environmental concerns does not translate into any discussion of the concepts of sustainability or SD. At best, we see an implicit 'sociology of the environment' approach rather than an engaged grappling with the concept of SD. The approach in Fulcher and Scott (1999) is similar. Again, there are references to environmental problems, the Green movement as an example of a new social movement, and an outline and critical review of official responses to the problems of the environment from Stockholm to the Earth Summit in Rio. The authors do, at least, define the concept of SD – following that of the Brundtland Commission in *Our Common Future* (World Commission on Environment and Development [WCED], 1987) – and highlight the different perspectives of rich and poor countries to environmental issues. This might have provided the basis for a more extended discussion of SD; but, ultimately, this is not forthcoming. For textbooks that aim to be, and in general are, challenging, stimulating, focused on recent debates within the discipline and that reflect the changes that are transforming society, the relative absence of SD from their pages is indicative of an ongoing marginalization of what should be a key concept for understanding the social changes that the respective authors claim to be a central concern.

In the latest edition of his text, Giddens's (2001, pxiv) aim is to 'keep the text at the cutting edge of the discipline'. While he does devote half a chapter and a number of other references to varying aspects of the environmental question, his approach, too, is ultimately more of a survey of existing sociological appropriations of the environment rather than an 'engaged' discussion of SD. Hence, we are introduced to familiar descriptive outlines of the nature of environmental threats/problems, discussion of the environmental movement as an example of a 'new social movement' and reference to the Brundtland Report and Rio Earth Summit of 1992. Discussion of the concept of SD does not proceed beyond the Brundtland definition: a summary of the major criticisms levelled at the concept does not provide the basis for further thought. Perhaps the most interesting aspect of Giddens's approach is the link drawn between environmental issues and the concept of risk in relation to, for example, climate change and genetically modified organisms (GMOs), and a brief concluding discussion linking SD to ideas of eco-efficiency and ecological modernization in the context of global inequalities. This last insight is not pursued, however, and Giddens's concluding justification of the environment as an appropriate topic for sociological investigation smacks more of 'incorporation' than 'engagement' or a 'cutting-edge' concern with SD.

There is, at least, some recognition of the significance of environmental concerns and some awareness of the issues in these texts. This is more than can be said for the two surveys of the discipline provided by the edited volumes of Taylor (1999) and Burgess and Murcott (2001). Taylor's collection purports to be informed by a conception of sociology as a discipline that develops ideas in order to help us understand societies as continually changing social processes (Taylor, 1999, p4). But the topics of the essays, defined as key areas of sociological research, equate to the established sub-disciplines, with no reference to sustainability or SD. Indeed, environmental change is mentioned as a key problem for research only by Sklair in his chapter on globalization (Sklair, 1999). Disquiet over environmental degradation, the influence of the environmental movement and the 1992 Earth Summit are mentioned as stimuli to this, and SD is mentioned only in passing without being defined or discussed. Other than this, one looks in vain for discussion of sustainability in this review. Burgess and Murcott's (2001) collection is part of a 'New Sociologies Series' that aims to provide an alternative to the standard texts and an account of major trends in British sociology (Burgess and Murcott, 2001, pxiii). While recognizing that such a volume cannot be comprehensive in its coverage, the volume, nevertheless, aims to focus on 'key issues and debates in sociology' and 'the light they can shed on the nature of contemporary society' (Burgess and Murcott, 2001, pxv). Emphasis is again given to the ubiquity of change, both in terms of substantive social change and the discipline of sociology. While accepting the 'unavoidable selectivity' of the collection, it is, however, disappointing to find that in a book with the above concerns and structured around developments in theory, methodology and methods, substantive areas, and policy and problems, there is no reference to sustainability or SD. Yet, this is an issue that reflects those central concerns and that cuts across all three sections of the book. The editors conclude that the collection exemplifies the vigour of UK sociology in moving the discipline forward. However, 'engaging with' SD would have provided the means for the volume to make a contribution to reconceptualizing the discipline in terms of theorizing and extending fields of study and inter-disciplinary studies, which it claims to do. Both of these collections, then, while no doubt providing a survey of the current state of mainstream UK sociology, exhibit the latter's myopia. Neither book deals with SD simply because mainstream sociology does not deal with SD. Hence, the collections can be seen as indicative of the current shortcomings of sociology.

Looking finally at the two texts that adopt an explicitly global perspective, one might intuitively expect these volumes to reflect a greater awareness of issues of sustainability. Both texts do, indeed, devote specific chapters to environmental issues. However, while Cohen and Kennedy (2000) entitle one of their chapters 'Toward a Sustainable Future', its subtitle is 'The Green Movement'. Hence, analysis tends to be focused more on environmentalism and new social movements instead of sustainability and SD. In addition to this particular chapter, scattered throughout the book is a plethora of references to different aspects of the environmental question. These demonstrate an awareness of, for example, the environmental impact of population pressure, tourism, global consumerism, poverty, the role TNCs and export-processing zones (EPZs), as well as environmental campaigns with regard to some of these issues. But none of this develops into a discussion on sustainability. The core chapter surveys the transboundary nature of environmental problems and recognizes the significance of North–South divisions on environmental matters. But key parts of the chapter then deal with the difficulties of mobilizing support, building alliances and developing strategies for action in defence of the environment at both local and transnational, grassroots and elite levels. Hence, the approach is grounded in the sociological analysis of social and political movements, rather than in debates on sustainability. Where the latter is addressed, we are presented only with a summary of the principles underlying the Brundtland definition, and a summary critique of the concept that is outlined simply, with no attempt to answer criticisms or to move the discussion forward. Engagement with the concept of SD is lacking. Macionis and Plummer's (2002) book is perhaps the most successful of these texts in terms of a focus on sustainability. Including a chapter on 'Social Change and the Environment' as 'a topic not always included in introductory sociology textbooks' (Macionis and Plummer, 2002, pxix) and as 'a fairly new topic for [sociologists] to study' (p625), the authors provide a good survey of its sociological significance. Following discussion of the changing nature of the environment and the social practices contributing to its degradation, and of the links between capitalism and the environmental deficit in terms of over-development and inequality – an 'environmental racism' that necessitates a more equitable distribution of resources – they discuss the possibilities for a sustainable world. Calling for the development of an 'ecologically sustainable culture' (Macionis and Plummer, 2002, p646) – or the Brundtland conception of SD – Macionis and Plummer introduce some basic explanations as to what this might mean (conservation of finite resources, reducing waste, bringing world population under control) before indicating the difficulties of achieving these aims through a comparison of technocentric and eco-centric approaches (p647). This could have provided the basis for a detailed discussion of the antinomies at the heart of SD; but this opportunity is passed up. Instead, they conclude with a call to recognize that the present is tied to the future, that all forms of life are interdependent and of the need for global cooperation. While these statements of moral principle are fine, one is left with a feeling of a missed opportunity to engage centrally with the issue of sustainability and social change.

While in no way exhaustive, this analysis provides sufficient grounds for arguing that the issues of 'sustainability' and 'sustainable development' remain of relatively marginal significance within mainstream sociology. Where these issues do appear, they tend to be addressed through the prism of an analysis of environmentalism as a movement. This points towards an 'incor-poration' of the environment as a further sub-discipline within sociology rather than an innovative interrogation of the issues at play. Where sustain-ability and SD are tackled head on, discussion is limited and fails to 'engage' with the topic in a way that its central significance for both social change and the discipline of sociology deserves.

Thus, an important starting point for reflecting on how sociology as a discipline may connect with the wider challenges of SD faced by higher education is to try and understand its limited engagement. Although one could root this explanation within the context of modern sociological fashion, it is important to also look at the ways in which these omissions are framed by a wider structuring of HE, whose priorities engender forms of knowledge that limit the types of engagement suggested above. Indeed, it is to these broader issues that we now turn.

SUSTAINABLE DEVELOPMENT AND THE HIGHER EDUCATION CONTEXT

As we have seen, mainstream sociology has largely avoided the question of SD. Established theoretical, empirical and sub-disciplinary concerns appear to hold sway over emerging issues and debates – however pressing. Yet, the higher educational context within which these debates often take place does not exist in a social, political and economic vacuum. Like any other social institution, HE itself succumbs to the ebb and flow of a range of broad external forces. In this sense, not only might it be seen as a place where educational debates about SD are lacking (certainly within the context of sociology), but, at the same time, as a place where the whole concept of education can be seen to be changing (Deem, 2002). What we argue in this final section is that, while at the level of the curriculum, issues concerning SD may well be marginalized in HE establishments in the UK, at the same time they may, paradoxically, be seen as central to the broader educational agenda.

Across the board, UK educational provision has changed dramatically during more recent years. Most powerful in this respect has been the desire of successive governments in the post-1979 period to regenerate a greater degree of intimacy between education and the economy. Of course, the explicit connections between these two social spheres are nothing new. In his book *Schooling for Work in Capitalist Britain*, Shilling (1989) maps the historical development of the education–economy link, clearly demonstrating that one of the ways in which governments have traditionally sought to alleviate political and economic pressure at times of crisis is by restructuring educational resources in line with specific kinds of needs.[1]

Within the context of our own society, it is perhaps schools that have suffered most as a consequence of the restructuring processes which have accompanied a political preoccupation with neo-liberalism and market reform (especially in the post-1988 period), and which have brought with them, amongst other things, changes to curricular requirements aimed at better preparing young people for the adult world of work. As Apple (1982, 1990) has often noted, education is a highly politicized sphere where different kinds of knowledge exist, some with a higher status than others. What Apple asserts is that the reason why some knowledge might be prioritized at any particular point in time is precisely because of its value within the broader political and economic sphere. In today's society, knowledge is a commodity. Education and educational resources are seen as the lynchpin of economic prosperity, a point continually re-emphasized by policy reforms and political manoeuvres.

Take the case of New Labour. In 1997 a recast and revitalized Labour party fronted their election campaign with the slogan 'Education, education, education'. Many assumed that this was the beginning of a return to social democratic ideals, comprehensive schooling and a refutation of educational inequalities. Yet, since that time New Labour has vehemently resisted the social democratic project, preferring, instead, to champion existing neo-liberal trends – pursuing assessment and accountability strategies in schools; driving adult participation and learning via the lifelong learning agenda; and encouraging an 'up-skilling' and 're-skilling' of the work force through notions of 'continuing professional development'. Strictly speaking, this is not simply a replication of Conservative policy and practice. This is 'third-way' politics: a set of ideas falling between notions of social democracy – where the state predominates in the distribution of goods and services and social welfare sits high on the political agenda – in contrast with neo-liberalism – where notions of social welfarism diminish and the market takes distributive precedence (see Giddens, 1998, 2000). Couched within these terms, post-1997 educational reforms have been characterized by New Labour's preoccupation with the knowledge-based global economy (Blair, 2000; Blunkett, 2000; Department for Education and Employment [DfEE], 1998).[2] Central to this overall project is the exploitation of human capital and resources. The logic in play here is that if the UK is to remain/become a global economic force, it must attract overseas investment. In order to do this, it must demonstrate a highly skilled (and continually re-skilled and up-skilled) labour force. Within the context of this model, the development of individual potential in terms of the acquisition of 'knowledge', education and skills is the key to a sustainable economic future, as Mulderrig (2002, p4) notes:

> *While it is possible to identify the general business-oriented thrust of New Labour education policy and its consonance with Third Way ideology, the policy should perhaps also be understood as an aspect of the government's relationship to more global and economic forces. Globalization sits in a complex relationship with the 'modernization' of public services; it is simultaneously the set of political and economic processes which modernization helps to construct, and the discourse by which it is legitimized. The theme of globalization and the imperative for economic competitiveness is the core rationale running through New Labour's educational initiatives.[3]*

Accordingly, such political and economic forces have witnessed the development of educational provision around public–private partnerships (PPPs) and private finance initiatives (PFIs). Again, there is a sense in which this idea is nothing new. The city technology colleges (CTCs) of the late 1980s were constructed around a similar idea. In the New Labour era, this drive has taken on a different guise with the emergence of specialist schools, academies, educational action zones (EAZs) and the management of educational institutions by private companies (Chitty and Dunford, 1999; Tomlinson, 2001). Indeed, a key feature of contemporary debates on the evolution of educational systems both nationally and internationally is that they must involve the business sector (Robertson, 2002). At the same time it is recognized that private intervention in the educational marketplace has the potential to open up a whole series of possibilities with regard to cross-boarder trade agreements (see Department of Trade and Industry [DTI], 2002; Rikowski, 2002a, 2002b; Ziguras, 2002).[4]

Perhaps not surprisingly, HE has rapidly followed suit. Proclamations on the importance of the of the 'knowledge economy', the 'learning society' and the 'information age' are all said to be based upon a particular model of higher educational provision that has its origins in international discussions on education and training during the post-1945 era – that is, those involving the influential structures of the Organisation for Economic Co-operation and Development (OECD), the United Nations Educational, Scientific and Cultural Organization (UNESCO), the International Labour Organization (ILO), the World Bank and the Council of Europe.[5] This model has regularly been presented as a blueprint for economic survival in the post-modern (post-Fordist) age by UK politicians and policy-makers (DfEE, 1996, 1998; Fryer, 1997; Kennedy, 1997; National Committee of Inquiry into Higher Education, 1997).[6] This is an 'instrumental' education in the sense that it is about the development of human resources and economic productivity much more than about notions of personal achievement, growth and fulfilment and the promotion of education for the social good. The Dearing Committee outlines this scenario better than most. For them, successful societies will, in future, be learning societies and will heavily depend upon higher education:

> *The expansion of higher education in the last ten years has contributed greatly to the creation of a learning society – that is, a society in which people in all walks of life recognize the need to continue in education and training throughout their working lives. . . But, looking 20 years ahead, the UK must progress further and faster in the creation of such a society to sustain a competitive economy. . . In a global economy, [the fact that] the manufacturers of goods and providers of services can locate or relocate their operations wherever in the world gives them greatest competitive advantage. . . When capital, manufacturing processes and service bases can be transferred internationally, the only stable source of competitive advantage (other than natural resources) is a nation's people. Education and training must enable people in an advanced society to compete with the best in the world.* (National Committee of Inquiry into Higher Education, 1997, p9)

Somewhat insightfully, Foster (2002) has called this the 'Tesco' model of education, where learning is packaged and sold along ever more 'flexible' lines in order to suit economic need and consumer demand (see also Levidow, 2002; Nunn, 2002).[7] In this sense, Foster (2002, p37) goes on:

> *Higher education. . .is directed to the continual recasting of knowledge and skills required to maintain the value of human capital in the technology-driven global economy. Higher education sub-serves the survival instinct of those societies (and within them, of those individuals) most ready to respond to change with cognitive and technological flexibility and self-reinvention.*

All of this has taken place within an increasingly 'marketized' higher educational climate where unprecedented growth, customer–client relations, and financial and commercial interests have been prioritized (see Henkel, 2000; Kogan and Hanney, 2000).[8] Accordingly, many of the structures of HE – both administrative and academic – have changed. Evidence of this can be seen in the adoption of 'new' managerial strategies, the increase in entrepreneurial activity, and the rapid development of systems of accountability (Deem, 1998, 2001, 2002; Delanty, 2001; Fuller, 2002; Slaughter and Leslie, 1997). Within all of this, the production, dissemination and management of knowledge have become increasingly important, as have the relationships between universities and private enterprises. The advent of virtual and corporate universities is evidence of this, taking their place amidst the widespread emergence of a global marketplace where higher educational provision may be bought and sold (Dodds, 2002; Kelk and Worth, 2002; Levidow, 2002; Nunn, 2002). Notwithstanding the fact that the HE sector has undergone this considerable restructuring, during more recent times it has become increasingly obvious that, as a whole, many UK universities have reached a point at which current levels of demand (in line with government targets) simply cannot be met by existing infra-structural arrangements – especially given the various pressures that academics find themselves under (Deem, 2001, 2002; Fuller, 2002; Slaughter and Leslie, 1997). In short, current forms of organization and delivery, it seems, are simply *unsustainable*.[9]

Where, we might ask, does all of this leave us with regard to issues of sustainable development? If this is the picture at the political and economic level, what can be done within the HE system to change the way in which the whole notion of SD is approached and considered? In terms of the recent past, of course, there are some positive points to draw upon here, some of which demonstrate at least a small amount of activity and interest in this area. The Toyne Report (Toyne, 1993), for example, discussed the relationship between HE and SD in a much less instrumental way, and in so doing set the scene for a 'greening' of the higher educational context.[10] Such events are being supplemented by promotional activity in other sectors of the education system. In primary education, for example, SD appears to be receiving a more rigorous treatment by those dictating curriculum innovation and change – despite the fact that its status remains somewhat marginal, its definitive underpinnings highly contested, and, following Apple (1982, 1990), the reasons behind its inclusion seem to link clearly with the broader economic agenda (see Chatzifotiou, 2002; Gough and Scott, 2001; Scott, 2002).[11] In this sense, the outlook over the longer term suggests that higher educational practitioners will at least have a conceptual basis with which to work when students arrive at universities, safe in the knowledge that their 'clients' will have had some exposure to SD, however distorted. Sociology (like any other disciplinary area) then has the task of facilitating and engendering student interest and concern in this area – a process which should be aided by the fact that, as a discipline, sociology is grounded in the analysis and critique of power relations and social inequality. If evidence of social inequality was ever needed, it can surely be found in the marginalization of SD and its associated social movements. The only problem which then remains is the one regarding academics themselves, and whether they come to accept SD as a serious sociological issue. As we have seen within this chapter, it is perhaps this issue more than any other that is at the core and not the periphery of the current sociological dilemma.

NOTES

1   Academic and non-academic writers alike have long since pondered the ways in which education might act as an 'apprenticeship' or socializing agency for later life. This is perhaps most famously evident in Rousseau's philosophical classic *Emile* (Rousseau, 1762). In turn, and from somewhat contrasting theoretical standpoints, Parsons (1961) and Althusser (1972) make a similar point. In terms of the way in which schooling might be seen to correspond to specific aspects of working life, Bowles and Gintis (1976) make some interesting observations.

2   There is much debate about what the term 'knowledge economy' actually means given the way in which it is often used interchangeably with a range of other descriptors (see Nunn, 2002).

3   For more detailed accounts of New Labour's educational policy and practice, see Ball (1999); DfEE (2001); Department for Education and Skills [DfES] (2001), Halpin (1999); Hatcher and Hirtt (1999); Hill (2001); Muschamp, Jamieson and Lauder (1999); and Tomlinson (2001).

4   For developments on issues relating to cross-border trade negotiations, see www.gatswatch.org. For more on the problems of global educational provision, see Global Campaign for Education: www.campaignforeducation.org.

5   For more detail on the historical groundings of these discussions, see Tight (1998a, 1998b).

6   For more recent discussion on these issues with specific reference to UK higher education, see Committee of Vice-Chancellors and Principals [CVCP] and Higher Education Funding Council for England [HEFCE] (2000), Warwick (1999a, 1999b) and Floud (2002).

7   For Foster (2002) this particular interpretation of higher educational provision opposes a more 'exploratory' or 'Heuristic' model, which promotes an altogether more responsible and moral outlook on education (see also Foster, 2001).

8   In the UK, the post-1980 period has seen the transition to a system of mass higher education in line with government desires and expectations (Henkel, 2000). Current government recruitment targets suggest that 50 per cent of 18- to 30-year olds should be in higher education by 2010.

9   It is widely acknowledged by academics and politicians alike that UK higher education is currently in a state of crisis. Ongoing negotiations between the two parties reflect this (see Clarke, 2002; Universities UK [UUK], 2002).

10 Further thoughts in this direction have also been provided by Alabaster and Blair (1997). Similar and, to some extent, more advanced considerations in this area are evident in other countries, (see, for example, Thomas and Nicita, 2002).

11 In terms of the marginalization of issues relating to SD in the UK primary school curriculum, Chatzifotiou (2002) notes that such topics form part of the non-statutory national curriculum guidelines within the context of 'value-based' subjects – that is, 'citizenship' or 'personal, social and health education' (PSHE). Of course, there is still a great deal of debate about what exactly SD actually means and how it should be addressed within the context of UK state education (see, Bonnett, 2002; Reid, 2002; Scott, 2002; Stables and Scott, 2002). Again, activities elsewhere provide an interesting comparison in this respect (see Hopkins and McKeown, 2001).

REFERENCES

Alabaster, T and Blair, D (1997) 'Greening the University', in Huckle, J and Sterling, S (eds) *Education for Sustainability*, London, Earthscan, pp86–104

Althusser, L (1972) 'Ideology and Ideological State Apparatus', in Cosin, B (ed) *Education, Structure and Society*, Middlesex, Penguin, pp242–280

Apple, M (1982) (ed) *Cultural and Economic Reproduction in Education*, London, Routledge and Kegan Paul

Apple, M (1990) *Ideology and Curriculum*, second edition, New York, Routledge

Ball, S J (1999) 'Labour, learning and the economy: a policy sociology perspective', *Cambridge Journal of Education*, vol 29, no 2, pp195–206

Beck, U (1992) *Risk Society: Towards a New Modernity*, London, Sage

Benton, T and Redclift, M (1994) 'Introduction', in Redclift, M and Benton, T (eds), Social Theory and the Global Environment, London, Macmillan, pp1–27

Bilton, T, Bonnet, K, Jones, P, Lawson, T, Skinner, D, Stanworth, M and Webster, A (2002) *Introductory Sociology*, London, Palgrave

Blair, T (2000) Speech to 'Knowledge 2000', Conference on the Knowledge-Driven Economy, available at www.dti.gov.uk/knowledge2000/blair.htm

Blunkett, D (2000) Speech to 'Knowledge 2000', Conference on the Knowledge-Driven Economy, available at www.dti.gov.uk/knowledge2000/blunkett.htm

Bonnett, M (2002) 'Education for Sustainability as a Frame of Mind', *Environmental Education Research*, vol 8, no 1, pp9–20

Bowles, S and Gintis, H (1976) *Schooling in Capitalist America*, London, Routledge

Burgess, R and Murcott, A (eds) (2001) *Developments in Sociology*, Edinburgh, Pearson

Chatzifotiou, A (2002) 'An imperfect match? The structure of the National Curriculum and education for sustainable development', *The Curriculum Journal*, vol 13, no 3, pp289–301

Chitty, C and Dunford, J (eds) (1999) *State Schools: New Labour and the Conservative Legacy*, London, Woburn Press

Clarke, C (2002) DfES Discussion Paper on Higher Education, Accessed 20 December 2002, www.dfes.gov.uk/highereducation/docs/discussion.pdf

Cohen, R and Kennedy, P (2000) *Global Sociology*, London, Macmillan

CVCP and HEFCE (2000) *The Business of Higher Education: UK Perspectives*, London, CVCP/HEFCE

Deem, R (1998) 'New managerialism in higher education – the management of performances and cultures in universities', *International Studies in the Sociology of Education*, vol 8, no 1, pp47–70

Deem, R (2001) 'Globalisation, New Managerialism, Academic Capitalism and Entrepreneurialism in Universities: is the local dimension still important?', *Comparative Education*, vol 37, no 1, pp7–20

Deem, R (2002) 'The Knowledge Worker and the Divided University', Professorial address, 28 October, University of Bristol, UK

DfEE (1996) *Lifetime Learning: A Consultation Document*, London, HMSO

DfEE (1998) *The Learning Age: A Renaissance for a New Britain*, Cm 3790, London, HMSO

DfEE (2001) *Schools: Building on Success*, London, DfEE

DfEE (2001) *Professionalism and Trust: The Future of Teachers and Teaching*, London, DfES

Dodds, A (2002) 'GATS, Higher Education and Public Libraries', *Information for Social Change*, vol 14, winter 2001–2002, www.libr.org/ISC/articles/14-Dodds.htm

Delanty, G (2001), *Challenging Knowledge: The University in the Knowledge Society*, Buckingham, Open University Press

DTI (2002) *Liberalising Trade in Services: A New Consultation on the World Trade Organisation GATS Negotiations*, October, London, DTI

Floud, R (2002) 'Higher Education, the economy and society: developing vocational relevance', Speech by Professor Roderick Floud, Universities UK President, 21 February, Cavendish Conference Centre, London

Foster, J (2001) 'Education *as* Sustainability', *Environmental Educational Research*, vol 7, no 2, pp153–165

Foster, J (2002) 'Sustainability, Higher Education and the Learning Society', *Environmental Education Research*, vol 8, no 1, pp35–41

Fryer, B (1997) *Learning for the Twenty-first Century*, Leicester, National Advisory Group for Continuing Education and Lifelong Learning

Fulcher, J and Scott, J (1999) *Sociology*, Oxford, Oxford University Press

Fuller, S (2002) *Knowledge Management Foundations*, London, Butterworth Heinemann

Giddens, A (1998) *The Third Way: The Renewal of Social Democracy*, Cambridge, Polity Press

Giddens, A (2000) *The Third Way and Its Critics*, Cambridge, Polity Press

Giddens, A (2001) *Sociology*, Cambridge, Polity Press

Gough, S and Scott, W (2001) 'Curriculum Development and Sustainable Development: practices, institutions and literacies', *Educational Philosophy and Theory*, vol 33, no 2, pp137–152

Halpin, D (1999) 'Sociologising the "Third Way": the contribution of Anthony Giddens and the significance of his analysis for education', *Forum*, vol 41, no 2, pp53–57

Hatcher, R and Hirtt, N (1999) 'The Business Agenda behind Labour's Education Policy', in Allen, M et al (eds) *Business, Business, Business: New Labour's Education Policy*, London, Tufnell Press, pp12–23

Henkel, M (2000) *Academic Identities and Policy Change in Higher Education*, London, Jessica Kingsley

Hill, D (2001) 'The Third Way in Britain: New Labour's neo-liberal education policy', Paper presented to Congress Marx International III, *Le capital et L'Humanité*, 26–29 September, Université de Paris-X Nanterre Sorbonne, Paris, France

Hopkins, C and McKeown, R (2001) 'Education for Sustainable Development: past experience, present action and future prospects', *Educational Philosophy and Theory*, vol 33, no 2, pp231–244

Jenkins, R (2002) *Foundations of Sociology: Towards a Better Understanding of the Human World*, Basingstoke, Palgrave Macmillan

Kelk, S and Worth, J (2002) 'Trading it away: How GATS threatens UK Higher Education', www.peopleandplanet.org/tradejustice/tradingitaway.asp

Kennedy, H (1997) *Learning Works: Widening Participation in Further Education*, Coventry, HEFCE

Kogan, M and Hanney, S (2000) *Reforming Higher Education*, London, Jessica Kingsley

Levidow, L (2002) 'Marketising Higher Education: Neoliberal Strategies and Counter Strategies', *The Commoner*, no 3, January, www.thecommoner.org/03levidow.pdf

Macionis, J and Plummer, K (2002) *Sociology: A Global Introduction*, Edinburgh, Pearson

Mellor, M (1997) *Feminism and Ecology*, Cambridge, Polity Press

Mulderrig, J (2002) 'Learning to Labour: the discursive construction of social actors in New Labour's education policy', www.ieps.org.uk.cwc.net/dec02.pdf

Muschamp, Y, Jamieson, I and Lauder, H (1999) 'Education, Education, Education', in Powell, M (ed) *New Labour, New Welfare State? The 'Third Way' in British Social Policy* Bristol, Policy Press, pp101–121

National Committee of Inquiry into Higher Education (1997) *Higher Education in the Learning Society*, London, HMSO

Nunn, A (2002) 'Interpreting the "Knowledge Economy" Cacophony: The extension of commodification to information production, dissemination and storage', *Information for Social Change*, vol 14, winter 2001–2002, www.libr.org/ISC/articles/14-Nunn.htm

Parsons, T (1961) 'The school class as a social system: some of its functions in American society,' in Halsey, A, Broadfoot, P, Croll, P, Osborn, M and Abbott, D (eds) *Education, Economy and Society*, London, Collier/Macmillan, pp434–455

Redclift, M and Woodgate, G (1994) 'Sociology and the environment: Discordant discourse?', in Redclift, M and Benton, T (eds) *Social Theory and the Global Environment*, London, Routledge, pp51–66

Reid, A (2002) 'Discussing the Possibility of Education for Sustainable Development', *Environmental Education Research*, vol 8, no 1, pp73–79

Rikowski, G (2002a) 'Schools: the Great GATS Buy', www.ieps.org.uk.cwc.net/rikowski2002c.pdf

Rikowski, G (2002b) 'Transfiguration: Globalisation, the World Trade Organisation and the National faces of the GATS', *Information for Social Change*, vol 14, winter 2001–2002, www.libr.org/ISC/articles/14-Glenn_Rikowski.htm

Robertson, S (2002) 'Changing Governance/Changing Equality? Understanding the Politics of Public–Private Partnerships in Education in Europe,' Paper presented to European Science Foundation Exploratory Workshop, Globalisation, Education Restructuring and Social Cohesion in Europe, 3–5 October, Barcelona, Spain

Rousseau, J-J (1762) (reprinted 1956) *Emile*, London, Heinemann

Scholte, J (2000) *Globalization: A Critical Introduction*, London, Palgrave

Scott, W (2002) 'Education and Sustainable Development: Challenges, responsibilities and frames of mind', *The Trumpeter*, vol 18, no 1, www.trumpeter.athabascau.ca/content/v18.1/scott.pdf

Seidman, S (1998) *Contested Knowledge: Social Theory in the Postmodern Era*, Malden, Massachusets, Blackwell

Shilling, C (1989) *Schooling for Work in Capitalist Britain*, Lewes, Falmer Press

Shove, E (1994) 'Sustaining developments in environmental sociology', in Redclift, M and Benton, T (eds) *Social Theory and the Global Environment*, London, Routledge, pp256–265

Sklair, L (1999) 'Globalisation', in Taylor, S (ed) *Sociology: Issues and Debates*, London, Macmillan

Slaughter, S and Leslie, G (1997) *Academic Capitalism*, Baltimore, John Hopkins

Stables, A and Scott, W (2002) 'The Quest for Holism in Education for Sustainable Development', *Environmental Education Research*, vol 8, no 1, pp53–60

Taylor, S (ed) (1999) *Sociology: Issues and Debates*, London, Macmillan

Thomas, I and Nicita, J (2002) 'Sustainability Education and Australian Universities', *Environmental Education Research*, vol 8, no 4, pp475–492

Tight, M (1998a) 'Education, Education, Education! The version of lifelong learning in the Kennedy, Fearing and Fryer reports', *Oxford Review of Education*, vol 24, no 4, pp473–485

Tight, M (1998b) 'Lifelong Learning: Opportunity or Compulsion?', *British Journal of Educational Studies*, vol 46, no 3, pp251–263

Tomlinson, S (2001) *Education in a Post-Welfare Society*, Buckingham, Open University Press

Toyne, P (1993) *Environmental Responsibility: An Agenda for Further and Higher Education* (the Toyne Report), Report of a Committee on Environmental Education in Further and Higher Education, appointed by the Department for Education and the Welsh Office, London, HMSO

UNCED (1992) *Earth Summit 1992*, UNCED, Rio de Janeiro, London, Regency

Universities UK (2002) 'Response to DfES Discussion Paper on Higher Education', December, Universities UK, Accessed 20 December 2002, www.universitiesuk. ac.uk/discussion/consultation_response_text.pdf

Warwick, D (1999a) 'Globalisation: the challenges and opportunities for UK Higher Education', Speech by Diana Warwick, CVCP Chief Executive to the Seventh Annual Association of University Administrators Conference, 29 March, www.universitiesuk.ac.uk/speeches/show.asp?sp=23

Warwick, D (1999b) 'The Future Business of Universities', Speech by Diana Warwick, CVCP Chief Executive to the Association of Business Schools, 23 March, www. universitiesuk.ac.uk/speeches/show.asp?sp=21

WCED (1987) *Our Common Future*, Oxford, Oxford University Press

Ziguras, C (2002) 'GATS goes to school', *New Internationalist*, no 349, September, p7

Chapter 15

Politics and Sustainable Development

Robert Garner

INTRODUCTION

Sustainable development is, pre-eminently, a political concept. Politics is centred on recognizing competing interests and values, and the mechanism whereby attempts are made at reconciliation. Finding a balance – between the interests of humans and the rest of nature; between present and future generations; between the North and the South; between economic prosperity and environmental protection – provides the crucial political context of, and the subject matter of the academic political science contribution to, sustainable development. There is still a tendency for issues of development to be separate from the study of sustainability or environmentalism in the study of politics. This is partly a result of academic turf disputes and the needs of specialization. Equally significantly, it reflects the uneasy relationship between development and environmental protection. Sustainable development represents a political compromise, offering the prospect of continuing development particularly in the South at the same time as sustainability or environmental protection. For some radical or 'dark' Greens, if development is taken to mean economic growth then it becomes incompatible with any meaningful sense of environmental protection.

SUSTAINABILITY IN THE POLITICS CURRICULUM

If we focus on the sustainability dimension, it is evident that the 'greening' of the politics curriculum has continued at a steady pace during the past decade or so. Students of politics had previously examined issues relating to the environment; but what distinguished this earlier work was its tendency to utilize environmental themes in order to illustrate mainstream preoccupations, such as the role of pressure groups (Kimber and Richardson, 1974) and theories of power (Crenson, 1971). During the later period, environmental politics emerged as a distinct sub-field of the discipline. Many politics departments now have at least one member of staff willing and able to offer environmental politics courses, and some, such as the department at Keele, have a particular strength in the area. Likewise, the Political Studies Association, the major professional body for political scientists in the UK, now has a specialist Green Politics group, and the number of panels focusing on the issue at the annual conference has increased. There is also a specialist journal called *Environmental Politics*, which has published four editions a year since 1992.

The study of environmental politics has emerged for obvious reasons. The intensification of perennial environmental problems – such as air and water pollution – the growing incidence of environmental disasters, and the relatively recent recognition of global problems such as climate change and ozone depletion have helped to push environmental issues to the top of the political agenda. Accompanying these problems, and at least partly caused by them, has been growing public interest in the quality of the natural environment. Thus, governments have been unable to ignore the staggering rise in the membership of new and old environmental groups during the last two decades or so, or the vociferous public concern over specific issues such as the building of new roads and the export of live animals. Political scientists, too, have, rightly, been unable to ignore these developments.

The study of environmental politics, however, still has something of a 'Cinderella' status. Typically, courses exist as options in the third year of degree programmes and as modules on MA courses. There has been less success in integrating environmental themes within traditional politics courses. This can be explained by two main factors. First, there is the simple generational point that older academics, who obviously provide the leadership in most departments, tend to work in more traditional areas of the discipline; some, at least, may be reticent to employ younger colleagues working in the environmental area and even more reticent to consider integrating environmental themes within the mainstream politics syllabus. Secondly, and more importantly, the subject matter of environmental politics cross-cuts the traditional demarcations in the discipline. In order to market themselves, young scholars are more often than not encouraged to specialize as political theorists or as political scientists or international relationists, and are thus less likely to be tempted into adopting the holistic approach that a study of environmental politics demands.

STRANDS OF ENVIRONMENTAL POLITICS

The fragmented nature of environmental politics is reflected in the fact that it is possible to identify four main dimensions, which this section explores in turn. It is useful that these four dimensions are now covered in a growing number of text books on the subject, the four best known being Carter (2001), Connelly and Smith (1999), Garner (2000a), and Young (1993).

The political sociology of the environment

The first strand involves the input of *political sociology*, a discipline that seeks to analyse the interface between the state and society. Here, the main aim has been to explain the rise of environmentalism as a political issue. Clearly, as was pointed out earlier, the role of objective environmental problems is an import- ant explanatory variable. What distinguishes a *social scientific* study of the environment from a merely technical preoccupation is that, at least to some degree, one can explain the rise of environmental concern independently of the objective facts of environmental degradation. Thus, sociologists have sought to emphasize the importance of changing cultural values (Inglehart, 1977, 1990), structural changes to post-war Western society (Cotgrove and Duff, 1980, 1981) and the activities of the media and environmental pressure groups in explaining the existence of a public much more attentive to environ- mental issues. Linked to this is the attempt to apply psephological techniques to explain the electoral record of Green parties (see, for instance, Rudig, 1985).

Work done on the environmental movement also occurs from a political sociology perspective. There are relatively few book-length texts (see Kimber and Richardson, 1974; Lowe and Goyder, 1983; Doherty, 2002). There is some focus on particular strands of the movement, leading one to ask whether 'movements' rather than a single unitary 'movement' are a more apt nomen- clature. Some of the literature is concerned with the question of whether the environmental movement is best regarded as an example of a new social movement (Jordan and Maloney, 1997); others concentrate on direct action as a particular tactic (Doherty, 1999), whereas still other choose to tackle the international environmental movement (McCormick, 1992). Following Man- cur Olson's groundbreaking study (Olson, 1965), which challenged the ability of cause groups to attract members because of their inability to offer selective incentives, recruiting and mobilizing members has been the preoccupation of some researchers (Jordan and Maloney, 1997).

Environmental public policy

The second dimension of environmental politics is best described as environ- mental public policy. Although interlinked, there is a distinction between the study of political processes, on the one hand, and the technical character of policy instruments, on the other. There is a *politics* of the environment precisely because widely perceived 'problems', however much they are scientifically validated, do not always result in a positive political response. The political scientist must seek to explain why decision-makers adopt one position rather than another. This involves examining the complex and often-concealed relationships between governmental and non-governmental actors and identi- fying the conflicts of interests that environmental decision-making inevitably produces. Furthermore, the interaction between these actors must be seen in the context of the particular historical, social, economic and scientific contexts within which it occurs.

Adopting particular general approaches (such as rational choice theory), macro-theories of the state (such as pluralism, elitism or Marxism) or micro- theories (such as policy network analysis) is useful here, although such theory application has so far been under-explored in the case of environmental decision-making. One strand that has played an increasingly important role in the environmental politics literature is the so-called 'ecological modernization' approach (see Dryzek, 1997, Chapters 7 and 8; Hajer, 1997; Weale, 1992). In some ways this approach is an attempt to operationalize sustainable development at a national level, its central pillar being a challenge to the assumption that there is a trade-off to be made between environmental protection and economic growth. Such a trade-off has been an article of faith for many radical Greens, influenced strongly by the *Limits to Growth* report published by a group of academics during the early 1970s (Meadows et al, 1972). By contrast, ecological modernization offers the prospect of sustainable growth through the greater use of renewable resources, increased conservation, the production of pollution-control technology and the recognition that environmental degradation has negative economic consequences.

The policy instrument's literature has tended to focus on the benefits of an integrated, holistic and precautionary approach as opposed to a fragmented and reactive one. Thus, building in an environmental dimension to the whole range of governmental activities, where environmental problems are addressed at the outset, is seen as preferable to a scenario where the environmental *consequences* of governmental decision-making are dealt with almost as an afterthought. Two other prominent policy instrument issues are worth mentioning here. First, there is the debate between exponents of informally imposed regulatory pollution standards, on the one hand, and the enforcement of minimum emission standards, on the other. The former (reliant upon a flexible and non-confrontational relationship between regulator and regulated) has traditionally been characteristic of the British approach, while the latter (emphasizing statutory and non-negotiable rules inevitably producing greater confrontation and often involving the intervention of the courts) is most evident in the US and, increasingly, Western Europe (Vogel, 1986). Second, the validity of a regulatory approach to pollution control has been challenged by advocates of economic instruments who argue that the environment can best be protected by providing incentives (a tax on leaded petrol being the obvious example) within market mechanisms (Pearce et al, 1989, 1993).

The environment and international relations

Given the distinctly cross-national nature of environmental problems, the international politics of the environment (including the nature of international agreements and the role played by the European Union) has, not surprisingly, produced a sizeable literature (see Brenton, 1994; Elliot, 1998; Hurrell and Kingsbury, 1992; Paterson, 2001; Porter and Brown, 1996; Vogler and Imber, 1996). Above all, of course, the environmental debate is supranational in character because it is inextricably interwoven with the relationship between North and South. If not quite representing a new theoretical approach to international relations theory, case studies of international environmental agreements do provide a means of further testing the validity of a variety of empirical theories, from the traditional realist approach through the more internationalist liberal institutionalist approach, to newer approaches based on feminism, political economy and critical theory.

The need for supranational agreements in the environmental field is obvious and urgent, particularly with the relatively recent identification of genuinely global problems, such as ozone depletion and global warming. Many multilateral environmental agreements do, of course, exist; but a judgement on the progress made so far ultimately depends upon the perceived severity of the problems, as well as the theoretical approach one utilizes. From a realist perspective, emphasizing the pre-eminence of nation states, such agreements are extremely difficult to establish (Dryzek, 1987, Chapter 6); therefore, the limited achievements made at international gatherings – exemplified by the 1992 Earth Summit held in Rio and the 2002 World Summit on Sustainable Development (WSSD) in Johannesburg – are wholly expected and may even have exceeded expectations.

An alternative pluralist or liberal-institutionalist model of international relations, on the other hand, points to an emerging centre of influence – based on international organization, non-governmental organizations (NGOs) and epistemic communities with an interest in particular environmental problems – that has emerged to challenge the influence of the nation state. One major study of global warming politics, for instance, argues that this alternative model is borne out by the empirical evidence (Paterson, 1996). The decline of the sovereign state, however, is not necessarily compatible with sustainability because it can lead to increased influence for globally organized economic interests (Williams, 1996).

Whatever the theoretical framework adopted, there are clearly a number of variables that help to determine the effectiveness of international environmental regimes. These include the identification of a problem that needs resolving; the scope of the problem; the sacrifices (particularly of an economic nature) that are required and the degree of flexibility built into a treaty; and the effectiveness of implementation and enforcement procedures. Added together, these variables go a long way towards explaining why, for instance, a reasonably successful agreement on ozone depletion has been negotiated, whereas a similarly rigorous agreement on global warming has remained elusive. Ozone depletion, unlike global warming, is universally accepted as a problem, is uni-causal in nature and involves a much lower level of economic sacrifice.

The environment and political theory

Political theorists have shown much more interest in the environment than other sub-sectors of the discipline (for general accounts see Barry, 1999; Dobson, 2000; Dryzek, 1997; Eckersley, 1992; Hayward, 1995, 1998). Indeed, Green political theory is now becoming an established part of the syllabus. The political theory of the environment involves a complex web of interrelated themes – involving both empirical and normative theory – and it is important to briefly set out what these are. Very basically, the political theory of the environment is grounded in a distinction between a reformist, so-called 'light green', approach and a radical, so-called 'dark green', approach. The light green position (sometimes described as 'technocentric' in orientation) sees environmentalism as a single-issue cause whose objectives can be achieved with modifications to existing industrial society. The dark green position (sometimes described as 'eco-centric' in orientation) rejects this reformist approach, arguing instead that only a radical restructuring of industrial society, and the creation of a new value system relegating the human species from its predominant position, can provide adequate protection for the planet.

Scholarly exchanges have occurred on various aspects of the light/dark divide. First, exponents of the dark green 'limits to growth' school have been challenged by the ecological modernizers, encountered above, who suggest that it is empirically incorrect to assume that there is an inevitable trade-off between economic growth and environmental protection. Dark green radicals retort by suggesting, on normative grounds, that a society based on Green values (egalitarianism, participatory democracy, respect for humans and the rest of nature) is preferable to one dominated by anonymity, materialism and acquisitiveness (Schumacher, 1973). A related debate concerns the viability of decentralized political forms, which most radical Greens seem to prefer. To what extent can self-sufficient egalitarian communities, approximating to an anarchist model, achieve the coordination necessary for the alleviation of environmental problems; and, if they are incapable of doing so, to what extent should the state be brought back in as a facilitator (see Goodin, 1992)?

Central to the dark green position is an 'eco-centric' ethic which seeks to impute 'intrinsic value' to nature (Fox, 1995; Naess, 1973). This can be contrasted with the 'anthropocentric' – or human-centred – ethic characteristic of light green environmentalism (Passmore, 1980). An eco-centric ethic is difficult to justify, not least because of the powerful argument that sentiency, the capacity to experience pleasure and pain, would seem to represent the most appropriate ground for moral standing or worth, thereby denying it to non-sentient parts of nature. Even if it can be justified intellectually, selling politically the idea that trees, rocks and mountains have intrinsic value presents even more problems. As a result, some Green political theorists, sympathetic to the radical agenda, have sought to challenge the necessity of an eco-centric ethic by attempting to put the case for an enlightened anthropocentrism in which it is in *our* interests to preserve the environment (Barry, 1999; Dobson, 2000; Hayward, 1998; Norton, 1991). Whether an enlightened anthropocentrism can completely eliminate the need for protecting nature for its own sake is a moot point (Garner, 2000b); but, clearly, it can take us a long way down the environmental protection road.

A final key question in this section is the extent to which Green political theory represents a distinct approach to politics, one that can be separated from traditional ideologies such as liberalism or socialism. Clearly, the status of Green political thought does depend a great deal upon answering this question affirmatively. The fact that advocates of a whole range of traditions – Marxism, feminism and conservatism included – have sought to incorporate Green themes and that there are now sub-divisions (such as eco-socialism and eco-feminism) within traditional ideologies would seem to indicate the absence of a distinct 'Green' political thought.

Whether there is a distinctive Green political thought would seem to depend upon the answers to two separate questions. The first concerns the extent to which Green thought has features that provide a challenge to mainstream political thinking. Two such 'blind spots' are apparent. The anthropocentric basis of traditional political ideology (of left and right) is fundamentally challenged by the eco-centric ethic of radical Green thinking, however difficult it may be to justify such a position. Furthermore, the emphasis on the limits to the Earth's resources and carrying capacity offers a distinct corrective to the productivist character of both liberalism and socialism.

The second question we need to ask is how far there are distinct social and political arrangements (for instance, centralization or decentralization; democracy or authoritarianism; common ownership or state ownership) that are mandated by a Green approach to politics. The answer to this second question is not so clear-cut. We saw above, for instance, that it is not apparent that decentralized political forms are appropriate from a Green perspective. The most that can be said here is that the choice of political structures available to Greens is by no means open (authoritarian solutions, for instance, must surely be rejected); but, conversely – at least without further, much more convincing, argument – the achievement of Green objectives does not point to a specific political solution.

CONCLUSION

The arrival and development of environmental politics and, more broadly, sustainable development as an academic discipline reflects the rise of problems which governments must grapple with if the human species is to survive. There is a *politics* of the environment because the existence of objectively defined problems is mediated through social and political processes. Technical and scientific solutions to most environmental problems are readily available to us. What has been lacking is the political knowledge necessary to provide us with the ability to utilize them to the best effect.

The future of the politics of sustainable development within academia is now assured, not least because of the increasing number of research students coming through the system who have chosen to focus on environmental themes within political sociology, public policy, international relations and, most notably, political thought. Just as the conventional wisdom holds that the integration of environmental concerns throughout the range of governmental activities is essential, at the academic level, too, integrating environmental issues within mainstream politics teaching is the best means of ensuring its continued growth and vitality.

REFERENCES

Barry, J (1999) *Rethinking Green Politics: Nature, Virtue and Progress*, London, Sage

Blowers, A (1984) *Something in the Air: Corporate Power and the Environment*, London, Harper and Row

Blowers, A (1987) 'Transition or Transformation? Environmental Policy Under Thatcher', *Public Administration*, vol 65, pp227–294

Brenton, T (1994) *The Greening of Machiavelli: The Evolution of International Environmental Politics*, London, Earthscan

Carter, N (2001) *The Politics of the Environment: Ideas, Activism, Policy*, Cambridge, Cambridge University Press

Connelly, J and Smith, G (1999) *Politics and the Environment: From Theory to Practice*, London, Routledge

Cotgrove, S and Duff, A (1980) 'Environmentalism, Middle Class Radicalism and Politics', *Sociological Review*, vol 28, pp333–351

Cotgrove, S and Duff, A (1981) 'Environmentalism, Values and Social Change', *British Journal of Sociology*, vol 32, pp92–110

Crenson, M A (1971) *The Unpolitics of Air Pollution*, Baltimore, The John Hopkins Press

Curtice, J (1989) 'The 1989 European Elections: Protest or Green Tide?', *Electoral Studies*, vol 8, pp217–230

Dobson, A (ed) (1991) *The Green Reader*, London, Andre Deutsch

Dobson, A (2000) *Green Political Thought*, third edition, London, Unwin Hyman

Doherty, B (1999) 'Paving the way: The rise of direct action against road building and the changing character of British environmentalism', *Political Studies*, vol 42, pp275–291

Doherty, B (2002) *Ideas and Actions in the Green Movement*, London, Routledge

Dryzek, J (1987) *Rational Ecology*, Oxford, Blackwells

Dryzek, J (1997) *The Politics of the Earth: Environmental Discourses*, Oxford, Oxford University Press

Eckersley, R (1992) *Environmentalism and Political Theory*, London, University College London

Elliot, L (1998) *The Global Politics of the Environment*, Basingstoke, Macmillan

Flynn, A and Lowe, P(1992) 'The Greening of the Tories: The Conservative Party and the Environment', in Rudig, W (ed) *Green Politics Two*, Edinburgh, Edinburgh University Press, pp9–36

Fox, W (1995) *Toward a Transpersonal Ecology: Developing New Foundations for Environmentalism*, Totnes, Resurgence

Garner, R (1993) *Animals, Politics and Morality*, Manchester, Manchester University Press

Garner, R (2000a) *Environmental Politics*, Basingstoke, Macmillan

Garner, R (2000b) 'The scope of green realism', *Contemporary Politics*, vol 6, no 2, pp185–190

Goodin, R E (1992) *Green Political Theory*, Cambridge, Polity Press

Haigh, N (1990) *EEC Environmental Policy and Britain*, second edition, London, Longman

Hajer, M (1997) *The Politics of Environmental Discourse: Ecological Modernization and the Policy Process*, Oxford, Clarendon Press

Hayward, T (1995) *Ecological Thought: An Introduction*, Cambridge, Polity Press

Hayward, T (1998) *Political Theory and Ecological Values*, Cambridge, Polity Press

Hurrell, A and Kingsbury, B (1992) *The International Politics of the Environment*, Oxford, Clarendon Press

Inglehart, R (1977) *The Silent Revolution: Changing Values and Political Styles Among Western Publics*, Princeton, Princeton University Press

Inglehart, R (1990) 'Values, Ideology and Cognitive Mobilization in New Social Movements', in Dalton, R J and Kuechler, M (eds) *Challenging the Political Order: New Social and Political Movements in Western Democracies*, Cambridge, Polity Press, pp43–66

Jordan, A (1993) 'Integrated Pollution Control and the Evolving Style and Structure of Environmental Regulation in the UK', *Environmental Politics*, vol 2, no 3, pp405–427

Jordan, G and Maloney, W (1997) *The Protest Business*, Manchester, Manchester University Press

Kimber, R and Richardson, J J (eds) (1974) *Campaigning for the Environment*, London, Routledge and Kegan Paul

Lowe, P and Flynn, A (1989) 'Environmental Politics and Policy in the 1980s', in Moham, J (ed) *The Political Geography of Contemporary Britain*, Basingstoke, Macmillan, pp255–279

Lowe, P and Goyder, J (1983) *Environmental Groups in Politics*, London, Allen and Unwin

Lowe, P and Rudig, W (1986) 'Review Article: Political Ecology and the Social Sciences – The State of the Art', *British Journal of Political Science*, vol 16, pp513–550

Martell, L (1994) *Ecology and Society*, Cambridge, Polity Press

McCormick, J (1991) *British Politics and the Environment*, London, Earthscan

McCormick, J (1992) *The Global Environmental Movement*, London, Belhaven

Meadows, D H, Meadows, D L, Randers, J and Behrens III, W (1972) *The Limits to Growth*: A Report for the Club of Rome's Project on the Predicament of Mankind, New York, Universe

Naess, A (1973) 'The shallow and the deep, long range ecology movement. A summary', *Inquiry*, vol 16, pp95–100

Norton, B (1991) *Toward Unity Among Environmentalists*, Oxford, Oxford University Press

Olson, M (1965) *The Logic of Collective Action*, Cambridge, Massachusetts, Harvard University Press

O'Riordan, T (1976) *Environmentalism*, London, Pion

Passmore, J (1980) *Man's Responsibility for Nature*, second edition, London, Duckworth

Paterson, M (1996) *Global Warming and Global Politics*, London, Routledge

Paterson, M (2001) *Understanding Global Environmental Politics: Domination, Accumulation, Resistance*, Basingstoke, Palgrave

Pearce, D, Markandya, A and Barbier, E B (1989) *Blueprint For a Green Economy*, London, Earthscan

Pearce, D et al (1993) *Blueprint 3: Measuring Sustainable Development*, London, Earthscan

Porter, G and Brown, J (1996) *Global Environmental Politics*, second edition, Boulder, Co, Westview

Rootes, C A (1991) 'Environmentalism and Political Competition: The British Greens in the 1989 Elections to the European Parliament', *Politics*, vol 11, no 2, pp39–44

Rudig, W (1985) 'The Greens in Europe: Ecological Parties and the European Elections of 1984', *Parliamentary Affairs*, vol 38, no 1, pp56–72

Rudig, W and Franklin, M N (1991) 'Green Prospects: The Future of Green Parties in Britain, France and Germany', in Rudig, W (ed) *Green Politics Two*, Edinburgh, Edinburgh University Press, pp37–58

Rydin, Y (1993) *The British Planning System: An Introduction*, Basingstoke, Macmillan

Sandbach, F (1980) *Environment, Ideology and Policy*, Oxford, Blackwell

Schumacher, E F (1973) *Small is Beautiful: Economics as if People Mattered*, London, Blond and Briggs

Vogel, D (1986) *National Styles of Regulation: Environmental Policing in Great Britain and the United States*, Ithaca, Cornell University Press

Vogler, J and Imber, M (eds) (1996) *The Environment and International Relations*, London, Routledge

Ward, H (1990) 'Environmental Politics and Policy', in Dunleavy, P et al (ed) *Developments in British Politics 3*, Basingstoke: Macmillan, pp221–245

Weale, A (1992) *The New Politics of Pollution,* Manchester, Manchester University Press

Williams, M (1996) 'International political economy and global environmental change', in Vogler, J and Imber, M (eds) *The Environment and International Relations*, London, Routledge, pp41– 58

Yearley, S (1992) *The Green Case,* London, Routledge

Young, S C (1993) *The Politics of the Environment,* Manchester, Baseline Books

Chapter 16

Geography

Phil McManus

Sustainable development presents a major challenge to geography to demonstrate its capability and relevance to what may be the most important public issue of our time. . . Geographers somehow missed the opportunity to be the central unifying discipline for the environmental movement in the 1960s. The opportunity has risen again in the sustainable development thrust. (Manning, 1990, pp290, 299)

INTRODUCTION

Geography is an ideal discipline for the academic advancement and promulgation of the concept of sustainable development. This is due to the long historical involvement of geographers in the investigating environmental processes and nature–society relations. There is, however, a sense that geographers have missed the opportunity to be at the forefront of research and teaching on sustainable development. In a recent review of geographical work on environmental issues from policy to political economy, Castree (2002a) omitted all discussion on sustainable development or sustainability. In fact, the terms were not used at all in the article. This omission, in an otherwise excellent and comprehensive review of current geographical research on the environment, speaks volumes about the failure of the sustainable development discourse to permeate the discipline of geography. It is a profound omission if we accept the claim by Castree (2002a, p359) that 'the most "practical" thing most of us do with our environmental research is to communicate it to our students'. Perhaps the relative absence of geographical input into sustainable development debates is symptomatic of a larger concern about the policy relevance of many sub-areas of geography (Peck, 1999; Martin, 2001; Cutter et al, 2002).

Despite the evidence of some important work by geographers on sustainability, this chapter commences from the position that geographers can and should be doing more. Why have geographers not engaged in sustainability debates as much as may be expected given its potential centrality to their discipline? Are there opportunities for geographers to contribute to education about sustainability in ways that are not happening currently in geography, and in ways that draw upon the strengths of geography *vis à vis* other fields of enquiry?

This chapter addresses the above questions by exploring the different approaches to studying nature–society relationships that are the basis of much work in geography, at least within the English-speaking world. This exploration demonstrates what work has been done by geographers, even if it is not under the banner of 'sustainable development'. This investigation, however, only partly reveals possible reasons why geography may not have been significantly altered by the discourse of sustainable development. It is necessary to understand how research on sustainable development and related environmental research within geography is currently translated into education about sustainable development. Importantly, it also raises questions about how these factors could be translated into education about the more radical notion of sustainability.

Before looking at the different approaches to nature–society relationships, it is worth noting that the discourse of sustainable development emerged from a history of eco-development (introduced at the Stockholm Conference in 1972); the *World Conservation Strategy* (IUCN/UNEP/WWF, 1980); and was popularized by the World Commission on Environment and Development (WCED, 1987). All of the above operate or are focused at the international level and address policy issues largely within the existing political structures. The language of sustainable development is the language of policy and of optimism (Manning, 1990). The WCED definition of sustainable development as 'development that meets the needs of the present without compromising the ability of future generations to meet their own needs' (WCED, 1987, pp8, 43) is adopted in this chapter. There are various national definitions of sustainable development or, in the case of Australia, the term ecologically sustainable development. The term sustainability often implies a more radical approach to questions about integrating ecology, society and economy than does the mainstream concept of balance between three equally sized circles, which is the WCED model. The latter part of this chapter looks in more detail about what type of sustainable development/sustainability education geography students are currently receiving, and discusses the normative question about what type of education they should be receiving.

GEOGRAPHICAL STUDY OF THE ENVIRONMENT

McKeown-Ice (1994) described four avenues of enquiry through which geographers study the environment. These are study of the natural environment, study of human impact on the environment, study of environmental influences on human behaviours and the study of the cultural perceptions of the environment. This chapter argues that these ways of studying the environment are often very different research agendas, undertaken by different types of geographers and using different ontologies, as well as different methods and techniques. They are not necessarily incompatible, and it is possible for an individual researcher to link the above avenues of enquiry in a single research project.

How could these different avenues of enquiry exist within a single broad discipline that ranges from fluvial geomorphology and biogeography to areas such as the new cultural geography of animals, the geography of music, transport geography and medical geography? The late 19th century saw the emergence of debates about what geography ought to be, and how geographers should work (Kropotkin, 1996). By the early 20th century, geography in the English-speaking world had become focused upon the study of regions. The main tool for geographers was the map. The work by geographers on human–environment relationships focused on studying the natural environment (what came to be called physical geography), and on studying human impact upon the environment and the environmental influences on human behaviour (both the realm of human geography). Cultural perceptions of the environment were not a major avenue of enquiry in the early 20th century. If anything, the work of geographers tended to stray into environmental determinism, as seen in the work of Friedrich Ratzel and the early work of Carl Sauer (see Herbert and Johnston, 1978; Livingstone, 1992). By the end of World War II, this form of geography, and geopolitics, was largely discredited. It was replaced by quantitative geography that was based upon positivism. The development of computers facilitated this quantitative movement in many sub-areas of geography. Systems thinking was the dominant trend by the late 1960s.

An important change in geography occurred in 1973 with the publication of David Harvey's book *Social Justice and the City* (Harvey, 1973). Whereas Harvey (1969) represented the zenith of systems thinking, his 1973 publication was grounded in Marxist theory and inspired many a generation of young human geographers to engage with Marxist ideas.

This was particularly important for geographical literature on the environment. Moving from a chronological approach to an overview of geographical literature on the building blocks of sustainable development (namely, environment, society/culture and economy), it is fair to say that the Marxist-inspired approaches to understanding the environment particularly influenced geographers during the 1970s and 1980s. Harvey (1974, p273) wrote that 'ideas about population, environment and resources are not neutral. They are political in origin and have political effects'. Smith (1984) updated Marx's belief that original nature no longer existed and that humans produced nature in the image of capital, a process he called 'the production of nature'. Geographical writing during this era tended to focus upon nature as being increasingly produced by humans in the image of capitalism (Fitzsimmons, 1989).

In 1989, Margaret Fitzsimmons's seminal article, 'The matter of nature' was published in the journal *Antipode*. Fitzsimmons (1989, p106) challenged geographers to address the 'peculiar silence on the question of social Nature'. She identified the silence in geographical literature as being due, in part, to the location of most academic geographers in cities, but noted that geographers had no such silence around the concept of space. Many geographers have addressed the challenge issued by Fitzsimmons. A number of geographers have focused on the social construction of nature (Castree, 1995; Demeritt,

1996; Gerber, 1997). Those works that could be said to be inspired by Marxist approaches, such as regulation theory and political ecology, include Bridge and McManus (2000), Bryant (1997), Howitt (2001) and Castree (2002b).

These are not the only approaches to understanding the foundations of sustainable development, nor are these the only areas of research. Since Fitzsimmons (1989), there have been many human geography articles that question nature and people's cultural perceptions of the environment. These range from business perceptions of the environment (Eden, 1998), and scientific and political perceptions of issues such as climate change (Bulkeley, 2001; Demeritt, 2001) to issues of environmental justice (Towers, 2000) and notions of hybridity (Whatmore, 1999). Geographers have also contributed to work on environmental history (Powell, 1996, McManus, 2002) and to work on environmental management (Bryant and Wilson, 1998, Howitt, 2001).

Gregory et al (2002) note that physical geographers have contributed significantly to environmental research. These authors argue that 'physical geography globally could have a pivotal role in the advancement of sustainable human systems' and go on to say that the advancement of sustainable human systems 'could provide a unifying theme for geography as a whole because it is embedded firmly in the unique qualities of a strong geographical approach to the solution of environmental problems' (Gregory et al, 2002, p137). It is important to note that these authors are using the word 'could' rather than 'have to' in identifying a role for geographers in relation to sustainable development. In summary, geographers have produced useful and important work on the building blocks of sustainable development, but have not embraced the concept despite being urged to do so by the presidents of various national geographical associations and by other individual academics. To understand why this may have been the case, it is useful to look at how the very influential report of the WCED (1987) was received by geographers.

OUR COMMON FUTURE AND BEYOND

By the time that *Our Common Future*, the report of the WCED, was released in 1987, geography had a long history of understanding human–nature relations. Given the timing of the WCED report in relation to the generational influence of Marxist geography, and the publication of Fitzsimmons's article between the WCED report and the 1992 Earth Summit in Rio, perhaps it is not surprising that geography were not as influenced as other fields of enquiry by the sustainable development discourse.

There were, however, other influences within and outside of geography that explain why geography has not embraced sustainable development, while impressive work has been done within geography on the components of sustainable development. A geographer at the forefront of sustainable development concern, Bill Adams, has neatly summarized the problem faced by many geographers who would otherwise adopt the concept of sustainable development:

> *Although it has exciting potential in policy terms, the concept of sustainability. . .has little rigour to offer geographers anxious to get an intellectual grip on issues of environment and development. Here, too, however, sustainability cannot be ignored, for it has few equals as a challenge to geographers to develop their theoretical ideas.* (Adams, 1999, p132)

Academic geography has tended to question the concept of sustainable development. Rather than presenting it as the goal posts for policy implementation, it has overwhelmingly perceived the Brundtland Commission concept of sustainable development as one environmental philosophy, albeit an important one given its impact upon the wider academic and policy environment, among competing environmental philosophies (McManus, 1996).

Work on sustainable development with an international development focus by geographers includes Adams (1995), Middleton et al (1993) and Kirkby et al (1995). Sally Eden (1996, 1998) has been at the forefront of critical analysis of business responses to the sustainable development discourse. Evidence of the incorporation of sustainable development within geography includes the addition of a chapter of sustainable development in later editions of books by geographers (for example, Johnston, 1996). Despite this work by geographers on researching, critiquing or promulgating the concept of sustainable development, and despite calls for specific work within sub-disciplines of geography (Lake and Hanson, 2000), arguably geographers have been more critical than many other disciplines about the components that comprise sustainable development – namely, the social, economic and environmental inputs.

If Sneddon (2000) and others are correct about geographers missing the sustainable development boat, the important question is why has geography not taken the lead in developing and promulgating the idea of sustainable development given that many leading geographers have seen this as a 'natural' area for geographers (Manning, 1990; Wilbanks, 1994)? This chapter argues that there are four main reasons for this failure. These reasons are the history of geographical ideas, the structure of geography departments, the focus upon new technologies in geography and the restructuring of the higher education sector in a number of countries.

As identified in the preceding section, leading geographers who may otherwise have been willing to embrace the concept of sustainable development as popularized by the Brundtland Commission were, in fact, most critical of this notion. Harvey (1996) wrote about 'mainstream' sustainable development and even the more radical notion of sustainability from a critical perspective. The 'standard view' of environmental management, according to Harvey (1996), rests upon the assumption that environmental problems are caused by market failure and intervention happens after the event. While sustainability discourse is proactive, the mainstream sustainable development discourse does not address the systematic issues within capitalism and is, therefore, dismissed by geographers such as Harvey (1996) in favour of an environmental justice approach to fight against the environmental inequities of capitalism.

Under the heading of 'geographical ideas', one could also incorporate the notions of normativity and scale. The concept of sustainable development, as popularized by the Brundtland Commission, balances the needs of the economy, society and the environment and is focused at the global scale. It is a normative concept about what the world *should* be aiming for. Geographers have tended to research the world as it currently exists (filtered through their own values). Even the more normative approaches, such as the Marxist-inspired geography of social justice, had an emphasis on demonstrating the existence of, and explaining the causes of, injustice, poverty and oppression (Harvey, 1973).

By the late 1980s, there was a growing reaction within human geography by younger researchers to universal doctrines, whether Marxist inspired or the social democracy of the Brundtland Commission. The recognition of cultural differences, the deconstruction of discourse and even the embryonic questioning of the human in human geography did not auger well for the acceptance of the universalist, normative discourse of sustainable development. This explanation fits with the observation by Johnston (1978, p197) that:

> *An academic discipline may reflect in its concerns and work the issues of contemporary society, but it is also a society itself, with its own norms of scholarly behaviour that determine how members react to the demands from the external environment.*

Far from being a common future, geographers appear to have moved away from universal approaches to understanding and changing the world. Cutter et al (2002) have expressed their concern about the various directions in geographical research by trying to refocus geographers upon what they consider to be important issues for geographical study. This is a major challenge, given the influence of geographical ideas about specificity and nuanced research, and the changes that have occurred within the discipline of geography and within the university sector in various countries.

GEOGRAPHY IN HIGHER EDUCATION

While the history of ideas within a discipline is important, it is not sufficient to explain the rejection of concerns regarding the external environment. In the case of sustainable development, geographers have not been at the forefront of sustainability research partly because of the structure of the discipline. Broadly divided into physical and human geographers, sustainability concerns about integrating the physical environment and the social and economic domains did not sit comfortably with either group of geographers. An appropriate image may be of a doubles' tennis team, both calling 'yours' as the sustainability ball passes between them.

Within geography, the introduction of geographic information systems (GIS) had a profound impact upon understanding geography, the structure of academic departments and the way in which resources were distributed within departments. Openshaw (1991) went so far as to suggest that GIS would be the new focus of unification for geographers. While events have subsequently proven Openshaw to be incorrect about unification, it is clear that GIS is often being introduced as a tool in many areas of geography, ranging from coastal studies to indigenous issues and sustainable development (see Engle, 2001; Open GIS Consortium Inc, 2002). There is considerable demand for GIS education from students because they believe, generally accurately, that this is a useful skill to assist their employment prospects. There have been debates in developing geographical curricula about the role of GIS, especially regarding whether all geographers should be required to learn at least basic GIS (similar to the requirement to learn statistics during the 1960s and early 1970s). To the best of my knowledge no such debates have occurred in geography about the need to incorporate sustainable development within the education of every geography student.

Finally, these factors have been compounded by recent challenges to universities to become more entrepreneurial and less reliant upon government funding. This has resulted in increased competition for fee-paying international students, the emergence of new courses to attract students and the decision of many students (or their parents) to enroll in courses that are likely to provide lucrative careers. In Australia it has resulted in the demise of each and every geography department and the emergence of merged departments/schools. These are often mergers with geology to create 'geosciences'; but more unusual mergers include the School of Anthropology, Geography and Environmental Science (SAGES) at the University of Melbourne. In the heightened competition for resources, these new structures were not always conducive to introducing sustainable development ideas.

In summary, while there are exceptions, overall, geography has not been a discipline that has expanded in a major way within the past 20 or so years. This has meant that a number of competing demands (such as GIS) on constant or reduced financial resources in real terms has limited the possibilities for the expansion of work on sustainable development. While GIS and sustainable development are not incompatible, little work has been done on their integration within geography. This scenario of constraint is exacerbated by the fact that most geographers who may otherwise have been strong advocates of the concept were, in fact, critical of the idea. At a time when universities were looking for entrepreneurial opportunities and courses, there was little chance that scarce resources were going to be allocated to employ and foster geographers who were critical of sustainable development and the institutions and structures from which the concept emerged.

Teaching Sustainable Development and Sustainability

Given the history of geography, the changing context of the discipline and the character of research within geography related to sustainable development, one would expect that geography has not changed markedly in response to the notion of sustainable development. Although other academic environments, such as the Centre for Urban Planning and Environmental Management at the University of Hong Kong and Architecture at the University of New South Wales (located in Sydney, Australia), have adopted sustainable development as their central concern and restructured their research and teaching accordingly, to the best of my knowledge this has not occurred in geography. While the ability of particular departments at different universities to embrace the concept of sustainable development and restructure their teaching and research is outside the scope of this chapter, it does suggest that further research on these departments may be useful for anybody interested in implementing sustainable development in higher education.

While there appears to be no previous study of the incorporation of sustainable development within higher education geography, or even literature in relevant geography-teaching oriented journals such as the *Journal of Geography*, it seems that geographers have incorporated the notion of sustainable development within their teaching in four main ways. These are to address it within an existing environmental course that is not focused on normative values; to address the concept within a course that is focused on wider development or management concerns; to develop new courses on sustainable development but to interrogate this notion within the course; or to develop a new programme (usually at the postgraduate level) that focuses on sustainable development.

It is common for geography departments to have at least one course that investigates society–nature relationships. This may be an environmental history/geography course or an ethics course that includes environmental issues. An example of an existing environmental course that includes some reference to sustainable development is a geography course on urban ecology led by Gavin Bridge at the University of Oklahoma. Bridge bases the course on the existing and past urban fabric of Norman, Oklahoma, and engages with urban environmental history and urban ecology to reveal the processes that have shaped the city of Norman (Bridge, 2001). Undergraduate teaching in geography at Staffordshire University, UK, includes courses on development, globalization and sustainability, and nature, environment and society. Courses are sometimes identified with a particular geographic location, as in, for example, a geography course at the University of Hong Kong called 'China: Environment and Sustainable Development'.

The second approach is to address sustainable development within a broader management or development-oriented course. Examples of this approach include:

- a second-year resource and environmental management course at the University of Sydney that addresses sustainable development as an idea among a variety of environmental philosophies, ranging from free market environmentalism through to eco-Marxism, eco-anarchism, eco-feminism and deep ecology; these concepts are then applied to environmental issues such as forestry, fishing, population growth and wildlife management;
- a postgraduate course at the University of Colorado in 'Comparative Environmental Studies: Cultural and Political Ecologies of Development and the Environment', which commences with the statement that 'a concern for the relationship between nature and society has been one of the pillars of geographic enquiry' (Bebbington, 2000).

The third approach is to create a new course on sustainable development. This approach was undertaken by me at the University of Bristol in the mid 1990s. It has since been developed in a third-year geography course at the University of Sydney called 'Sustainable Cities and Regional Change'. The notion of sustainability is introduced and interrogated at the beginning of the course; then environmental histories of cities, examples of previous normative approaches to cities and current ideas ranging from urban consolidation to bioregionalism are introduced so that students can think critically about the general desirability of these approaches and their suitability in particular contexts.

The fourth approach is to create a new academic programme that is based upon, or incorporates, the notion of sustainable development. When this does occur, it is usually at the postgraduate level and it may build upon the strengths of a department or school that is formed from a merger of geography and an environment-oriented department. Examples include masters programmes in sustainable development and in sustainability and environmental management at Staffordshire University, and the 'Disaster Management and Sustainable Development' programme run by the Division of Geography and Environmental Management at the University of Northumbria, UK.

As previously mentioned, a number of geography departments have been merged with environmental science and environmental management departments. The implications for geographical education are, often, that an environmental scientist or manager is appointed to the staff to teach, for example, environmental theory, ethics, impact assessment, sustainable development and environmental law. Geography appointments within these merged structures therefore tend to be in areas other than the environment, often to avoid overlap and to ensure that a wide range of geography is offered to students. This gives rise to a situation where students may obtain a broader education about environment and sustainability issues than if the traditional geography departmental structure had continued to exist, while at the same time there may be lingering concerns by some academics about policing the boundaries of disciplines such as geography.

The other major way in which geographical education about sustainability occurs is through the publishing of textbooks and dictionaries. Even if students may not be studying that particular part of the textbook or dictionary, the very existence of chapters devoted to sustainability gives the concept geographical legitimacy in the minds of many students. Recent textbooks where sustainability has figured prominently, and has not simply been pushed to the end of the book, include chapters by Adams (in Cloke et al, 1999) and Urich (in Le Heron et al, 1999). The fourth edition of the widely used *Dictionary of Human Geography* (Johnston, et al, 2000) has a major section on sustainable development (McManus, 2000). Students often use this resource and may follow up on the references used and the suggested reading. These resources are important to legitimate and further the concept of sustainable development within geography.

The above examples of courses and textbooks are not exhaustive. I accept that I have probably overlooked the pertinent work of a number of geographers. In considering the normative part of this chapter (how should sustainable development/sustainability be translated into geography education?) I am conscious that, perhaps, this is already being done far more than I have communicated above.

How Should Sustainable Development Be Taught in Geography?

Given the relative paucity of units of study within geography that focus upon sustainable development, it is worth considering how this concept should be taught. There are many possible answers to the question. Similar to the debates in environmental education about whether education should focus on the environment, the answer is strongly influenced by the value position of the individual academic. Unlike high/secondary school geography, there is no centralized examination, and therefore curricula development in universities is likely to be driven by factors such as the research interests of individual staff; an overall departmental vision of what geography students should be learning; a sense of what potential employers are demanding; and the availability of resources to meet competing demands. The result of combining these factors, and allowing for the various stages in the careers of individual geographers, is a mixture of ideas, content and approaches all coming under the label of 'geography'.

Given the history and nature of the discipline, it is likely that sustainable development will probably be no different than other 'new' areas of geography. Even among the geographers explicitly teaching about sustainable development, there will be a variety of approaches, especially given that some geographers are oriented towards international development while others focus on specific resources in a developed country.

This chapter suggests that teaching sustainable development in geography should involve:

- understanding the history of geographical thought in relation to the environment;
- understanding that the discourse of sustainable development emerged from specific power relations in response to particular concerns at an identifiable moment in history;
- understanding that there are various ways to conceptualize relationships between the environmental, socio-cultural and economic inputs into sustainability;
- understanding that the above terms are themselves meta-terms and open to interrogation;
- understanding how other disciplines have approached the concept and how geographers have incorporated, influenced or ignored this work;
- appreciating the concept of scale in discussions about sustainability.

This list raises questions about the current work that geographers do on nature–society relationships. If the term 'sustainable development' is not used, but the research and teaching of geographers focuses on the components of sustainable development, is this appropriate or sufficient? Should geographers move beyond their comfort zone of exploring and explaining existing nature–society relations (which includes new challenging work on animals and biotechnology) and enter into normative debates about what should be, rather than what is; and even more challenging for some geographers, should they enter debates about how to implement a desired vision?

The list also raises questions about the use of current geographical education on sustainable development/sustainability. If geographers, such as Bill Adams (1999), who research and teach sustainable development believe that the sustainable development literature lacks sufficient rigour, and if past presidents such as Iain Wallace (2002, p105) can critique sustainable development for 'the emptiness of the concept in a world system that remains structurally committed to unlimited economic growth', then there is a gulf between geography and sustainable development thought. This gulf will be reflected in the education of geographers. The question of bridging this gulf suggests three possibilities: geographers adopt the sustainable development concept as it currently exists; other academic disciplines and policy-makers take on board the geographical critiques of sustainable development; or there is a move towards some new ground by both geographers and sustainable development advocates. This last option recognizes the contribution of geographers to providing additional academic rigour to the concept of sustainable development/sustainability, while also making geography more policy relevant (Peck, 1999; Martin, 2001; Cutter et al, 2002) and having an impact beyond teaching our students (Castree, 2002a).

CONCLUSION

The idea of sustainable development is known to many geographers; but it has not been embraced by the discipline as a whole, nor by many of the individual geographers whom one would, perhaps, expect to embrace this concept. As this chapter has demonstrated, the reasons for this situation include the history of geographical thought, the structure and culture of geography departments at universities, the introduction of other appealing geographical ideas and tools, and the changing context of universities in relation to governments and funding models.

The research on sustainable development that has been done in geography is important. This research is incorporated within teaching; but there is no consistent pattern or level of incorporation due to the structure and *modis operandi* of geography departments within universities. A number of geographers have noted that geography is, however, well positioned to engage with the idea of sustainable development. As Adams (1999) recognized, despite its lack of rigour, the notion of sustainable development can contribute substantially to the discipline of geography. Geographers can reciprocate by significantly contributing to the development of thought on sustainability, and to the education of future generations of geographers through the inquisition and promulgation of this important concept. Sustainable development is a challenge to higher education and, possibly, to geography more so than many other disciplines.

ACKNOWLEDGEMENTS

Thank you to Ron Johnston, Gavin Bridge and Eleanor Bruce for their constructive comments on an earlier version of this chapter. Thank you also to Iain Wallace for his assistance with providing a recommended reference. Any remaining errors of fact or interpretation are my responsibility.

REFERENCES

Adams, W (1995) 'Sustainable Development', in Johnston, R, Taylor, P and Watts, M (eds) *Geographies of Global Change: Remapping the World in the Late Twentieth Century*, Oxford, Blackwell: pp354–373

Adams, W (1999) 'Sustainability', in Cloke, P, Crang, P and Goodwin, M (eds) *Introducing Human Geographies*, London, Arnold, pp125–132

Bebbington, T (2000) *Comparative Environmental Studies: Cultural and Political Ecologies of Development and Environment*, www.colorado.edu/geography/courses/geog_6402, accessed 10 March 2003

Bridge, G (2001) 'Everyday ecologies: cities, nature and teaching urban ecology', *Journal of Geography*, vol 100, pp154–165

Bridge, G and McManus, P (2000) Sticks and stones: environmental narratives and discursive regulation in the forestry and mining sectors', *Antipode*, vol 32, pp10–47

Bryant, R (1997) 'Beyond the impasse: the power of political ecology in Third World environmental research', *Area*, vol 29, pp5–19

Bryant, R and Wilson, G (1998) 'Rethinking environmental management', *Progress in Human Geography*, vol 22, pp321–343

Bulkeley, H (2001) 'Governing climate change: The politics of risk society?', *Transactions of the Institute of British Geographers*, NS, vol 26, pp430–447

Castree, N (1995) 'The nature of produced nature', *Antipode*, vol 27, pp12–47

Castree, N (2002a) 'Environmental Issues: From policy to political economy', *Progress in Human Geography*, vol 26, no 3, pp357–365

Castree, N (2002b) 'Marxism and the production of nature', *Capital and Class*, vol 72, pp5–36

Cloke, P, Crang, P and Goodwin, M (eds) (1999) *Introducing Human Geographies*, London, Arnold

Cutter, S, Golledge, R and Graf, W (2002) 'The big questions in geography', *The Professional Geographer*, vol 54, no 3, pp305–317

Demeritt, D (1996) 'Social theory and the reconstitution of science and geography', *Transactions of the Institute of British Geographers* NS, vol 21, pp484–503

Demeritt, D (2001) 'The construction of global warming and the politics of science', *Annals of the Association of American Geographers*, vol 91, pp307–337

Eden, S (1996) *Environmental Issues and Business: Implications of a Changing Agenda*, Chichester, John Wiley and Sons

Eden, S (1998) 'Environmental issues: knowledge, uncertainty and the environment', *Progress in Human Geography*, vol 22, pp425–432

Engle, S (2001) 'Negotiating technology: (Re)considering the use of GIS by Indigenous Peoples', *New Zealand Geographer*, vol 57, pp27–34

Fitzsimmons, M (1989) 'The Matter of Nature', *Antipode*, vol 21, no 1, pp106–120

Gerber, J (1997) 'Beyond dualism: the social construction of nature and the natural and social construction of human beings', *Progress in Human Geography*, vol 21, pp1–17

Gregory, K, Gurnell, A and Petts, G (2002) 'Restructuring physical geography', *Transactions of the Institute of British Geographers New Series*, vol 27, pp136–154

Harvey, D (1969) *Explanation in Geography*, London, Edward Arnold

Harvey, D (1973) *Social Justice and the City*, London, Edward Arnold

Harvey, D (1974) 'Population, resources, and the ideology of science', *Economic Geography*, vol 50, pp256–277

Harvey, D (1996) *Justice, Nature and the Geography of Difference*, Oxford, Blackwell

Herbert, D and Johnston, R (1978) 'Geography and the urban environment', in Herbert, D and Johnston, R (eds) *Geography and the Urban Environment*, vol 1, London, John Wiley, pp1–33

Howitt, R (2001) *Rethinking Resource Management: Justice, Sustainability and Indigenous Peoples*, London, Routledge

IUCN/UNEP/WWF (1980) *World Conservation Strategy: Living Resource Conservation for Sustainable Development*, Gland, International Union for Conservation of Nature and Natural Resources

Johnston, R (1978) 'Paradigms and revolutions or evolution. Observations on human geography since the second world war', *Progress in Human Geography*, vol 2, pp189–206

Johnston, R (1996) *Nature, State and Economy: A Political Economy of the Environment*, second edition, Chichester, John Wiley and Sons

Johnston, R, Gregory, D, Pratt, G and Watts, M (eds) (2000) *The Dictionary of Human Geography*, fourth edition, Oxford, Blackwell

Kirkby, J, O'Keefe, P and Timberlake, L (eds) (1995) *The Earthscan Reader in Sustainable Development*, London, Earthscan

Kropotkin, P (1996, originally published in 1885) 'What geography ought to be', in Agnew, J, Livingstone, D and Rogers, A (eds) *Human Geography: An Essential Anthology*, Oxford, Blackwell, pp139–154

Lake, R and Hanson, S (2000) 'Needed: Geographic research on urban sustainability', *Urban Geography*, vol 21, no 1, pp1–4

Le Heron, R, Murphy, L, Forer, P and Goldstone, M (eds) (1999) *Explorations in Human Geography: Encountering Place*, Auckland, Oxford University Press

Livingstone, D (1992) *The Geographical Tradition*, Oxford, Blackwell

Manning, E (1990) 'Presidential Address: Sustainable Development, The Challenge', *The Canadian Geographer*, vol 34, no 4, pp290–302

Martin, R (2001) 'Geography and public policy: The case of the missing manifesto', *Progress in Human Geography*, vol 25, no 2, pp121–137

McKeown-Ice, R (1994) 'Environmental education: A geographical perspective', *Journal of Geography*, vol 93, pp40–42

McManus, P (1996) 'Contested Terrains: Politics, stories and discourses of sustainability', *Environmental Politics*, vol 5, no 1, pp48–73

McManus, P (2000) 'Sustainable development', in Johnston, R, Gregory, D, Pratt, G and Watts, M (eds) *The Dictionary of Human Geography*, Oxford, Blackwell, pp812–816

McManus, P (2002) 'Your car is as welcome as you are: a history of transportation and planning in the Perth Metropolitan Region', in Trinca, M, Haebich, A and Gaynor, A (eds) *Country: Visions of Land and People in Western Australia*, UWA History/WA Museum, Perth, pp187–211

Middleton, N, O'Keefe, P and Moyo, S (1993) *The Tears of the Crocodile: From Rio to Reality in the Developing World*, London, Pluto Press

Open GIS Consortium Inc (2002) *Geographic Information for Sustainable Development*, www.ip.opengis.org/gisd/docs/20020630_GSDI_TS.htm, accessed 20 January 2003

Openshaw, S (1991) 'A view on the GIS crisis in geography, or, using GIS to put Humpty Dumpty back together again', *Environment and Planning A*, vol 23, pp621–628

Peck, J (1999) 'Grey geography?' *Transactions of the Institute of British Geographers NS*, vol 24, pp131–135

Powell, J (1996) 'Historical geography and environmental history: an Australian interface', *Journal of Historical Geography*, vol 22, pp253–273

Smith, N (1984) *Uneven Development: Nature, Capital and the Production of Space*, London, Basil Blackwell

Sneddon, C (2000) 'Sustainability in ecological economics, ecology and livelihoods: a review', *Progress in Human Geography*, vol 24, no 4, pp521–549

Towers, G (2000) 'Applying the political geography of scale: grassroots strategies and environmental justice', *Professional Geographer*, vol 52, pp23–36

Urich, P (1999) 'Sustaining Environments', in Le Heron, R, Murphy, L, Forer, P and Goldstone, M (eds) *Explorations in Human Geography: Encountering Place*, Auckland, Oxford University Press, pp261–285

Wallace, I (2002) 'Past President's Address: Sustaining Geography; Sustainable Geographies. The Linked Challenge', *The Canadian Geographer*, vol 46, no 2, pp98–107

Whatmore, S (1999) 'Hybrid geographies', in Massey, D, Sarre, P and Allen, J (eds) *Human Geography Today*, Cambridge, Polity Press, pp22–40

Wilbanks, T (1994) 'Presidential Address: Sustainable Development in Geographic Perspective', *Annals of the Association of American Geographers*, vol 84, no 4, pp541–556

WCED (1987) *Our Common Future*, Oxford, Oxford University Press

Chapter 17

Sustainability and Philosophy

Clare Palmer

INTRODUCTION

There are many ways in which a chapter on the discipline of philosophy and sustainability in higher education might be approached. This chapter considers only two relevant intersections between philosophy and sustainability. These are, first, an outline of the contributions that philosophical debate has made to exploring the meaning – or meanings – of sustainability and the ethical and political ideas associated with it; and, second, a discussion of the place of sustainability in Anglo-American philosophy, more broadly, including a brief consideration of some of the hurdles faced by those working on philosophy and sustainability in higher education. The chapter will, primarily, be referring to work in the tradition of 'Anglo-American' rather than continental philosophy, which deserves a separate chapter (although it is not clear that the development of ideas about sustainability faces any fewer problems in the continental tradition). The chapter will also not be considering feminist contributions – substantial though they are – since they are discussed in Chapter 8.

PHILOSOPHY AND THE MEANING OF SUSTAINABILITY

As Myerson and Rydin (1996, p103), amongst others, point out, 'sustainability' and 'sustainable development' are inherently ambiguous and contested terms, used in a variety of different contexts to encourage and to legitimate some policies and practices, while discouraging and de-legitimating others (indeed, Myerson and Rydin's study indicates one way in which some philosophers have engaged with discussions about sustainability – the work of discourse analysis and the study of sustainability as a rhetorical trope). In almost all contexts, though, sustainability is a value-laden concept. As McNeill (2000, p11) suggests, it is important to consider these broader value issues alongside bare definitions of sustainability. But a definition is a good place to begin, and the most well-known one stems from the World Commission on Environment and Development (WCED) report *Our Common Future* (WCED, 1987, p8) where sustainable human development is described as development that 'meets the needs of the present without compromising the ability of future generations to meet their own needs'.[1]

Immediately, two of the ethical issues usually related to sustainability – hunger and poverty (the needs of the present), and the needs of future generations – are raised. It is worth noting, though, that at first sight present generations and future generations seem to have different relations to the idea of sustainability. Future generations of humans are logically necessary to the sustainability of human society. It is less clear why the needs of the present – or at least the needs of *all* present people – should be so. It is at least *possible* that a highly inequitable society (a slave society, for instance), or a society where many people were hungry and poor, could continue into the indefinite future. Countering this, various arguments – from quite different perspectives in political philosophy – have been used to maintain that sustainability and equity are closely related (because of population increase and resource limitation; because poor individuals may destroy their environments in order to maintain themselves; or because inequitable situations usually require military capacity, which is, in a variety of ways, unsustainable).[2] Even if one does not accept such arguments, however, concerns about poverty should not be regarded as irrelevant to concerns about sustainability. In a broader value context, as suggested above, sustainability can signal concerns about integrating environmental protection with concerns about the economy, future generations, poverty and equity, quality of life and democratic participation (see Jacobs 1999, p26). Philosophical responses to some of these concerns are considered below; although only a relatively small body of philosophical work has been published specifically relating to sustainability, a considerable body of philosophical work exists that relates to need and poverty, future generations and the environment.[3]

Further questions about the meaning of sustainability have been generated by economists' distinction between 'strong' and 'weak' sustainability, a distinction that has also been of some philosophical significance. Turning on a proposed difference between 'natural capital' and 'human-made capital', weak sustainability 'stipulates an undiminished capital bequest [to future generations] irrespective of how it is composed'; while strong sustainability 'stipulates an undiminished bequest of natural capital' (Holland, 2001, p396). But some philosophers, in particular Alan Holland – have questioned these distinctions. Holland, for instance, questions the posited distinction between weak and strong sustainability and between natural and human-made capital; interrogates the supposed relationship between *natural* capital and the natural world; and asks whether it is morally appropriate to think of the natural world as capital – that is, solely or primarily as a human asset – at all, an issue discussed further below (see Holland 1997, 1999, 2001).

PHILOSOPHY, SUSTAINABILITY AND POVERTY

Discussion about distributive justice has been central to political philosophy for generations. However, more recently a specialized philosophical literature relating to hunger and poverty, and the obligations of richer nations, organizations and individuals to those who are hungry and poor, has been growing.

One of the earliest, and still most well-known, contributions to this debate appeared in the paper 'Famine, Affluence and Morality' by the ethicist Peter Singer in 1972. Singer based this paper on a utilitarian approach to ethics – maintaining that ethical behaviour is behaviour that minimizes pain and maximizes happiness in the world. Based on this approach, Singer began his article with the assumption 'that suffering and death from lack of food, shelter and medical care are bad' (Singer 1972, p23). He followed this with the claim that 'If it is within our power to prevent something bad from happening, without thereby sacrificing anything of comparative moral importance, we ought to do it' (Singer, 1972, p24). Based on this, Singer argued that affluent individuals have moral obligations to give aid to those in need. The fact that the poor are a considerable physical distance from the affluent is, for Singer, quite irrelevant; just as it would be wrong to walk past a drowning child because to rescue the child would mean dirtying one's trousers, so it is wrong to live a life of affluence while others are starving. The harm to an affluent person of giving up their wealth is much less than the harm to an absolutely poor person from starving; the two are not comparable harms. The logic of Singer's argument is that affluent individuals should impoverish themselves to the point where their becoming worse-off would leave them worse-off than the destitute they were trying to relieve. Recognizing, though, that no one would, realistically, go this far, Singer adopted a compromise position: the best outcome would arise from the affluent tithing one tenth of their income.

Singer's paper triggered debates about poverty and morality from a variety of ethical perspectives. Some philosophers, like Singer, argued that giving aid to the poor is a moral obligation, but based this on different moral foundations – arguing, for instance, that having enough to eat is a basic human *right*, and that those who are hungry have the right to claim food, or the means to grow food, from the affluent.[4] Other philosophers argued the case that, assuming one was not directly responsible in any sense for the poverty, one could offer aid as an act of beneficence, rather than as an overwhelming obligation to impoverish oneself (see, for instance, O'Neill, 1977). Yet others maintained that giving aid itself would only exacerbate problems of poverty by increasing the size of hungry populations – a modern version of Malthus's 19th-century arguments now associated with Garrett Hardin (1977). Although Hardin did not himself, during the 1970s, use the language of sustainability, this kind of argument is premised on the view that aid to the poor is unsustainable because the resulting increase in human population will ultimately destroy both the poor and the affluent. Of course, many have argued vehemently against this case on a variety of grounds; but what is interesting here is the argument (the inverse of the more common one) that the relief of poverty threatens, rather than improves, the prospect of human sustainability.[5]

Philosophy, Sustainability and Future Generations

Philosophers have for many years puzzled over intrinsically interesting and difficult questions relating to future generations. For many, such questions are set in an ethical context, asking what present generations might owe (if anything) to future generations, and whether it makes sense to talk of 'intergenerational justice'. This concern is clearly central to human sustainability. After all, a necessary condition for human sustainability is that future people can meet their basic needs and reproduce successfully – which requires at least a minimal level of care by today's people.

One might, though, question whether sustainability, in this sense, is desirable. For instance, some philosophers (although not explicitly in the context of sustainability) have questioned whether there is any moral obligation to produce future generations at all; is it good that human beings continue to exist and, if so, why?[6] Suppose we all voluntarily decided to be sterilized, would any wrong be done?[7] In response, other philosophers – utilitarians, for example – might argue that in failing to create new generations, the possibility of many future happy people existing in the world has been lost. This chapter does not go into this debate further here; it merely suggests that it is possible to question the idea that sustainability in the sense of the continuation of human beings is necessarily good.[8]

Most discussions of sustainability, however, are premised on the view that there will, at least in the normal course of events, be future generations; so what is of interest is how the actions of present people could impact upon the well-being of future people – and whether this is a matter for moral concern.[9] As philosophers have pointed out, lying behind these questions is the asymmetric relationship between present and future generations. Present people will never meet members of future generations beyond their own offspring, nor will they know anything about them. Conversely, however, while our existence is necessarily independent of theirs, theirs is necessarily dependent upon ours – both absolutely with regard to there being future individuals at all, and, relatively, with regard to which future individuals there are.

A number of moral and political philosophers find it hard to account for moral obligations towards future generations.[10] Some of those who base human obligations on rights theories, for instance, have found it difficult to ascribe rights to future generations since no particular, identifiable, individual future individuals yet exist, a difficulty compounded by the fact that our very actions will determine which future individuals come into existence at all.[11] The rights theorist Richard De George (1988) goes so far as to say that 'we owe future (people) nothing and they have no legitimate claims on us, for the simple reason that they do not exist'. While other philosophers such as Joel Feinberg and Robert Elliot have argued that it is at least coherent to speak of individuals of future generations as having rights that could constrain our behaviour in the present, the question is by no means resolved.[12]

For those philosophers who accept that present people do have moral obligations towards future people, one central problem is how to weigh what is owed to the future against the present. The logic of some philosophical positions – some forms of utilitarianism, for instance – seems to be that, since there may be a vast, even infinite, number of generations to follow, we end up owing the future everything![13] Interpretations like this seem to imply a strong 'bias to the future', with important implications for policy – in particular, one might assume, for resource consumption.[14] Of vital significance in making such judgements, in relation to the Brundtland definition of sustainability, at least, must be what is considered to be a 'need' – and the constant creation of new human 'needs' – a subject that has also generated a substantial philosophical literature. Some philosophers, writing more recently about obligations to future generations, have moved away from basing their discussion either on the rights, or on the happiness, of future individuals. They maintain, instead, that future generations can be regarded as being, in some sense, a community with present people – albeit a transgenerational community – and that as members of a community, we have obligations to them (for instance, not to poison them) just as we have to present people.[15]

This brief survey of debates within philosophy about future generations has served to emphasize that philosophers have argued for a wide range of positions, including both that present humans do, and do not, have obligations to generate future people; that assuming they exist, present people have no obligations towards future people or, alternatively, very heavy obligations towards future people; or that obligations are stronger toward immediate than toward more remote future generations; and, indeed, every position in between.[16] Whatever one may think of this, it is clear that philosophical debate opens up some key questions about future people that are relevant to sustainability – questions which all too often are ignored or to which the answers are assumed in much political and academic discussion of sustainability.

PHILOSOPHY, SUSTAINABILITY AND THE ENVIRONMENT

Definitions of sustainability, such as the WCED definition, do not explicitly mention the environment. However, the environment is clearly vital to human sustainability since it is central in meeting the needs – and allowing for the flourishing – of both present and future generations of humans. This was certainly the interpretation of the significance of the environment taken in the Rio Declaration, emerging out of the 1992 Earth Summit in Rio de Janeiro: 'Principle 1: Human beings are at the centre of concerns for sustainable development. They are entitled to a healthy and productive life in harmony with nature.'

Similar principles emerge in the Johannesburg Declaration on Sustainable Development, from the 2002 Johannesburg World Summit. Here, environmental degradation is viewed as a cause of human 'indignity and indecency', and environmental problems such as loss of biodiversity, desertification, climate change and pollution are seen as 'continuing to rob millions of a decent life'.[17] Alongside harms to present humans, future people may be endangered by present people in a variety of environmental respects: for instance, by depleting resources; by the generation and unsafe storage of radioactive waste; by loss of biodiversity; by genetic modification of living organisms; by climate change and by other kinds of pollution. Environmental practices in the present are some of the most important ways in which present people can impact upon future generations, and some philosophical discussions of sustainability – as well as most prominent policy documents – have focused on these kinds of environmental concerns. However, this is not the only way in which the environment is regarded as important in philosophical discussions of sustainability. For those working in what has become known as 'environmental ethics' or 'environmental philosophy', a range of other questions about the environment is also raised.

Environmental ethics – as a sub-discipline of philosophy – began to emerge during the early 1970s with a series of important papers on ethical problems relating to animals and the environment. Of course, consideration of these issues was not new – there were a number of forerunners (such as in the 'land ethic' of the American forester Aldo Leopold, and the principle of 'reverence for life' adopted by Albert Schweitzer). During the 1970s, though, philosophers began, more systematically, to examine questions about the value of the environment and organisms within it. In particular, a number of philosophers questioned the idea that the environment should be regarded solely as having instrumental value – value as a means to another end: meeting human needs. This 'instrumental' approach, they maintained, is anthropocentric or human-centred; it sees the environment merely as a collection of human resources or as natural capital providing humans with benefits. Interpretations of sustainability such as those considered above appear to be anthropocentric in this way, suggesting, for instance, that if means could be found to meet the needs of present people, and not to damage the prospects for future people, environmental protection would not be needed; or that it is possible to substitute human capital for natural capital without there being a loss of value.

Many environmental ethicists instead argued that the environment, or some aspects of it, is of non-instrumental, or *intrinsic*, value. This position was famously maintained in Richard Routley's 1973 paper 'Is There a Need for a New, an Environmental Ethic?' Routley uses a thought experiment in which one person, a last person, is left in the world. The last person sets about painlessly eliminating every living thing, animal and plant in the world, leaving behind a completely barren planet. Routley asks whether this person is doing a wrong thing; from an anthropocentric position, he maintains, such behaviour is harmless. To think that there is something wrong with this behaviour is to think that there is some other value or values in the natural world, aside from that of usefulness to humans: values that anthropocentric accounts of sustainable development cannot take into account.

From this position, the value perspectives endorsed in much discussion of sustainable development are either wrongheaded or importantly incomplete in focusing value entirely on human beings. As Rolston (1991), one of the best-known environmental ethicists, comments, 'Let's face it, sustainable development is irredeemably anthropocentric.' For this reason, some environmental ethicists – while acknowledging ethical obligations both to current needy people and to future generations – reject the idea of sustainable development altogether. Others have attempted to develop different ways of understanding sustainability that incorporate the value of individual non-human organisms and/or species, ecological systems, ecosystemic processes and biodiversity, even where they are not directly useful to present or future human beings (Andrew Dobson, 1998, discusses some such models of 'environmental sustainability' in his book *Justice and the Environment*).[18] Donald Scherer (2002, p343), for instance, argues for an 'ecosystemic concept of sustainability' maintaining that 'sustainability, if understood ecosystemically, includes the recognition of goods other than human well-being and the resources that conduce thereto'. Including the good of ecosystems in considerations of sustainability may produce rather different policies from models based entirely on human interests, even where those interests include the living poor and future generations (it might, for instance, raise questions about 'development' in the case of wild ecosystems – the good of which might be best served by being left alone).[19]

Indeed, the very multiplicity of ethical concerns encompassed within a wider interpretation of sustainability is sometimes seen as leading to conflict. Of course, there are many occasions where the interests of present and future generations of humans, and those of ecosystems or the integrity of the natural world, coincide.[20] But might there not also be occasions of conflict between, for instance, the needs of humans and the maintenance of wild areas or the habitats of endangered species? The philosopher Holmes Rolston (2001, p413) in his controversial paper 'Feeding People versus Saving Nature' argues that there are occasions when it is right to 'save nature' rather than 'feed people'. While eradicating poverty may be indispensable, Rolston (2001, p406) argues, it 'may not always be prior to conserving natural value'. Where loss of tiger habitat due to human population increase and a black market for tiger organs threatens the continuance of the tiger species, Rolston (2001, p413) suggests, we are 'left wondering whether the tigers should always lose and the people always win'. Other environmental ethicists have resisted this whole way of construing the problem, arguing that dilemmas of this kind cannot be taken out of the context of complex international and corporate responsibilities for threats to natural values, and that analyses like this privilege the rich North over the poorer developing countries.[21] In a broader sense, conceptions of the human good and quality of life that incorporate concern for nature for its own sake would make human and natural values less easy to prize apart (see Holland, 2001; O'Neill, 1993). However, one might respond to this debate, the inclusion of intrinsic natural values – whether these are attached to non-human living organisms, species, ecosystems or ecological processes – clearly complicates discussions of sustainability, both philosophically and in terms of its practical policy-making implications.

THE PLACE OF SUSTAINABILITY IN ANGLO-AMERICAN PHILOSOPHY

There are a number of philosophical centres, organizations and fora in which these debates about hunger and poverty, future generations and the environment have developed. For example, the International Society for Environmental Ethics (ISEE) is an established organization with international membership, a web-based bibliographic search capacity, a regular newsletter with details of a wide range of recent articles published on environmental ethics, frequent specialist meetings at American Philosophical Association conferences, and an electronic mailing list. Of the three areas considered in this chapter – poverty, future generations and the environment – environmental ethics is unquestionably the largest; arguably, it has made the biggest contribution to discussions about sustainability, more broadly. As a philosophical sub-discipline, environmental ethics seems to be flourishing, with a range of dedicated philosophical journals, a steady stream of new anthologies, textbooks and monographs, and regular conferences. Environmental ethics is widely available to study in colleges and universities across the US, both as part of philosophy programmes and as a more general contribution to interdisciplinary education, while a flourishing Center for Environmental Philosophy and MA programme in philosophy have been developed at the University of North Texas, from where the leading journal *Environmental Ethics* is published. Although, in the UK, environmental ethics is much less widely studied in philosophy departments, a popular MA degree in values and the environment is run at Lancaster University, and is available as a distance-learning degree to students internationally.

Clearly, a number of professional philosophers are actively engaged with issues relating to sustainability. Many attempt to link their philosophical concerns to current policy debates in their local area, nationally and, indeed, internationally. In making these connections, philosophers have worked with those in other academic disciplines, including the natural and social sciences, as well as liaising with local and national governmental policy-makers, local peoples and representatives of non-governmental organizations (NGOs). One example of this has been the discussion relating to the establishment of an Earth Charter, a proposed charter of international principles focusing on the environment and on sustainability, with the ultimate aim of endorsement by the United Nations (UN). Philosophers have played an important part in the development of this charter by engaging constructively and critically in the process of its formation, and in subsequent consultation about the principles adopted.

However, this picture of flourishing philosophical interest in poverty, future generations and the environment may present a misleadingly positive picture of study in philosophy and sustainability, and its location within Anglo-American philosophy, as a whole. Problems certainly exist for the development of work in philosophy and sustainability on a number of levels.

First, until very recently, much philosophical interest has tended to focus on a narrow range of concerns. In environmental ethics, for instance, a central concern has been the theoretical discussion about 'intrinsic value' in nature and what this might mean. While this is an important and interesting question philosophically, the focus has been criticized. One criticism is that discussions of this kind are abstract and obscure, just philosophers talking to themselves, in language impenetrable to non-philosophers and at a level that provides little practical guidance with respect to pressing environmental concerns. A second criticism concerns the insistence by many environmental ethicists that some kind of attribution of intrinsic value to nature is a requirement if it is to count as an environmental ethic at all. This has alienated some – both within philosophy and outside it – individuals who are interested in sustainability issues from a human-centred perspective. A further, related criticism has concerned the focus within environmental ethics on wilderness and 'untouched' nature as the locus for intrinsic value. Many issues relating to sustainability concern human practices in the environment – such as waste production and transportation – that do not directly relate to wilderness. Furthermore, most humans live in urban areas, and it is here, some have argued, that philosophical discussion of sustainability should focus

Although it is true that philosophers have, in the past, tended to focus on abstract questions about, for instance, intrinsic value and wild nature, most recently, research on more practical and urban issues has developed. In the US, in particular, there has been a growth in philosophical forms of 'environmental pragmatism' – while there has also been development in urban ethics, and ethics of the built environment.[22] Furthermore, a number of philosophers have concentrated on arguing that the natural world is fundamentally important for human understanding of 'the good life' – making the discussion of 'intrinsic value' in nature less central (Holland, 2000, p4). Such explorations of sustainability in relation to philosophy look likely to grow and to become increasingly important. This suggests a positive outlook for the development of philosophical work on sustainability.

Philosophers working on sustainability-related issues have, then, encountered a number of *practical* criticisms about the focus of their work, particularly where it is primarily abstract and conceptual. However, precisely the opposite criticism is frequently made from within professional philosophy as a discipline, where applied work on the environment and on issues such as poverty and sustainability is often regarded as insufficiently rigorous and lacking in theoretical sophistication. The heart of Anglo-American philosophy is usually seen as lying in difficult and often highly technical problems in the study of mind, language and knowledge. Applied ethics, in general, and ethics of environment and development, in particular, fall far beyond this perceived heartland in the borderlands of philosophical acceptability. Philosophers who have specialized in the area, for example, of environmental ethics find it difficult to secure academic positions on this basis (though such an interest may be accepted as a teaching sideline) and often end up locating themselves in other disciplines or in interdisciplinary units. Working primarily on philosophical questions in sustainability or the environment certainly creates enormous difficulties for someone wishing to pursue a career in academic philosophy, although a few individuals have done so. There seems to be little sign of this difficult career situation changing, particularly in the UK. So although debates about the environment, poverty and future generations are philosophically vigorous, such issues are generally regarded as being of marginal significance by the wider body of Anglo-American philosophers.

CONCLUSIONS

This chapter has outlined some philosophical contributions to debates about poverty, future generations and the environment. These debates are important in helping to clarify the possible meanings of sustainability, in considering its ethical remit, and in examining problems that might be generated by ethical commitments to it. What such philosophical debates do not do, however, is unite to put forward a 'received view' on the desirability of certain commitments in relation to sustainability. Philosophers disagree about what sustainability might mean, what ethical commitments might be entailed by it, how any commitments should be prioritized or implemented and, indeed, whether sustainability is a good aim at all. Although many philosophers are committed, for instance, to poverty relief, to the protection of the environment or to the interests of future generations, not all are; and entering into philosophical debates on such matters does not necessarily imply that one should be. One role of philosophy has always been as the irritating gadfly and this context is no exception – the idea of sustainability is not a sacred good beyond question.

But, nonetheless, sustainability – in the form of concerns about, for instance, species extinction, climate change, global inequality and resource use – is, and will remain, central to national and international policy-making, both for those in government and those in pressure and protest groups seeking to influence the policy-making process. It seems likely that careful philosophical work can make an important contribution here to debates that are absolutely central to the nature and direction of both human and non-human futures. If this is right, a crucial step forward would be greater acceptance of philosophical work in this area within professional philosophy, as well as further work by philosophers of sustainability in making their arguments accessible and useful to policy-makers without sacrificing philosophical rigour and sophistication.

ACKNOWLEDGEMENTS

My thanks to Doris Schroeder and John O'Neill for comments on drafts of this chapter.

NOTES

1   Alan Carter (2000, p451) suggests another definition again – sustainable development could be taken to mean 'the attainment of a certain level that is viewed as a precondition for sustainable lifestyles': in other words, development for sustainability.

2   See Dobson (1999, p3) and Carter (2000, p459).

3   But see, for instance, Dobson (1998, 1999) Carter (2000), Goodin (1999).

4   Aiken (1977, pp85–102) argues something like this.

5   Many central philosophical papers – including work by Singer, Onora O'Neill and Hardin relating to issues of hunger and poverty – are collected in Aiken and LaFollette (1977).

6   A view argued by Golding (1972) and Delattre (1971).

7   An example discussed in more detail in Kavka (1981).

8   Of course, some other groups have adopted the misanthropic argument that the continuance of human beings is bad because of their negative impact on other life forms.

9   As expressed by Feinberg (1980, pp147–148).

10   Contractarian philosophers, such as John Rawls, often find this problematic. See Rawls (1972, p292) and Attfield (1987, p9).

11   See Norton (1982, p320).

12   See Feinberg (1980) and Elliot (1989).

13   See Narveson (1978); see also Parfit (1984) and Narveson (1967).

14   Passmore (1980, p78) argues that concern about using up resources for future generations is fruitless because if we think into the far future, there are so many people involved that, for example, reducing our petrol consumption to a thimbleful apiece would not mean our remotest descendents get any.

15   See, for instance, de-Shalit (1995); O'Neill (1993).

16   Golding (1972, p98), amongst others, adopts the position that 'the more distant the generation we focus on, the less likely it is that we have an obligation to promote the good'.

17   See the Johannesburg Declaration on Sustainable Development, paragraphs 1 and 18, www.johannesburgsummit.org.

18   Dobson (1998) suggests that three kinds of environmental sustainability exist: a 'natural capital' conception that is anthropocentric; an 'irreversibility' conception that is concerned for aspects of non-human nature which might be irretrievably lost; and a 'natural value' conception that ascribes intrinsic value to nature. For a critique of Dobson's approach, see Carter (2000).

19   It should be noted that there is some dispute amongst environmental ethicists as to whether it makes sense to talk about the 'good' of an ecosystem at all.

20   A point also made by Holland (2001, p394).

21   See, for instance, Brennan (1998); Brennan also asks, significantly, to whom Rolston's 'we' corresponds here.

22   See Light and Katz (1996), a special supplement to the *Journal of Social Philosophy*, January 2003, on urban environmental ethics and Fox (2001).

REFERENCES

Aiken, W (1977) 'The right to be saved from starvation', in Aiken, W and LaFollette, H (eds) *World Hunger and Moral Obligation*, Englewood Cliffs, NJ, Prentice-Hall, pp85–102

Aiken, W and LaFollette, H (eds) (1977) *World Hunger and Moral Obligation*, Englewood Cliffs, NJ, Prentice-Hall

Attfield, R (1987) *A Theory of Value and Obligation*, New York, Croom Helm

Brennan, A (1998) 'Poverty, Puritanism and Environmental Conflict', *Environmental Values*, vol 7, no 4, p305–331

Carter, A (2000) 'Distributive justice and environmental sustainability', *Heythrop Journal*, vol XLI, pp449–460

Delattre, E (1971) 'Rights, Responsibilities and Future Persons', *Ethics*, vol 82, no 3, pp254–258

Dobson, A (1998) *Justice and the Environment*, Oxford, Oxford University Press

Dobson, A (ed) (1999) *Fairness and Futurity*, Oxford, Oxford University Press

Elliot, R (1989) 'The Rights of Future People', *Journal of Applied Philosophy*, vol 6, no 2, pp159–169

Feinberg, J (1981) 'The Rights of Animals and Unborn Generations', in Partridge, E (ed) *Responsibilities to Future Generations*, Buffalo, Prometheus, pp139–149

De George, R (1988) 'Do We Owe The Future Anything?, in Sterba, J (ed) *Morality in Practice*, Belmont, CA, Wadsworth, pp108–115

Fox, W (2001) *The Ethics of the Built Environment*, London, Routledge

Golding, M (1972) 'Obligations to Future Generations', *The Monist*, vol 56, no 1, pp85–99

Goodin, R (1999) 'The Sustainability Ethic: Political, Not Just Moral', *Journal of Applied Philosophy*, vol 16, no 3, pp247–254

Hardin, G (1977) 'Lifeboat Ethics: the case against helping the poor', in Aiken, W and LaFollette, H (eds) *World Hunger and Moral Obligation*, Englewood Cliffs, NJ, Prentice-Hall, pp 12–21

Holland, A (1997) 'Substitutability: or why strong sustainability is really weak and absurdly strong sustainability is not absurd', in Foster, J (ed) *Valuing Nature?*, London, Routledge, pp119–134

Holland, A (1999) 'Sustainability: should we start from here?', in Dobson, A (ed) *Fairness and Futurity*, Oxford, Oxford University Press, pp46–68

Holland, A (2000) 'Introduction', in Holland, A, Lee, K and O'Neill, D (eds) *Global Sustainable Development in the 21st Century*, Edinburgh, Edinburgh University Press, pp1–8

Holland, A (2001) 'Sustainability', in Jamieson, D (ed) *Companion to Environmental Philosophy*, Oxford, Blackwell, pp390–401

Jacobs, M (1999) in Dobson, A (ed) *Fairness and Futurity*, Oxford, Oxford University Press, pp21–45

The Johannesburg Declaration on Sustainable Development (1992) www.johannesburg summit.org

Kavka, G (1980) 'The Futurity Problem' in Partridge, E (ed) *Responsibilities to Future Generations*, Buffalo, Prometheus, pp109–123

Light, A and Katz, E (eds) (1996) *Environmental Pragmatism*, London, Routledge

Light, A and Rolston, H (eds) (2002) *Environmental Ethics*, Oxford, Blackwell

McNeill, D (2000) 'The concept of sustainable development', in Holland, A, Lee, K and McNeill, D (eds) *Global Sustainable Development in the 21st Century*, Edinburgh, Edinburgh University Press, pp10–29

Myerson, G and Rydin, Y (1996) *The Language of Environment*, London, UCL Press

Narveson, J (1967) *Morality and Utility*, Baltimore, Johns Hopkins University Press

Narveson, J (1978) 'Future People and Us', in Sikora, R I and Barry, B (eds) *Obligations to Future Generations*, Temple University Press, Philadelphia, pp38–60

Norton, B (1982) 'Environmental Ethics and the Rights of Future Generations', *Environmental Ethics*, vol 4, no 3, pp319–335

O'Neill, J (1993) *Ecology, Policy, Politics*, London, Routledge

O'Neill, O (1977) 'Lifeboat Earth', in Aiken, W and LaFollette, H (eds) *World Hunger and Moral Obligation*, Englewood Cliffs, NJ, Prentice-Hall, pp148–164

Parfit, D (1984) *Reasons and Persons*, Oxford, Clarendon Press

Partridge, E (1980) *Responsibilities to Future Generations*, Buffalo, Prometheus

Passmore, J (1980) *Man's Responsibility for Nature*, London, Duckworth

Rawls, J (1972) *A Theory of Justice*, Oxford, Oxford University Press

Rolston, H (1991) 'The Wilderness Idea Affirmed', *The Environmental Professional*, vol 13, pp370-377

Rolston, H (1977; edited in 2001) 'Feeding People versus Saving Nature', in Schmidtz, D and Willott, E (eds) *Environmental Ethics: What Really Matters, What Really Works*, Oxford, Oxford University Press, pp404–416

Routley, R (later Sylvan) (1973; edited in 2002) 'Is there a need for a new, an environmental ethic?', in Light, A and Rolston, H (eds) *Environmental Ethics*, Oxford, Blackwell, pp 47–52

Scherer, D (1995; edited in 2002) 'Is sustainability possible?', in Light, A and Rolston, H (eds) *Environmental Ethics*, Oxford, Blackwell, pp334–358

de-Shalit, A (1995) *Why Posterity Matters: Environmental Policies and Future Generations*, London, Routledge

Sikora, R I and Barry, B (eds) (1978) Obligations to Future Generations, Philadelphia, Temple University Press

Singer, P (1972) 'Famine, Affluence and Morality', *Philosophy and Public Affairs*, vol 1, no 3, pp229–243

United Nations Conference on Environment and Development (UNCED) *Rio Declaration*, Rio de Janeiro, Brazil, UNCED, 3–14 June 1992, Principle 1

WCED (1987) *Our Common Future: Report of the WCED*, Oxford, Oxford University Press

Chapter 18

Conclusion: The Future – Is Sustainability Sustainable?

Cedric Cullingford

There are two levels to the concept of sustainability. One is scientific. This is the issue of climate change or the greenhouse effect, of pollution and the threat of environmental disaster due to the determination to pursue immediate gratification without caring about the long-term results of such greed. The second level is moral. This is the issue of globalization, of the widening distinctions between the rich and the poor and the tensions between the concept of sovereignty and intervention.

The two levels are intimately connected. Whatever the scientific arguments about cause and effect, the decisions to cut down rain forests, to make paper and clear land for agriculture have clear consequences. The disasters of the past have clearly demonstrated the way in which over-exploitation can have unforeseen consequences. The Roman Empire turned the bread basket of North Africa into a desert. The example of the ruin of the Great Plains of North America is more immediate. Both are representative of the typical consequences of unsustainable policies and actions. In a time of clear communication, there is no excuse not to learn from past mistakes.

The issue that people do not wish to learn is a moral one. The consequences of action do not always fall on the perpetuator, either for reasons of geography or for reasons of time. Immediate gratification is of greater concern for most people and the responsibility to care for the environment too heavy. The fact that the possibilities of great natural disaster constantly exist make such calamities unconvincing. Like weapons of mass destruction or the possibility of worldwide nuclear conflagration, people become accustomed to living in the shadow of threats and 'learn to love the bomb'.

Since the development of nuclear power, scientific research has not been able to protect itself from moral consequences. Those who argue for the inevitability of scientific advance, as in genetic engineering, cannot be unaware of the moral issues. Their very stance, suggesting that where there is a problem there will always be a solution, acknowledges the seriousness of the issue. In scientific terms, every invention and new insight has an effect. We do not need to have chaos theory to remind us of the intricate connections between one act and another.

Sustainability is usually discussed in scientific terms, with the awareness that greater drought in certain parts of Africa or more flooding in parts of South-East Asia are a direct consequence of environmental change. Sometimes, as in over-irrigation, the results are localized. Occasionally, as in air pollution, there are far-reaching consequences. This pattern of collective decision-making and its costs is, however, a moral issue. Those who cause environmental damage are not those who reap the consequences. The issue is, therefore, one of responsibility. To what extent should we take heed of other people and other nations? Should our conscience be affected as we hear of people starving? Can we remain psychologically 'an island, entire of itself'? If we do so, if we deny the existence of society, then we have made a moral, not a scientific, choice.

There has never been a time before when the possibility of self-destruction and of mutability has been so constantly before us. This should make a difference. We cannot any longer project a simple self-centered optimism that mankind will keep 'progressing'. Yet, we are not haunted by these thoughts. For most people, the concept of sustainability is merely associated with personal inconvenience. For many, the only time that they come against sustainability is in the ensuite bathrooms of hotels where the management pleads with guests, for the sake of the environment, not to demand new towels or new sheets.

The more expensive the hotel, the more urgent is the warning that making use of the laundry has a catastrophic effect through the application of so much washing powder. The reminders of the cost to the environment – bottle banks and the separation of rubbish into different coloured bins, or, for some, a greater frequency of flooding – are still comparatively trivial and are matters of more inconvenience than urgency.

All social and psychological analyses of the relationship of the individual to politics have commented on the ambiguous connections between one and the other. The journalistic formula of one death next door holding as much weight as 1000 deaths in another country sums up the natural self-centredness of the individual. Politics matter in so far as they impinge upon everyday behaviour, and there are concentric rings of concern from the personal to the more general, from taxes to the state of transport. An awareness exists of other global issues, especially if they threaten to involve the interests of the individual, as in war; but generally these are of a different level of concern. This is partly because the world of politics is strident and separate; the personalities rather than the policies dominate the interest of all within the various factions of political parties and newspapers in such a way that they do not impinge upon what they laughingly term 'ordinary people'. A political party without power and without the prospect of power might be of huge interest to politicians because of the fascination with internecine strife; but they have no connection with the currents of individual and social life.

There is a tendency to distance oneself from larger issues, to withhold curiosity about what is happening elsewhere ('Besides, that was in another country and the wench is dead'). But everyone is affected by the politics of the environment. This is not a game of power, of interpersonal or international argument. All are involved in the consequences of other people's actions.

Sustainability involves issues that are about competing interests and values, but not from a position of choice. The need to work together is mandatory. We might argue about the rights of the sovereign state as we assert the rights of the individual; but these rights can have consequences for other people. The nuclear disaster of Chernobyl might have been dismissed as a Soviet problem; but its impact was not just local. North Koreans attempt to retain an immutable independence; but the country's very insularity is a threat – let alone its possession of nuclear weapons. Knowing when and at what level to intervene is the new great issue for the international world, one in which all people are involved. The very concept of international responsibility, like the 'United Nations', is a new one, but one that we are forced to take seriously.

In terms of political globalization, there are quite distinct and separate camps of suspicion and hatred. Various groups distrust each other's motives and intentions. They seek enemies against whom to define themselves. For them, the issues of intervention are loaded with difficulties of cultural takeovers and subtle domination, of terror in one form or another. Sustainability, like the environment, is of a different dimension. It cannot be reduced to political argument in the same way as the hegemony of states or the rights of dictators. The need for responsible political action was never greater; and this involves a serious readdressing of the large issues of human life – not only those of physical survival but of meaning and cultural identity.

The problem with the contemporary and increasingly volatile awareness of international interdependence and interference is that it has still not been fully developed. The concept of international relations, like that of nationalism and territorial aggrandizement, like the 'scramble for Africa', has changed.

Increasing industrialization and its effects – delineated and dealt with up to a point in act after parliamentary act years ago – is now too big for individual action. This is well illustrated by the way in which areas beyond national boundaries are dealt with – international waters and fish stocks are a good example. Underlying these aspects of internationalism is a far more challenging one that has been ignored. This is the, as yet, inability to define what it is to be human. The 'meaning of life' is forced to take on new meanings. It can no longer be defined in terms of the exclusivity of one religion, the exquisite differentiations of the class system or the artifacts of nationalism.

The sense of a New World, of a new climate of opinion, is becoming apparent. When the phrase 'the end of history' was coined, it was immediately latched on to with relief: something was changing; there would be a marked shift in the patterns of life. Clearly, those politicians who are empowered to deal with it are better suited to the status quo. People will always be more comfortable with the familiar; and, yet, there is a tense, almost new language that accompanies the inexorable rise of technology. With this, there should be a new concern for human beings themselves. The discoveries of science drift inwards into the philosophy of mind, as well as outwards, into technological applications. An undercurrent of a real shift, of something waiting to be born, is felt as much as the sense of mere anarchy set loose upon the world. The 'war to end wars' was the final cry of a particular strand of optimistic universalism. The sense of powerful undercurrents prevails. At the end of the 20th century, that sense was curbed into a rational, technological guise. The sense of an inescapable challenge remains. It is very difficult to separate an awareness of rapid technological change from an underlying feeling of unease at the unchanging behaviour of human beings. The confidence of politicians is shadowed by their limitations.

Naturally, and all too humanly, the challenges and the possibilities of a more sustainable world are frequently ignored. The desire for a genuine new start, the hope for a better world, is replaced by the immediate, or by the despair expressed by Yeats in *The Second Coming*. We are left with the many invocations of change, from the popular to the arcane, as if the changes themselves, like fashions, were all that counted, rather than their meaning. This indicates both ignorance and an awareness of something unknown 'slouching towards Bethlehem to be born'.

Although there are changes taking place that give a new challenge to relationships, we live in a time of relentless individualism. The dominance of market forces, of competition, and of distinctions between success and failure reflect the disparities between the rich and poor. This is not a society that is ready to embrace collective responsibility for the well-being of others. The underlying *modus operandi* is of thinking specifically of oneself, as if this is some kind of primary virtue (Sennett, 2002). This affects universities.

Universities are caught up in the competitive ethos, as if they have to use all of their possible advantages to raise themselves above (and denigrate) others. Their histories and their prestige, their relevance and their popularity, and, above all, their income are all fodder to competition. They fight for numbers of students and sizes of research grants. They compare their retention rates and job placements. They look with sceptical fascination at the league tables. They know that they are being constantly divided into groups in terms of prestige and research money. In a parody of the education system as a whole, they are not only subject to inspection and to league tables, but also to the fear of being 'named and shamed', to the threat of closure, to the financial struggles of private industry. Their main task is to survive, to make money. Their secondary task is to become a leading private enterprise.

This sense of fighting for distinction is a new phenomenon, although it is given greater resonance by a tradition of superciliousness within universities. Just as schools are divided by their socio-economic intake, so universities are struggling to justify themselves as having a more advantaged or more deprived clientele, or both at the same time. This change to universities, with the concomitant low morale, loss of self-confidence, enforced managerialism and insecurity, has come about subtly and for a number of reasons. Some would argue that the loss of authority and status and the abandonment of the principle of independence were inevitable; indeed, the loss of a sense of common purpose in universities is palpable. This does not imply that nothing good is going on, or that, during the past, all was as perfect as it could be in an imperfect world. It does, however, suggest a concern for the future.

Universities have always needed a mission, a deeper sense of purpose than mere survival. This has often taken the form of an unspoken acknowledgement of a shared vision of their place in the world. This is not the same as surviving financially, adding more managers and entrepreneurs, shedding academic staff, increasing administration and making the acquisition of research funds the fundamental judgement of scholarship. The diurnal scramble to survive means fire-fighting rather than long-term development. The question is: what particular part do universities play beyond being large employers and trainers for the job market?

At the heart of universities, the idea of one subject has always prevailed. Universities, for better or worse, create, define and advance a particular form of knowledge. It is called a 'discipline' since a subject has the purpose both of enlarging and defining a body of knowledge and teaching styles of thinking. The application of a discipline is through the development of logic.

Professors are there to develop their subject. It is in the awareness of what subjects entail, as well as their demarcation lines, that universities reveal their particular purpose. Subjects have naturally evolved over the years. They have moved from theology and classics, through science, to humanities and social science. Every new entrant has been subject to hostility and suspicion until allowed to join the pantheon. The changing nature of subjects and their struggles for recognition, some decaying, some evolving and some forcing themselves on the field, is well documented (see, for example, Becher and Trowler, 2001). What is clear, for all the changes and arguments, is that it is in the idea of a subject – an academic discipline and all that this entails – that universities have their being. They are not places of one single collective vision any more then they have one definable product. Subjects vary and impose their own rules and expectations, but the idea of a subject is central.

Sometimes the importance of a discipline is shown up by the arguments within it. Subjects keep redefining themselves. Some no longer seem to be relevant, or they are questioned as having no scholarly coherence. Some are more fashionable and more highly considered than others. It is the arguments within subjects, however, that demonstrate their resonance. Let us take a relatively new and 'respectable' subject as an example. When Robert Graves was at Oxford, he recalls his tutor at Wadham saying to him: 'I understand, Mr Graves, that the essays, which you write for your English tutor, are, shall I say, a trifle temperamental. It appears, indeed, that you prefer some authors for others' (*Goodbye to All That*, 1929). There was a canon of respectable literature. The Anglo-Saxon school flourished and attempts to replace 'The Owl and the Nightingale' with 19th-century literature are still firmly in place. The influence of the literary critic F R Leavis, and the resistance to him at Cambridge, as well as the mutual disparagement of his colleagues at Oxford, all suggest what some would call a healthy antipathy founded on self-interest. In fact, it is all a sign of an emerging, changing idea of what constitutes a 'discipline'.

Today, the notion of books as offering moral insights and revealing the development of social mores is replaced by books as sites for deconstruction, as sources of academic discourse rather than inspiration. The fact that the moral imperative is overtaken by the academic is in itself revealing. It demonstrates that the idea of a discipline is not simply a moral prerogative. The passions that fuel academic discourse are fuelled by the interpretation and the boundaries of what constitutes a subject, as well as who has the authority to make such judgements.

At the heart of universities is perhaps unfortunately, the notions of the subject. Interdisciplinarity might be fostered and practical applications frowned upon, but the notion of what promotes learning and what constitutes scholarship remain. The idea of a subject can be interpreted in several ways. At one level, it is a discipline, a mode of thought within a narrow enough body of knowledge to make the possibility of complete command significant. At another level, a subject is an accumulation of facts and their interconnection for their own sake. At the same time, subjects also offer employment, a way of making money. Further down these levels of distinction is the idea that a subject creates wealth.

When a university uses a subject simply as a means to create money, it resembles any other enterprise, with patents and marketing. If the only point is the outcome, the exploitation of students and their subsequent success, then universities act as a private firm of headhunters. The discomfort felt by universities is partly a result of the dichotomy between the new pressures to be entrepreneurial and the deep-seated instinct that their purpose is somewhat more complex.

Universities' primary function is usually defined as teaching and producing graduates; and, yet, this is not really the case. Other institutions can do this. While academic status and validity are important, there is something else about the idea of a university that nourishes both the best and worst of academic life. In fact, at the nebulous core of universities is the notion of a discipline that puts forward something independent of moral designs.

Sustainability is both a practical and moral subject. It is interdisciplinary, as much a matter of concern to the humanities (Said, 1993) as to the sciences. It is, at once, an inescapable dilemma of our time, a matter of study and reflection, and a challenge to action. It raises questions about globalization and personal responsibility. It constitutes, in fact, all that a discipline calls for: a greater understanding and a basis for the moral authority of knowledge.

Politics have never been too far away from universities and their causes. Politics should not interfere with universities; but as they are the universal means of action, universities cannot be kept at a distance. The politics of the environment are not just about day-to-day issues. It is even less about issues of party positioning or personal grasps of power. The politics that involves universities deals with equality, responsibility and justice; in international terms, it deals with the inequalities in the global distribution of wealth. Poverty is another way of defining it. It is not a matter that universities can avoid simply by making money.

Sustainability is essentially a physical manifestation of the same central issue: the inequality of power. It is put into resource terms at a time when resources equal power more than ever before. The challenge for civilization, if we ever get there, is not the creation of great works of art that are appreciated by an elite, but the widespread appreciation of the most challenging levels of cultural demands. Universities have always been thought of as ivory towers, above the hurly-burley of the everyday. Bourdieau (1984) even suggests that all cultural standards are a form of elitism.

Universities in their spread of subjects and their wide clientele cannot afford to serve the notion of an elite. They will be forced to engage in the debates and struggles of the time. Furthermore, they cannot afford to lose their idea of standards – of real dialogue, of the proper use of knowledge and the ability to make distinctions, holding onto the notion of truth.

This is where the idea of a discipline is so important. The Earth's future has always been uncertain; but we cannot say that we are not forewarned. Global challenges will not go away. It is possible that human beings will, as usual, muddle through, half-blinded by narrow-mindedness, uncertain as to how much to think about others and coming to the right conclusions only after trying all of the other options.

The alternative is for universities to be engaged in the central debate of our time by making sustainability more central in the extant curriculum and by making sure that the argument that it entails is carried forward in an authoritative and civilized manner. Universities should, ideally, be engaged in improving conditions in the world, in enhancing sympathetic conduct and in spreading enlightenment. Of course, this is an ideal and the reality is sometimes quite different, with careers to be made and rivalries to be overcome. By understanding the place of sustainability as a global issue, both the ideal and the actual status of universities will be enhanced. Universities will also be more clearly seen as having an international role, not just in competition but in their shared mission.

The issues addressed in this book affect all subjects and are also subjects in their own right. The examples of universities could have a deeper effect on schools, not just in environmental education but in dealing with controversial subjects – for example, in scientific knowledge. Universities must also take action.

Pupils in schools need to learn to overcome the divide between right and wrong, and the sense that events are 'unchangeable'. They need to learn to be critical. If universities do not deal in an intelligent way with the central questions of our time, who will? The question goes beyond whether capitalization and democracy will survive (Emmott, 2003). It is about the nature of survival itself and what constitutes a genuine civilization.

The future of universities depends upon the purpose that they serve. The fact that they will survive is not in doubt. What is in doubt is whether they will have the kind of influence on people that gives them meaning. Universities nurture particular attitudes. These can be negative, as well as creative, self-centred and prejudiced, as well as enlightened and understanding. Universities can become self-enclosed private companies, competing, marketing and turning out products. They can also become something more, assuming a role in the shaping of individuals as members of academic communities, as educators of teachers and as international collaborators.

This is where sustainability could have an important role in giving universities a sense of purpose. As a globalized concept, sustainability is both a subject in itself and covers subject boundaries It is not marred by religious or political affiliations. It is significant at a scientific and moral level. The problems with the concept of sustainability lie not in the issues that it deals with, but the way in which it is treated. Sustainability can be reduced to a series of catch phrases. It can sound like little more than scolding and cajoling. The problem is that it can be so little fun.

Every subject should have depth and depth includes humour. This is what universities should be able to bring, turning an unexamined phrase such as 'lifelong learning' on its head and interrogating it, asking what the alternatives are. The independence of universities lies in encouraging their staff to work with each other with a purpose that gives true satisfaction. All people are born curious. Most survive their educational experiences with a yearning for more knowledge. Universities should be for those who foster curiosity about the meaning of life. At the heart of this is the subject of sustainability in all its contexts – a sustainability of the human spirit, as well as of the environment.

REFERENCES

Becher, T and Trowler, P (2001) *Academic Tribes and Territories*, Buckingham, Open University Press

Bourdieu, P (1984) *Distinction: A Social Critique of the Judgment of Taste*, London, Routledge

Emmott, W (2003) *20:21 Visions: The Lessons of the 20th Century for the 21st*, London, Allan Lane

Graves, R (1929) *Goodbye to All That*, London, Jonathan Cape

Said, E (1993) *Culture and Imperialism*, London, Chatto and Windus

Sennett, R (2002) *Respect: The Formation of Character in a World of Inequity*, London, Allen Lane

Index

Page numbers in *italic* refer to Tables, Figures and Boxes